THE POWERFUL CONSUMER

THE POWERFUL CONSUMER

Psychological Studies
of the American Economy

GEORGE KATONA

Survey Research Center,
The University of Michigan

McGRAW-HILL BOOK COMPANY, INC.

New York   Toronto   London   1960

THE POWERFUL CONSUMER

To my wife

To my wife

Preface

This book is a product of work done at the Survey Research Center of the University of Michigan. The underlying notions presented in the book have grown and have been modified in the course of close contact with colleagues at the center. The Economic Behavior Program of the Survey Research Center, directed by the author since its establishment in 1946, has provided the setting in which his ideas have developed and have been tested.

The sample interview survey, which represents the methodological tool for research in economic psychology, is a large-scale enterprise in which a great number of people participate. Regrettably, it is impossible to recognize the contributions of everyone who helped to carry out the surveys; however, a few persons must be singled out to whom the author feels particularly indebted. Rensis Likert, director of the Institute for Social Research—of which the Survey Research Center is a division—and Angus Campbell, director of the center, are foremost among those who made the surveys possible and stimulated the studies in economic psychology. Leslie Kish, director of the sampling section, and Charles Cannell, director of the field section of the center, devised methods and upheld standards without which the surveys could not have been carried out.

Three colleagues in the Economic Behavior Program have shared the author's work for many years. The book could not have been written without a continuous exchange of ideas with Eva Mueller, James Morgan, and John Lansing. All three, as well as Richard L. Waddell, senior editor of *Business Week* magazine, read the manuscript of the book and made many valuable suggestions. The book also profited a great deal from the conscientious work of several research assistants and many interviewers located all over the country.

Sample interview surveys not only require the participation of experts in several areas; they are also expensive. The author is greatly indebted to those who have provided the funds, substantial in comparison to the usual standards of social science research, although small in relation to the costs of research in natural sciences and technology. The Ford Foundation, through its grant for studies on the origin and effects of economic attitudes, made a three-year panel study possible. Grants by the Rocke-feller Foundation contributed greatly to the theoretical analysis of eco-nomic behavior. Several grants by the Foundation for Research on Human Behavior made the exploration of new approaches to economic psychology possible. Funds from the University of Michigan, partly through the Institute for Social Research and partly through faculty grants made by the department of economics, filled the gaps on numerous occasions.

Research on practical problems with the aim of providing data of imme-diate usefulness is not remote from basic research. Therefore it has been possible to utilize substantial funds from government agencies and private business corporations for the surveys in which material relevant to eco-nomic psychology has been collected. The Board of Governors of the Federal Reserve System has not only financed the Surveys of Consumer Finances, conducted by the Survey Research Center, but economists at the Board have also greatly contributed to devising the objectives and analyzing the findings of those surveys. Several large business corporations entrusted the center with research which frequently concerned new, pre-viously uncharted areas in which the practical payoff was not assured in advance. The author regrets that it is not possible to list the names of these business firms and associations. Suffice it to say that he is indebted not only for the funds received but also for the opportunity to discuss findings and ideas with business economists and business leaders.

Cross-disciplinary activity has become much more accepted during the last few years than it was in earlier years when the author's work on economic psychology began. It is therefore necessary to mention that as early as 1947, the University of Michigan, through giving the author appointments as both professor of economics and professor of psychology, and permitting him to give interdisciplinary courses listed in both depart-ments, greatly contributed to cross-disciplinary research and to the training of students and research assistants in the interlocking aspects of both disciplines.

One of the tasks which the author could not have carried out without assistance concerns the form of presentation of his ideas. He is most grateful for the editorial assistance of Sylvia M. Kafka, whose suggestions were invaluable. He also wishes to express his thanks to Nancy McAllister for her secretarial assistance and typing.

Thanks are due finally to the ten thousands of respondents who were interviewed in nationwide surveys and supplied the data which serve to support the ideas and propositions presented in the book. These studies cover the period from the end of World War II until the beginning of 1959. Additional surveys, aimed at a better understanding of develop-ments in 1959 and 1960, are under way at the Survey Research Center.

Contents

Contents

PART ONE

Introduction

CHAPTER 1

Income and Confidence

Economic Instability

Instability of the economy is still one of our most pressing problems. In the early fifties in this most fortunate of all countries, many people had thought that depressions, and even recessions, belonged to the past. They believed it to be inevitable that they would have more and better material things as years would go by, for wages and incomes could move in one direction only—up. Then during the recession of 1958 some people were cut off overtime pay or worked shorter hours, while others were laid off or even lost their jobs. They learned that it was not possible to count without question on a household budget based on current income as providing the lowest possible standard of living. Incomes could go down, and there was no guarantee of permanent good times. Something could happen to the economy which would deeply affect all of us; it could cause great suffering to some and make it impossible for others to gratify their fondest desires and dreams.

The realization of the instability of our economy brought a second old truth to the foreground. This truth is perhaps most simply expressed in the words of the newsletter of a major bank to its customers in March, 1958, when the decline in demand was a well-established fact: "Demand depends on income and confidence." [1] Lip service has long been paid to "waves of confidence" or "waves of mistrust" which may play a role along with changes in financial conditions in the fluctuations of the economy. Up to the present time, however, this consideration has hardly influenced either government or business policies aimed at counteracting unfavorable or spurring favorable economic trends. Only in recent years has any serious effort been made to subject the role of the psychology of the people in economic matters to scientific study. This book is basically a report on that study.

Demand depends both on ability to buy and on willingness to buy. Fluctuations of demand, whether by consumers or by business firms, may originate in changes either in the former or in the latter. It goes without

[1] First National City Bank of New York, *Monthly Letter*, March, 1958, p. 26.

saying that nobody can buy if he has no income, assets, or credit. It does not follow, as some would seem to believe, that if people have sufficient income, assets, or credit they will necessarily buy. Ours is a complex economy in which the situation of different consumer and business groups varies greatly. Looking at the entire economy, rather than at individuals, in the short run only minor upward or downward shifts in ability to buy occur, and they may be either preceded or followed by similar or divergent shifts in willingness to buy. Which change comes first is a matter to be studied—not to be decided *a priori*. The origin of depressions as well as of booms must be looked for both in financial and in psychological developments. Similarly, measures intended to avert or remedy depressions may be influential in changing either ability to buy, or willingness to buy, or both—or may be futile because one impact may cancel out the other.

As we have said, this is hardly new. What is new is that the psychological factors are susceptible to study, analysis, and measurement. Some people think that incomes, assets, debts, and their changes can be determined with ease and exactitude while the intangible state of confidence or anxiety is a matter of nonscientific feelings and opinions. During the last ten or fifteen years it has, however, been demonstrated that changes in the American people's optimism or pessimism, in their feelings of security or insecurity, in their degree of confidence or mistrust and uncertainty, are measurable. Changes in motives, attitudes, and expectations represent scientific data as reliable as changes in incomes, assets, and debts. How psychological tendencies can be measured, what progress has been made in such measurements, and what conclusions may be derived from them—to answer these questions is one major objective of this book.

Economic instability, whether it be inflation or depression, does not differ from other major issues of our times in being of double origin. The interaction of psychological with environmental factors is readily acknowledged as being relevant to the widespread incidence of neuroses, psychoses, alcoholism, juvenile delinquency, and the manifold interpersonal problems that arise at home, at school, and at work. Political instability in democracies also stems from both the environment of the voters and their personalities, for, as has been demonstrated in repeated studies, voting behavior depends on the voters' reactions to new political issues and candidates as well as on old established patterns and group belonging. In all these areas the importance of both sets of factors is clearly recognized, and efforts to solve the problems usually approach them from both directions.

Two major areas remain—economic instability and international conflict—in which solutions are still sought largely on the basis of changing the environmental factors alone—in the former instance, financial; in the latter, military or political. The attitudes and motives of the peoples involved are largely ignored. We must grant that in the matter of inter-national affairs, the task of changing the attitudes, expectations, and opinions of the peoples of other countries is formidable; in the case of Soviet peoples with whom our communications are minimal, perhaps even impossible. But in domestic economic matters, is it not time to try to learn as much as we can and then make use of what we know about the economic psychology of our own people in an attempt to keep our econ-omy on an even keel?

What we must know, then, is how human behavior—motives, attitudes, hopes, and fears of consumers and businessmen—contributes to bringing about prosperous times or inflation or recession. Thereby we may learn how to mitigate or even avert economic instability. What we know thus far about this great problem is far too little. The time has not arrived to promise infallible remedies. But the little we know and the promising leads we have are worth discussing and writing about.

Interaction between Financial and Psychological Factors

The very fact that demand depends, partly, on willingness to buy means that the buyers, businessmen and consumers alike, have some latitude of action. Their discretion, to be sure, has limits, but within these limits much that is beneficial and much that is damaging may be done. Before turning to the study of willingness to buy, we must face the fact that the notion of human discretion in economic matters is not generally accepted. What are the alternatives? First of all, of course, there is the old theory of the invisible hand: Businessmen and consumers, and gov-ernments too, are presumed to be marionettes moved about by some higher design; free will and discretion in action are illusions. In somewhat more scientific terms it is the impersonal market which is accepted as governing our economic fate. An individual may have some latitude in promoting his own personal success. But the influence of any individual on the total economy is negligible since the economy is affected by market processes only. The laws of the market may not suffice to predict the reactions of each individual to changes in supply or demand or the quantity of money, but the reactions of all individuals, determining what happens to the entire economy, are governed by inexorable laws of the market. According to this theory psychological factors represent, at most, short-range deviations and aberrations from what must happen because of objective laws of the market place.

Let us say here, briefly, what will be made clear later, that economic psychology does not represent the opposite extreme of thought which would deny any influence to market factors. Psychological factors, such as motives, attitudes, expectations, and group belonging, are intervening variables operating between the stimuli of market conditions and the responses to them in the form of economic decisions. The psychological factors do not alone determine the final decision, but under certain conditions they are powerful enough to alter individual as well as mass reactions and thereby influence the entire economy.

The starting point of any analysis of consumer demand must be the enabling conditions represented by income, assets, and debts, as well as by such demographic facts as population growth and the age distribution of the population. Over a period of several years these conditions may vary substantially. From one quarter to the next, however, changes in them are usually insignificant. Consumer sentiment, on the other hand, though sometimes unchanged over fairly long periods, may occasionally undergo swift changes. What is the origin of these changes? Do they originate exclusively in financial considerations, either national or personal? Or may the origin sometimes lie elsewhere? It will be shown that changes in consumer attitudes and expectations may be unrelated to changes in consumer incomes. In addition to their origin, the effects of changes in consumer sentiment on the economy must be studied. It is necessary to find out which types of consumer demand are and which types are not influenced by perceptions, attitudes, hopes, and fears of consumers.

Short-term variations in economic activity represent our major but not our exclusive concern. Our interest extends to the influence of motives and attitudes on the growth of our economy over longer periods. How does the post–World War II economy, psychologically speaking, differ from the economy of earlier periods? This inquiry suffers from the lack of reliable scientific data on the economic psychology of earlier times. Nevertheless, it will be possible to point to some crucial differences and thus to provide further evidence of the role of human behavior on the economic scene.

Economic Behavior

Economic psychology is a behavioral science. The latter expression, although quite new, is already widely used and also frequently misunderstood. It is assumed that behavioral science is equivalent to social science and encompasses all of psychology, sociology, economics, political science, and some other disciplines as well. Behavioral science has, however, a distinctive meaning. It studies action of man (or groups of men) by applying the scientific method—observation, measurement, testing—to man himself. Therefore it includes only parts of the social sciences. Economic psychology is that behavioral science which studies the economic behavior of man. Not all of economics does so. The expression "economic behavior" has been used in three difference ways, the first two of which fall outside the realm of economic psychology.

One meaning of the term "economic behavior" is the behavior of the "economic man," that is, the behavior postulated in economic theories of rationality. Basic assumptions are set forth: maximization of utility by each individual, perfect competition, full knowledge of and control over the means of achieving the postulated ends—these are the most important ones. From these assumptions a deductive science is derived which establishes the forms of behavior required under the given circumstances and their implications for the economy. That people frequently, or even generally, do not behave according to what has been deduced from the postulates is not viewed as a cause for concern. The theory aims at establishing how rational businessmen and consumers ought to behave in order to achieve the postulated goals. It is frequently assumed that individual deviations from the norm would cancel out and would therefore not influence the average behavior and the total market. Or it is maintained that by a process of elimination only those businessmen would survive who behave in the stipulated, optimal manner.

This traditional form of economics is not behavioral science. It does not apply the scientific methods of empirical research to economic behavior. This of course does not mean that it is unimportant. Economic theory performs invaluable service by providing guideposts and hypotheses to be tested by empirical methods.

Second, in the realm of positive or analytical economics the term "economic behavior" is often used to mean the behavior of prices, or incomes, or the economy. Economists are then concerned with relationships that exist between changes in production, prices, incomes, consumption, and investment. Statistical and econometric analysis in the form of correlations, or regression equations showing functional dependence, is applied to the observed results of behavior. The concern in this case is with the relationship among amounts saved, spent, and invested, and prices rather than with the behavior of people, that is, with the human factors making for saving, spending, producing, or price setting. As a leading economist put it recently, "It is the behavior of commodities not the behavior of men which is the prime focus of interest in economic studies." [2] Thus a recent volume on the "behavior of unemployment" deems the analysis of the relation of different rates of employment and unemployment to production, profits, and inventories sufficient for an understanding of unemployment, without any studies of the behavior of

[2] K. E. Boulding, *The Image*, p. 82. Only brief titles of books and articles will be given in the footnotes; for complete references, see the Bibliography at the end of this book.

producers and consumers which may cause unemployment, or the behavior of the unemployed themselves.

This type of economic analysis serves a very useful purpose. Like the behavioral sciences it makes use of the scientific method of observation and measurement, applying it however to economic processes rather than to the behavior of man.

Economic behavior in the third and last sense of the term, the sense used in this book, refers to the behavior of the people whose actions play a role in determining economic trends. Economic psychology holds that in order to understand the behavior of commodities, that is, the interrelationship between supply, demand, income, and saving, it is necessary but not enough to analyze the results of human behavior. It is necessary also to study the decision makers and the process of decision making, because motives, attitudes, and opinions influence actions and thereby what happens in and to the economy.

The crucial question of economic psychology is a pragmatic one: Do we gain a better understanding of economic processes, and are we able to predict economic processes with greater accuracy, if we make psychological studies of economic behavior in addition to the more traditional financial studies? At first, economic psychology started out by answering this question in the affirmative on *a priori* grounds. Later it produced empirical evidence supporting its contention.

The Scope of This Book

That some powerful leaders may influence the economy has always been recognized. Since time immemorial, kings, presidents, and parliaments have interfered with supply and demand by such acts as levying taxes and duties or instituting public works. Business leaders have also influenced the course of the economy, for instance, by introducing technological innovations or new institutional practices. Yet the psychological studies which form the basis of this book were directed neither to political leaders nor to entrepreneurs. Our interest lay primarily in studying the discretion in decision making and in action of consumers, the unorganized masses, who in the past have been considered passive factors rather than powerful forces influencing the stability or instability of the economy.

The two basic propositions, "Demand depends on income and confidence" and "Changes in confidence are measurable," are applied to consumers. We shall show that millions of households may step up or reduce their purchases, not only because their ability to buy has increased or decreased, but also because their attitudes have changed. Information on changes in consumer sentiment contributes to an understanding of economic processes and to our ability to predict the future course of the economy.

What conclusions emerge from a study of the influence of consumer motives, habits, attitudes, and expectations on consumer spending? Is today's American economy made more stable or less stable by the millions of decision makers who may change its course? The conclusion that will be drawn from our studies is that consumer thinking is inherently conservative and sane, and not inclined toward sudden and excessive fluctuations. While far from fully rational, consumers are not puppets in the hands of unscrupulous manipulators. Rumors and unfounded statements do not sway consumers easily because they have a fairly sound, if unsophisticated, picture of the workings of the economy.

This book, then, has a thesis. It presents propositions, arguments, and conclusions which are not generally accepted. At the same time it sets forth the findings on consumer behavior obtained through quantitative research. Data do not, of course, *prove* a theory; they do lend it support and probability.

Psychological economics is a fairly new discipline which stems from the requirements of our time. Therefore, the findings on consumer behavior and its relation to psychological factors refer to developments of the last fifteen years. Most of the data reported in this book have been collected in interview surveys carried out since the end of World War II by the Survey Research Center of the University of Michigan and directed by the author and his associates.[3]

A few years ago the author attempted a first systematic presentation of economic psychology. In his book *Psychological Analysis of Economic Behavior,* he said that the work was premature in the sense that not enough was known to present a theory of economic psychology. Yet the book was written to make certain specific notions and findings available to others and to stimulate them to study psychological problems of the economy. In this hope the author was not disappointed. Theorizing has made some progress since 1950, and a fair amount of new research has been carried out since then. Although this book has the same starting point as the other, there is practically no duplication. With only brief references to what was shown earlier, ideas and arguments not available in 1950 are presented here. The empirical material which constitutes the bulk of this book was not presented in the earlier one.

[3] The methods of these surveys, conducted with representative samples of consumers, will be described in the Appendix.

CHAPTER 2

Consumer Latitude

Elementary textbooks of economics teach us that the purpose of all production is consumption. "The consumer is king"—so goes an old saying. Yet during the past fifty years, scholars have assigned the consumer a minor role in the economy. Of the three major sectors of the economy, two, the business and government sectors, have been recognized as having power and influence to generate income and thus to contribute to the growth of the economy. These functions have been denied the consumer sector. More specifically, fluctuations in business activity have been thought to originate in injections of money into the economy through business investment and government deficits, or in the diminution of money flow through reduced business spending and government surpluses. New trends arising through business or government activities have been thought to be transmitted to the consumer sector, but it has been assumed that changes may not originate there.

Two propositions are implicit in much of modern economic analysis and make it understandable why little attention has been given to consumer behavior. The first says that consumer incomes depend on the activities of business and government; the second, that consumer expenditures depend on consumer incomes. The first proposition appears obvious on the basis that, with the exception of relatively small payments for services, consumers do not derive their incomes from other consumers. Overwhelmingly, wages, salaries, and profits paid out by business firms make up consumers' income.

The second proposition was most clearly formulated by Lord Keynes, who postulated that the propensity to spend is a fairly stable function of income. Statistical studies have confirmed that in the aggregate consumers spend most of what they make and that the proportion of total personal incomes spent does not vary greatly over the long run.

Objections to the second proposition will constitute the major topic of this chapter, even though we shall also raise the following question regarding the first proposition: Is it not possible that consumers who have great needs work harder and raise their income? If this were the case, not only would consumer expenditures depend on incomes but, to

10

some extent, incomes would also depend on consumer expenditures. First, however, we shall be concerned with the fact that over the short run the proportion of income spent on certain consumer goods may fluctuate greatly.

Economies are conceivable in which consumer expenditures do depend solely on consumer income. Indeed, as of fifty or one hundred years ago in the United States, and even today in many countries, this may constitute a fair approximation of the actual situation. We may think of a poor economy in which most people devote all their income to subsistence. Whatever people earn they spend on food, shelter, and clothing in order barely to survive. In such a situation consumer discretion is absent. In feudal societies it is the landowning gentry, and in early industrial societies the few great entrepreneurs, who direct the economy. But in the United States today the role of the consumer is fundamentally different. Several major recent developments have substantially increased the power of American consumers by allowing them freedom to ~~advance~~ *speed up* or delay their purchases and to spend either above or below their current incomes.

Recent Changes in the Role of the Consumer

First, there has been what some analysts have called an income revolution. We now have broad middle- and upper-middle-income groups rather than masses of poor people and a few very rich ones. Whether or not the proportion and influence of the very rich have diminished, as some believe, is not important for our purposes. What is relevant is that millions of families now have "supernumerary incomes." They are in a position to spend money on things other than necessities. If they so choose they can increase or decrease their rate of spending.

In 1957 over 38 per cent of the 53½ million American families (and unattached individuals) had an annual income of over $6,000. Their total income represented almost two-thirds of the nation's total personal income of $332 billion. Does this represent any substantial difference from earlier years? Unfortunately survey research, which provides the information on income distribution, is of fairly recent origin. Yet data are available for 1944 and indicate the effects of recent developments. A problem arises, of course, because of inflation: the 1944 dollar was worth much more than the 1957 dollar. To compensate for this difference, $4,000 was considered to be the lower limit of supernumerary income in 1944; $6,000, in 1957. On this basis 20½ million families are found to have had supernumerary incomes in 1957 as against 12 million in 1944.

Since retail prices rose by about 60 per cent from 1944 to 1957, the $220 billion total annual income of the 20½ million families in 1957 might more appropriately be compared with $135 billion rather than $84 billion for the 12 million families in 1944. Even so, there can be no doubt that the number of families in a position to make discretionary expenditures, and the amount of money at their disposal, have increased very substantially in the course of but twelve years. And this increase has not been due to the very rich. It is not the number and resources of people with very high incomes alone which have grown. The major difference is in the number and resources of families who in 1957 had an annual income between $7,500 and $15,000.

Beyond this important change, American consumers today have a larger amount of reserve funds than ever before. Prior to the Second World War

TABLE 1. INCREASE IN FAMILIES WITH SUPERNUMERARY INCOMES

Year	Limits set for supernumerary income	Number of families* with supernumerary income	Total annual income of these families
1944	Over $4,000 annual income	12 million	$ 84 billion
1957	Over $6,000 annual income	20.5 million	220 billion

* A family consists of related people living together; a single person may constitute a family.

NOTE: These calculations, made through adjusting data from the Surveys of Consumer Finances and from Census Bureau surveys through the use of Internal Revenue Service data, are more complete than the survey distributions in later parts of this book. In survey distributions somewhat fewer family units are considered.

SOURCE: S. F. Goldsmith, *Survey of Current Business*, April, 1959.

total liquid assets of American families—bank deposits, bonds, currency, and the like, exclusive of business funds—were estimated at $45 billion with most families having no bank deposits or government bonds. During World War II about three out of every four families acquired some government savings bonds or savings accounts, and total personal liquid assets rose to $145 billion. During the following twelve years of substantial consumer spending the rate of growth of savings was much slower. Yet liquid reserves did not decline. In 1957 approximately $175 billion were available in savings or reserve funds. About one-fourth of all American families had no such funds in 1957, and about 30 per cent had less than $500 worth. But at least 20 per cent had between $500 and $2,000 and close to 25 per cent more than $2,000 in reserve funds.

Next there is the fact that buying on credit is today a generally accepted and widely practiced form of behavior. Homes purchased for owner occupancy are paid for over many years by obtaining mortgage credit, automobiles are paid for over two to three years by buying on installment, and many other larger purchases are likewise frequently financed through borrowing. The number of one-family houses owned by their occupants rose by 10 million from 1946 to 1957, and the majority of home purchases are financed by a mortgage. Ownership of automobiles, washing machines, refrigerators, and the like increased greatly, and close to two-thirds of the cars and one-half of the other durables, altogether over one-fifth of total retail purchases, are made on credit.[1] In 1957, 47 per cent of all families had some installment debt; 30 per cent, some other personal debt; 35 per cent, mortgage debt. Eliminating duplications, about two-thirds of all families had some kind of debt.

The easy availability of credit and the psychological acceptance of credit buying mean, of course, that consumers may, if they so choose, spend more in any given year than their current income and their current liquid reserves.

Still another significant change in consumer spending over the past fifty years is the importance attached to durable and nonperishable goods by consumers. The automobile is, of course, the most important single item, nonexistent in the nineteenth century and now an inevitably necessary possession and expenditure for most families. So are television sets, refrigerators, and some other household appliances.

When a society spends all its income on perishable goods, such as food; on semidurables, such as clothing; and on services covering short periods, such as rent; its discretion in postponing purchases or in buying in advance of immediate needs is severely limited. This is not true of the purchases of durable goods, nor of many other discretionary expenditures. Some of what we spend on services and many of our expenditures on recreation, vacations, and luxuries are postponable. Alternatively, these expenses may be increased substantially depending both on our resources and our frame of mind.

Finally, it is important for any consideration of the greater influence of the consumer on the economy to note that the economic intelligence of the American people has increased greatly. Through the media of mass communication—some of which, radio and TV, are fairly new—people all over the country and in all walks of life now receive some economic news. News, whether good or bad, spreads rapidly and, because of the centralized nature of news sources, fairly uniformly. Consumer discretion could hardly be exercised so as to influence the economy if broad masses of people were entirely uninformed about economic events.

[1] These statistics do not reveal the full scope of buying on *credit*. Many of the houses and cars not bought on credit were not bought for cash either but represented an exchange (in the case of cars much of the payment consisted of trade-ins). In addition, many cars fully paid in cash are jalopies costing less than $250.

Different Forms of Consumer Behavior

It is possible, then, for American consumers to have substantial discretion of action in the United States today. Because of (1) the existence of broad groups of consumers with income in excess of what is needed for bare necessities, (2) liquid-asset holdings, (3) the availability of credit, and (4) the spending of substantial amounts on durable goods—and also because they may all be influenced by the same economic information at the same time—consumers are potentially an important factor in the economy and may influence its fluctuations. The extent to which consumers actually exercise their discretionary power is subject to limiting factors. These may best be explained by distinguishing types of expenditures which differ from one another from the behavioral point of view. Some forms of consumer behavior are much more susceptible to change under the impact of changing attitudes and expectations than other forms of behavior.

According to traditional notions, consumers may dispose of their incomes in either of two ways: they may spend or they may save. In analyzing consumer money outlays we cannot rest content with this simple distinction. Both spending and saving may be contractual or habitual, and therefore not subject to a genuine decision at the time of the transaction. Alternatively, there are outlays of choice both among amounts spent and amounts saved.

Many outlays by consumers are contractually set and do not require a new decision to be carried out. Many of these are classified as amounts saved rather than amounts spent. The repayment of mortgages, of installment and other debts, as well as payments of life insurance premiums, when the debts and the insurance policies are already in effect, are major examples of contractual outlays which may not depend on developments during the period of the payments. Only under catastrophic conditions does the possibility of choice and decision making arise (should I or should I not pay the amounts due?). Defaults of such payments are rare during most cyclical fluctuations. Similar contractual payments, classified as expenditures rather than savings, are represented by a multitude of dues and charges, as well as by rent and by real estate taxes and interest on the part of homeowners.

Expenditures on necessities are in many respects similar to contractual obligations. Even though it cannot be determined exactly what is and what is not a necessary expenditure, it is no doubt true that basic outlays, not only for shelter but also for food and clothing, will continue to be made except under catastrophic circumstances. The same applies to payments for such services as gas and electricity and for many medical expenses. In other words, the leeway of consumers to restrict a great portion of their money outlays is severely limited. Limitations exist also regarding the possibility of a substantial increase in these expenditures, partly because some of these outlays are not indefinitely expandable and, more important, because expenditures on food and clothing and on many other things are frequently habitual. Some consumer outlays are subject to the influence of relatively enduring and slowly changing habits, while others are not.

In addition to money outlays that are contractual, necessary, or habitual, there are discretionary outlays. Some of these represent expenditures, some savings. We thus arrive at the following fourfold division of consumer money outlays: [2]

CLASSIFICATION OF CONSUMER MONEY OUTLAYS

Kind of outlay	Spending	Saving
Outlays determined by past decisions or habits	Necessities, convenience goods, habitual and contractual expenditures	Contractual and habitual saving
Outlays of choice........	Discretionary expenditures	Discretionary saving

Outlays determined by past decisions or by habits are less variable and are easier to predict than outlays of choice. Of money spent on food or rent and of money saved by repaying debt or paying life insurance premiums, it holds good that the outlays made in the preceding period represent a fair prediction for estimating the outlays in the next period. There will, of course, be some differences from year to year in the amounts involved, but the changes will depend primarily upon changes in income. These two segments of our classification are, typically, a function of income. It is not here then that we can look for a clue to consumer discretion and consumer contributions to promoting or impeding economic activity.

A third way of disposing of income is in discretionary saving. We shall show in Chapter 7 that this, too, is an unrewarding field in which to search for the key to the problem. Additions to bank accounts and purchases of securities, or real estate, are usually discretionary decisions, but they do not initiate cyclical fluctuations and are not systematically connected with them. There remains but one area in which to search for the source of consumer influence on the economy—discretionary consumer spending.

[2] See G. Katona, in L. R. Klein (Ed.), *Contributions of Survey Methods to Economics.*

Consumer Investment Expenditures

Discretionary consumer expenditures are postponable, and the goods purchased through such expenditures are storable. The timing of these expenditures is not fully determined by developments in the environment; they can be made later than needed or, alternatively, in advance and in excess of needs. They include many purchases of automobiles, household appliances, and furniture, as well as additions and large repairs to homes, vacation trips, some educational expenses, and a variety of luxury items in connection with hobbies, recreation, and travel. Not all expenditures on cars, appliances, or repairs are discretionary. For example, a person may buy a car because his car has been stolen or because he habitually buys a new car every two years. But these are exceptions—as there are, of course, some discretionary purchases of clothing items and even of food.

Statistical data about the total of discretionary consumer expenditures are not available. In our quantitative studies, therefore, we shall deal with consumer expenditures on durable goods—automobiles, appliances, and furniture—or, alternatively, with what has been called consumer investment expenditures, which include durable goods as well as additions and large repairs to homes.

Purchases of homes for owner occupancy represent, of course, most important genuine decisions. They are not included under investment *expenditures* because money put into the purchase of a house is viewed as money saved. Nevertheless, we shall be concerned with consumer decisions to buy or build a house, and also to move. Consumer discretion is exercised in most of these decisions. Also, they are frequently connected with an array of discretionary expenditures, such as additions and repairs, and purchases of furniture and other durable goods.

Discretionary expenditures are characterized by the following three features:

1. There is no compelling need to make these expenditures at a given time. Most purchases of automobiles and large household appliances are replacement purchases and are usually made before the old piece of equipment becomes unusable. Articles in fairly good condition and even in excellent condition are replaced by newer and better ones, the timing of replacements being a matter of discretion. Even when the occasion for a purchase is the inadequate functioning of an old piece of equipment, the consumer usually has the choice between repairing or buying. First purchases of automobiles and first purchases of traditional household appliances, usually made by young people, are likewise often discretionary

in their timing. Purchases of newer durable goods—room air conditioners, garbage disposals, or clothes dryers, for instance—depend by their very nature on something other than compelling need.

2. Discretionary expenditures are usually not governed by habit. Since habits generally derive from frequently repeated performance and most durable goods are usually bought once in several years, this point needs little elaboration. There are people who habitually trade in their cars every year or, more frequently, every second or third year. But even in these cases there usually exists an element of deliberate choice. In the case of vacations, to mention another example, the timing may be habitual, and yet there is usually considerable discretion regarding their nature and duration which determine the amounts spent.

3. Discretionary purchases are usually not made on the spur of the moment, but rather after considerable deliberation and discussion among family members. The planning period may, of course, be fairly short. Usually several months, rarely as long as a year, elapse between the arousal of the idea and the conclusion of the purchase. When there were much shorter intervals between first thinking about buying a car or a refrigerator, for instance, and actually doing so, it was found that either the purchase was not discretionary or there were special opportunities for making an advantageous purchase. Exceptional circumstances characterize most transactions in which a single visit by a salesman or one advertisement are successful both in awakening a need and in clinching the sale. Also, relatively inexpensive items—a piece of occasional furniture or a table radio, for instance—are often bought without any extensive planning period. Yet the question Should I or should I not buy?, the decision about which of several conflicting needs should have priority, and above all, concern about the timing of the purchase occur in most durable-goods purchases. The same is true, of course, of large repairs, improvements and additions to the house and of the purchase of a number of expensive luxury items, such as a yacht, a motorboat, a summer home, or power tools.

Discretionary expenditures, then, are not inevitably necessary, not habitual, and not made on the spur of the moment. It follows that there is no clear and direct relationship between the circumstances or occasions of such purchases and the purchases themselves. Intervening variables mediate between the stimulus and the reponse. The buyer, as a result of his past experience, his personality, and his group belonging, plays a role both in evaluating the circumstances and in shaping his reactions to them. It therefore becomes essential to study changes in motives, opinions, attitudes, and expectations in order to understand changes in discretionary expenditures.

Close to one-half of all American families made a major expenditure for durable goods in every year between 1950 and 1957.[3] The lower the age and the higher the income of the buyer, the more frequent are these expenditures. But the proportion of income spent on durable goods does not rise with income. As J. N. Morgan has shown, unlike any other country and period, in postwar America people spent a constant proportion of their income on consumer investment items at all income levels—except for the very lowest (under $1,000 annual family income) and the very highest (over $7,500 income). If summer cottages, motorboats, and other luxury items—for which no statistical data were available to Morgan— had been included among investment expenditures, probably the proportion of income spent would not have been lower even at the highest levels of income. However this may be, durable expenditures today have similar importance in the budget of fairly affluent people as in that of people with moderate means. In this respect they differ from necessities as well as from luxuries (and also differ from amounts saved, since the proportion of income saved goes up with income).

The Commerce Department in setting up the national accounts divides consumer expenditures into three categories—durables, nondurables, and services. The first category is somewhat too inclusive for our purposes because it contains a fair number of small items—toasters, china and tableware, linen, floor coverings and other home furnishings—which represent substantial amounts in the aggregate but rarely in terms of a single purchase by an individual family. Tires, tubes, and parts for automobiles are also included among durable goods, although these are mostly necessary rather than discretionary purchases. On the other hand, the category of durable goods is not broad enough to represent discretionary expenditures, because it excludes improvements and additions to homes and, naturally, vacation and travel expenses. Nevertheless, it is worth mentioning that over the last few years durable goods expenditures, as defined by the Commerce Department, represented about 13 per cent of all consumer expenditures and fluctuated much more widely than other consumer expenditures. The proportion of income spent on nondurables remained fairly stable over several years while the proportion of income spent on services showed a steady increase. The increase was due partly to a disproportionate advance in the cost of services and partly to larger spending on the home, education, and travel, as well as other discretionary items.

[3] Detailed statistical data on expenditures for durable goods, taken from the Surveys of Consumer Finances, have been published in the *Federal Reserve Bulletin* of July, 1958. See also, J. N. Morgan, "Consumer Investment Expenditures" and Chapter 11 of this book.

The Dynamic Elements of the Economy

We have found that in order to understand variability in consumer behavior the traditional dichotomy of spending and saving and the uniform treatment of all consumer expenditures do not suffice. Similarly, in order to focus our attention on the dynamic factors that make for instability of our economy, we cannot remain satisfied with the usual division of Gross National Product (GNP) into three sectors—consumers, business, and government. In our national accounts as prepared by the Commerce Department, GNP, the total of all money spent on goods and services, is broken down into those three sectors of the economy. This breakdown for 1957, for instance, is shown in Table 2.

TABLE 2. NATIONAL ACCOUNTS FOR 1957

Receipts	In billion dollars	Expenditures	In billion dollars
Personal disposable income....	300	Personal consumption expenditures	280
Business gross retained income..	44	Gross private domestic investment.....................	64
Government net receipts.......	88	Government purchases	87
Statistical discrepancy.........	2	Net foreign investment.......	3
Gross National Product......	434	Gross National Product......	434

SOURCE: U.S. Department of Commerce.

The expenditures of the consumer sector represent close to two-thirds of all expenditures, much more than the expenditures of the business and the government sectors. It is hardly surprising that quarterly or annual fluctuations of this great proportion of the total usually correspond closely with the fluctuations of GNP. Further, it is seen in Table 2 that most of what consumers make they spend. Except during years of war, consumers year after year spend at least 90 per cent of their incomes, and a proportion of 90 per cent necessarily correlates quite closely with the total of 100 per cent.

What has been said about habitual actions and genuine decisions of consumers applies to business behavior as well. Naturally, a substantial proportion of expenses of business firms is contractual, and further proportions represent expenses necessary to stay in business as well as those which are habitual. The table presented above which divides the Gross National Product omits most of these payments since, to avoid duplications, it considers outlays from gross retained earnings of business rather than outlays from total business receipts.

Not all the expenditures included in the Gross National Product are equally relevant for the study of cyclical fluctuations in economic activity. We may single out from the three sectors of the economy five principal areas of discretion and variability. It is in these areas that behavior is most susceptible to the influence of changing motives, attitudes, and expectations:

> Increases or decreases in government receipts or expenditures
> Increases or decreases in business inventories
> Expenditures for business plant and equipment
> Expenditures for residential construction
> Expenditures for consumer durable goods

Changes in the amount of money the government injects into the economy have traditionally been accepted as a major factor in economic fluctuations. More recently fiscal policy has been viewed as a method through which the government may exert a countercyclical influence. Through increased spending, say, for defense or public works, through tax reductions or, contrariwise, through economizing and increasing taxes, the government may expand or restrict the flow of income. Fiscal policy is, of course, influenced by many considerations not connected with business cycles, as for instance, by increased or decreased defense requirements. Additional expenditures may add fuel to the fire if they occur in inflationary times and may act in the proper direction if they occur in times of recession. Furthermore, some of the changes in the government's contribution to stabilizing the income flow are automatic rather than discretionary. Tax receipts rise when profits and incomes go up and fall when profits and incomes decline. Both of these automatic effects are desirable, as are the effects of other "automatic stabilizers," primarily, the social security legislation. Unemployment benefits increase the money available to people when money is needed most, namely, when there is depression with a high degree of unemployment. Thus many of the fluctuations in the relation of government receipts to expenditures must be viewed as nondiscretionary. There remains nonetheless substantial latitude of financial action on the part of the government.

The same is true of business inventory policy. Involuntary changes in inventories do occur since business stocks grow when sales fall unexpectedly and decline when sales increase unexpectedly. But genuine decisions to cut down on the volume of inventories or to build up the pipelines are often taken by manufacturers, wholesalers, and retailers alike. The changes involved may amount to as much as several billion dollars within a relatively short period of time.

Business capital expenditures—amounting to about $30 billion in 1957 —represent, in part, carrying out previous decisions or following habitual practices. Nevertheless, again in the order of magnitude of a few billion dollars, swift changes in the pace of capital outlays may be made according to the sentiment of business leaders.

In the important field of construction, certain potentially variable elements, such as the erection of public buildings and schools or the construction of highways, depend upon the government sector of the economy, be it Federal, state, or local. Other elements, such as the construction of factories and office buildings, which are also subject to sudden expansion or contraction, represent business investments. There remains the area of residential construction, which is likewise frequently viewed as an activity of business, the fluctuations of which depend on the ability and willingness of builders to invest and to speculate. Yet the willingness of consumers to purchase new houses certainly plays a role. Speculative builders determine their rate of activity according to both past consumer demand and their views about prospective consumer demand. That demand, in turn, is influenced by consumer sentiment, for instance, by people's notions as to whether a given moment represents a good or a bad time to buy a house. Certainly, of the recent annual expenditure of approximately $15 billion on nonfarm residential construction some portion was necessary or habitual. It is equally certain that this economic activity may be stepped up or lowered to a significant extent as the result of genuine decisions of consumers regarding their housing needs and the appropriate time to gratify them.

Turning, finally, to discretionary spending by consumers we find that consumer expenditures on durable goods amounted to $35 billion in 1957. Among these there were, of course, some which were habitual, necessary, or even inevitable, as for example, replacing a wrecked car which is needed for commuting to work. Yet annual fluctuations in such expenditures, again in the order of magnitude of several billion dollars, must be assumed to be discretionary. They may or may not follow the trend either of consumer incomes or of business activity.

On the economic scene the marginal effect matters. Relatively small changes may make the difference between an upturn and a downturn. Any one of the three sectors of the economy—government, business, or consumers—may provide the spark for a change of direction or may transmit changes originating in any other sector. While the role of business and government in initiating changes in economic activity has been given wide recognition, the influence of consumers and of consumer sentiment has been neglected in the past. Before presenting empirical findings on changes in consumer sentiment and their relation to changes in economic activity, we shall discuss briefly the various theoretical approaches to an explanation of fluctuations in consumer expenditures on durable goods.

Theories of Fluctuations in Expenditures on Durables

Three theories may be distinguished. Traditionally, increases or decreases in consumer demand have been attributed to changes in *income*. In addition, changes in *needs* may be thought to account for fluctuations of consumer spending. We shall discuss these theories briefly and contrast them with the theory of psychological economics which attributes to the *willingness to buy* a role in determining changes in expenditures on consumer durables.

According to the first theory, all consumer expenditures, including expenditures on durables, are a function of income. Income differences explain the differences in the behavior of different families at the same time: the higher the income, the larger the absolute amount of expenditures. More important, in studying the behavior of all people at different periods, durable-goods purchases are assumed to increase when income goes up and to decline when income is reduced. Consumers are marionettes who do their spending according to what they make. Individual families may behave differently, but these differences cancel out and do not influence the economy.

If this were the entire explanation, changes in the *proportion* of income spent on durables, as they occur from one period to the next, would not be accounted for. We turn therefore to a more sophisticated theory as expressed in the famous "psychological law" of J. M. Keynes (see his *General Theory*). In simplest terms, the law says that when a family's income increases or decreases, the rate of expenditure will not immediately be adjusted to the new income level because spending habits change slowly and gradually. Since what is not spent is saved, it follows that for a time at least the proportion of income saved would increase with an increase in income and vice versa. This would be true not only of individual families but of the nation, and Keynes formulated his theory in terms of the entire economy: when national income rises, the temporary stability of sticky expenditures causes the proportion of income spent to decrease, and the reverse is true when national income declines. Although this "law" introduces the factor of a lag in adjusting to income changes, it leaves untouched the basic theory that income and its changes alone are relevant to explain fluctuations in spending.

Three major counterarguments may be raised against the Keynesian position.[4] First, Keynes' view that habitual practices influence all consumer expenditures may have been correct fifty or one hundred years ago when incomes were spent mostly on nondurables and services. But today in the United States expenditures on durables are important and are usually not habitual. Possibly, then, these expenditures should behave in the same manner as savings are assumed to behave: an increment in income, not used for habitual expenditures, would then be used either for durable goods or for saving; when income declines, habitual expenditures are not immediately adjusted downward and therefore less money remains either for durables or for saving. In other words, it might be held that either amounts saved or expenditures on durables would increase disproportionately when national income goes up and decrease disproportionately when it goes down. Such a view, which would represent a substantial departure from Keynesian principles, would not differentiate between expenditures on durable goods and amounts saved.

The second major objection to Keynes' psychological law is that adjustments to income increases cannot be considered as merely the reverse of adjustments to income decreases. The effects of reward are usually not just the opposite of the effects of punishment. It is conceivable that delay in adjusting habitual expenditures to income changes may prevail in the one case, but not in the other. Part of the Keynesian argument appears well supported by studies of noneconomic behavior: habits are sticky under the impact of adverse developments; it is a hardship to abandon pleasurable practices which have become part and parcel of a person's manner of living. Therefore it would be understandable if adjustments of usual expenditure patterns to income declines, subjectively a most difficult process, were delayed as long as possible. When, however, income goes up, habits acquired during a period of previous lower-income levels may not be sticky. Upward adjustments of living standards are pleasurable and easy. Such adjustments may be instantaneous or may even occur prior to the income increases as an effect of expectations. This possibility brings us to our third objection to Keynes' psychological law.

Although he places great weight on the role of expectations in business behavior, Keynes disregards expectations in explaining consumer behavior. He argues that while some people expect income increases, others expect decreases, and the two expectations will usually cancel out and therefore not affect the economy. This again may have been justified in the nineteenth century when most people who were not entrepreneurs were uninformed about business developments and were not subjected to fairly uniform news transmitted by mass media. Today, however, changes in

[4] Arguments presented in Chapter 7 of *Psychological Analysis of Economic Behavior* by G. Katona are summarized here.

consumer expectations tend to be uniform and to spread rather than to cancel out. Therefore we cannot accept a theory which explains fluctuations of durable goods expenditures in terms of past income changes alone and ignores expectations.

A second theory purporting to explain fluctuations in expenditures on durable goods maintains that they are a function of *needs*. Income, of course, remains important as an enabling condition; needs without resources cannot be transformed into demand. But given income, it is need which makes for purchases and absence of need which causes abstention from buying. Need is assumed to be absent after it has been gratified and to be pronounced when it has not been gratified for a prolonged period. This is a dynamic theory in the sense that it could well serve to explain reversals in trends of business cycles. But the theory could hardly explain the fact that occasionally demand for durable goods remains stable over prolonged periods. Most important, the psychological basis of the theory cannot be accepted.

Prosperous times are characterized by frequent large purchases, that is, by thousands and thousands of people satisfying their needs for automobiles and other goods. In other words, according to the theory, in prosperous times people's needs become saturated. Prosperity would then be its own gravedigger. Following the satisfaction of very many people's needs, the inevitable result would be an absence of needs and a depression. By the same token, a depression would automatically generate forces to overcome itself. After a prolonged absence of satisfaction, needs would necessarily arise, set off a buying spree, and restore prosperity.

But is it generally true that after we have what we want our needs are saturated? Yes, if a hungry man gets a big meal the need for food disappears. But what is true of biological motives is not necessarily true of social motives. Accomplishment tends to raise levels of aspiration. Having achieved what we want, we often raise our sights. It is not the gratification of needs but failure and frustration which make us renounce further goals and ambitions. If we repeatedly fail to achieve what we want, our drives and motives tend to wither away and we cease to strive for more.[5]

To be sure, after buying a car, for some time to come we shall not need or desire another car. But usually we desire many things and not just one. After buying the car, the other needs may come to the fore. The satisfaction of one need may lead to striving to satisfy other needs or desires. Prosperity may then continue and need not automatically reverse itself.

Depression, on the other hand, is characterized by failure and disappointment. When thousands of people fail to satisfy their needs, even

---

[5] The problem of saturation will be discussed more extensively in Chapter 8.

strivings and desires may be impaired. Since it is not the have-nots who feel the greatest need for automobiles, household appliances, and the like, and since it is not those who have the least who transform their needs into demand, recovery from depression is, unfortunately, not automatic.

Willingness to Buy

The need theory does not suffice. It does not explain the circumstances under which the gratification of needs does lead to saturation and those under which it does not. For the third explanation of fluctuations in discretionary expenditures we turn then to the theory that they are partly a function of the willingness to buy. Psychological economics, of course, recognizes the function of income and resources, that is, of the ability to buy and of variations in such ability. It goes further, however. It says that there may also be fluctuations in willingness to buy, independent of fluctuations in ability to buy, and that they, too, influence demand.

Needs are widespread. Few of us have everything we need, and practically none of us everything we want. The crucial questions concern the subjective saliency of needs and the transformation of needs into demand. Under what circumstances will desires push us strongly toward action? When we are optimistic, confident, and secure. When will we feel saturated and cease to strive for more and better things? When we are pessimistic, distrustful, and insecure.

Consumers' discretionary expenditures are a function of attitudes in several areas. Attitudes toward one's personal financial situation are important but do not tell the whole story. It is relevant whether we feel that our income and personal situation have improved and will improve further. But beyond that, each of us is a member of a group. We feel that our own well-being and progress are influenced by what happens to others with whom we are personally associated, as well as by what happens to our community and country. Even if we ourselves are not directly affected, unfavorable developments in the broader systems to which we belong make us uneasy and favorable developments stimulate us. Therefore, if we are to understand the factors influencing consumer behavior, we must study the attitudes of the people toward the entire economy and their expectations as to what will happen to the economy.

The theory of willingness to buy is a refinement of, rather than a substitute for, the first two theories. It presents the conditions under which changes in expenditures do lag behind changes in income as Keynes has postulated. It also discloses the conditions under which the opposite result takes place, and actions may even precede income changes. The psychological theory will indicate that saturation with goods is an attitude which may arise under certain conditions but need not arise even when there is repeated gratification of needs. Thus the theory aims to show the scope as well as the limits of consumer discretion in economic behavior.

What psychological economics postulates is that changes in consumer attitudes and expectations are capable of influencing the proportion of income spent on discretionary purchases and sometimes, often at crucial times, do so. It does not assume that changes in discretionary expenditures are always independent of changes in income. On the contrary, it will be shown that at certain times the rate of discretionary purchases seems to be governed by income alone. These are times when attitudes primarily reflect income developments and are not of crucial importance. But there are also times when changes in sentiment and confidence due to other factors govern the economic scene.

Postwar Conditions and Attitudes

Up to now we have been concerned with short-run fluctuations in economic attitudes as related to expenditures on durables. Yet there is more to the study of attitudes than is relevant to studies of business cycles. It appears that several phases of one business cycle, possibly even several consecutive cycles, though varying in degrees of optimism and pessimism, are characterized by similar sociopsychological sets and attitudes.

Three sets of conditions have influenced American society and economy in the decade after World War II, a period characterized by a high level of durable-goods purchasing. All three differ fundamentally from conditions existing before the war.

First, following World War II the American people on the whole were optimistic and confident. They believed that they were moving ahead. Regarding what their economic situation would be in five or ten years, only two opinions were widespread: income and standard of living would either remain the same or go still higher. With the exception of older people, practically nobody expected his situation to get worse. Severe depressions were thought not to be in the cards. People trusted that government and business had learned how to prevent depressions. Therefore people became "thing-minded." They were anxious to acquire more and more of the good things of life and to upgrade their possessions.

Higher incomes went hand in hand with shorter working hours. Long week ends became the rule, paid vacations commonplace. Leisure time stimulated a great variety of activities, practically all of them expensive. Instead of sitting at home with a book or newspaper, the common pastimes became driving around by car and eating out, going on fishing trips and staying in motels, and working with power tools to make furniture or to improve the home. Watching television was one of the least expensive of the leisure-time activities.

Desires and needs for more and more things and more and more expensive activities had their impact on striving for higher incomes. Husbands looked for higher pay or second jobs, and wives returned to work when their children grew up. Ruth Mack presented convincing arguments indicating that consumer interests and standards did influence income. Consumer enterprise and thing-mindedness made income a function of expenditures on the part of some, perhaps many, families.[6]

Second, the baby boom and the rapid growth in population, begun in 1940, continued apace. In the fifties, the great new development consisted of a substantial increase of three- and four-children families and a decrease in the number of families with no children or an only child. The population increase was far from uniform throughout the country. Internal migration was very substantial. In the fifties, 85 per cent of the population growth occurred in what statisticians call metropolitan areas (cities with 50,000 population and the environs). There was practically no population increase in rural areas and small towns not adjacent to large cities. And within metropolitan areas the central cities did not grow. A significant postwar event was the growth of suburbs.

The impact of suburbia on consumer behavior can hardly be overstated. We refer now not to such things as the increased demand for casual wear which caused a change in the clothing industry, but to the very greatly increased demand for durable goods. Young people chose to marry early, to have several children in the early years of marriage, to live in what they call nice neighborhoods, and to have cars, washing machines, refrigerators, television sets, and several other appliances at the same time. That they did so decide was, of course, not unrelated to their optimistic and confident mood. That they did not raise the question Should we have babies or the material things we want? but embarked on having both was made possible primarily by installment buying, which came to be seen as a necessary part of the American way of life. Moving to suburbs or new subdivisions and having several children created new needs and again stimulated striving for higher incomes.

The third lasting characteristic of the postwar years was inflation. Not only did most prices rise much of the time, but most people were fully aware of everything having become much more expensive than five or ten or twenty years earlier. People disliked and resented the price increases. They considered the raise in their wages, salaries, and profits as rewards for their accomplishments, as something due them. The higher cost of living took away from the fruits of their work. Price increases were seen as "bad," price stability as well as price declines as "good." These

[6] R. P. Mack, "Trends in American Consumption and the Aspiration to Consume."

beliefs led to unfavorable reactions, especially in the purchase of durable goods, at times when prices were felt to have increased rapidly. Optimism and confidence were occasionally weakened or even interrupted by inflationary experiences. Then consumers hesitated and postponed buying. Their behavior thus helped to arrest galloping inflation, though it did not suffice to avert creeping inflation.

PART TWO

Attitude Change

CHAPTER 3

Consumer Attitudes and Demand for Durable Goods

How did the economic attitudes of the American people change in the course of the years following World War II? How were these changes related to fluctuations in economic activities? Let us look at the answers to these questions as revealed by the interview surveys conducted by the Survey Research Center during those years.

Obviously, it is impossible to give a full account of the economic fluctuations from 1945 to 1958 in a brief chapter. Attention will be given primarily to changes in consumer purchases of durable goods, while other aspects of business cycles will be neglected. The purpose of the chapter is to present an overview of the evidence which supports the thesis about a relationship between changes in attitudes and in discretionary expenditures by consumers.

After the End of World War II

Early in 1945, after more than three years of desperate struggle and heartbreak, victory appeared certain and the end of war imminent. The rapid reconquest of France during the second half of 1944 was followed by a last desperate attack by the Nazis. When that attack fizzled out in the Argonne Forest, economists and statisticians in a multitude of Washington offices stopped worrying about problems of the war economy. Even though it was generally assumed that the war against Japan would not end quickly, all thoughts turned toward problems of reconversion. What would happen to the American economy when the war was over? How would the transition to a peacetime economy be accomplished? These were the big questions in the spring of 1945.

Most experts came forth with the same definite prediction: there would be an economic crisis; there would be substantial unemployment. After the surrender of the enemy, soldiers, sailors, and airmen would be demobilized quickly. Orders for tanks, ships, and planes would be canceled, and American industry would discharge millions of workers. The reconversion

31

of plants to the production of civilian goods would take time, and demand for civilian goods, even though it would rise, would not compensate for war orders.

There were a few dissenting voices. Some economists predicted rapid inflation. During the war unprecedentedly large proportions of income had been saved. For several years in succession people had saved approximately one-fourth of what they had earned, and most of this money had been put into war bonds and bank deposits which could be cashed or withdrawn without delay. When people would be spending both their incomes and their accumulated liquid assets, demand would exceed the supply of goods and runaway inflation would develop.

Both predictions proved to be false. True, war production did cease after Japan's surrender, and demobilization proceeded at a fairly rapid pace. The reconversion of plants, making possible the resumption of output of consumer durables, took a long time. Still postwar unemployment did not come near the predicted level of 6 to 10 million. Many women and older workers were glad to stop working, and many factories, remembering their wartime struggle with a shortage of workers, kept on some of their employees during reconversion. Civilian demand grew much more rapidly than expected—and still inflation was kept within bounds.

Legally the approximately $100 billion worth of savings accumulated by the American people during World War II were liquid; psychologically they were not. It was shown through wartime surveys that people did not feel that they were forced to save during the war. On the contrary, they felt happy that higher incomes made it possible for them to accumulate some reserve funds after the terrible depression of the thirties. Reserves against future contingencies were thought to be necessary and not to be spent lightheartedly. Such reserves were considered to be exchangeable against permanent possessions—to buy a house or a business, for instance, was seen as a legitimate use of savings—but were not to be spent for daily needs or even for automobiles and household appliances.

Yet there was change from war to peace. A survey conducted early in 1946 revealed that the desire to spend and to acquire consumer goods had become much stronger and the desire to save weaker. Within a short time after the end of the war the proportion of income saved fell greatly. But for the total population spending never exceeded incomes. In none of the postwar years were the aggregate liquid asset holdings reduced. The greater rate of spending promoted prosperity and restricted unemployment, but without causing runaway inflation. There was some inflation when the patriotic restraint to spending disappeared and price controls were lifted, but nothing comparable to what happened in many countries in other continents. The people's spending spree was limited by their desire to keep their savings intact and by their undisturbed confidence and trust in the value of the dollar.

One further finding of survey research obtained toward the end of the war, as well as in the first few postwar years, is of particular interest. In contrast to the experts, people on the whole were optimistic about the economic developments which would take place after victory was achieved. They believed that the end of war could have only good consequences. They believed that their income, held down by wage controls during the war, would rise when the war was over. In 1946 and 1947 they maintained their confident attitudes. They expected to improve their standard of living and did not fear recession.[1]

At that time, however, most experts attached little importance to economic attitudes. When consumer purchases rose greatly after the end of the war, the increase was generally attributed to pent-up demand. It was argued that people were rushing to eat steak and take long drives because meat and gas were no longer rationed; that they were anxious for that first new car after having had an old one or none at all for so long. Some experts devoted much ingenuity to calculating the size of the pent-up demand in order to predict when it would be exhausted and when what they called a temporary spending spree would end. But was deferred demand the only factor relevant to the increased spending? Or were consumer optimism and confidence enduring reasons for postwar prosperity? These questions could be answered in 1949.

1948–1949

Makers of wrong forecasts rarely admit that their theories and methods are incorrect. They usually place the blame on accidental factors or on errors of timing. By the fall of 1948 they lifted their heads and predicted that the postwar depression was just postponed and would take place at last. Wartime rationing and price control had given birth to two years of the rule of deferred demand which in turn had stimulated employment. But the basic factors which cause depressions necessarily to follow after wars could not be denied for long. In time of war industrial capacity is artificially overextended; a cleansing process is therefore inevitable to bring industrial capacity back to normal. Prices must fall sooner or later to wipe out advances caused by the wartime need for raw materials, purchased then without regard to cost. The inevitable substantial retrenchment of government spending must have its effect on the entire

[1] Further information on consumer attitudes immediately after the end of the war as well as in 1948–1949 has been presented in G. Katona, *Psychological Analysis of Economic Behavior.*

economy as soon as the pent-up demand has been satisfied and business has filled up its inventory channels. This was the reasoning of many experts toward the end of 1948 when shortages in consumer goods and sellers' markets came to an end.

Impressed by the decline in government expenditures and a rise in their inventories, many business leaders became doubtful and uncertain. Production was therefore restricted and workers were laid off. Yet the predicted postwar depression did not come. A year later, in the fall of 1949, business was again on the upgrade. The recovery was accomplished primarily by the American consumer, who remained optimistic and continued to purchase at a very high rate.

One of the annual surveys of the Survey Research Center was conducted early in 1949 when business sentiment was shaky and production declining. The survey disclosed that in one respect the masses of consumers were in agreement with business leaders. They, too, expected inflation to end. While a year earlier the majority of the people had thought that prices would go up during the succeeding twelve months, toward the beginning of 1949 the great majority expected them to go down. "What goes up must come down" ran the reasoning; people felt that the time had come for a reversal of wartime trends. At the same time, there was an increase in the proportion of people whose income declined. Nevertheless, early in 1949 more people said that their financial situation had improved than had said so early in 1948. While during the preceding years of rising prices many people whose income had risen had felt worse off, in 1949 even people whose incomes had remained stable professed to be better off. Expectations regarding the business outlook remained optimistic: people argued that declining prices would ensure a continuation of large consumer demand and therefore of good times.

Early in 1948 a smaller proportion of the people expected their incomes to go up than expected prices to go up. Early in 1949, the opposite was true: a larger proportion expected higher incomes than expected higher prices. Most important, in 1949 the proportion of people expressing intentions to purchase automobiles as well as such large household goods as refrigerators, television sets, and washing machines had increased over 1948 (see Figure 1). People did not appear to be saturated, nor was their buying mood impaired.

It was in early March of 1949 that the data compiled from the just-completed survey had been fed into the IBM machines and had come out revealing the improvement in consumer attitudes, the increased public confidence and intentions to buy. A friend, aware of the factual economic picture at the time, looked askance at the survey results and advised the author to save his reputation and refrain from publishing them. His reasoning sounded logical: most people are unaware of economic facts. They don't realize that production and wages go up when prices go up and down when prices go down. When production cutbacks put more people out of work, all those attitudes just uncovered will

Figure 1. Change in attitudes from early 1948 to early 1949

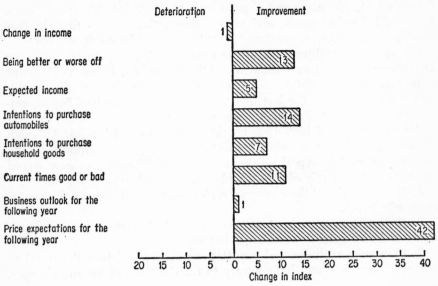

NOTE: For each question an index was constructed, separately for early 1948 and early 1949, by deducting the unfavorable responses from the favorable ones. The figure shows the difference between the two indices in percentage points. For example early in 1948, 29 per cent said they felt better off and 39 per cent that they felt worse off, giving an index-value of −10; early in 1949, 33 per cent said better off and 30 per cent worse off, giving an index of +3; the figure shows an improvement of 13.

The change of price expectations is not strictly comparable to the other data. The figure is drawn on the basis of the assumption, explained in the text and analyzed in detail in Chapter 12, that an expected small increase in prices (of things people buy) represents a deterioration and an expected decrease in prices, an improvement of attitudes.

The figure shows the change in the frequency of expressed buying intentions in per cent from 1948 to 1949. To the proportion of people expressing definite intentions to buy, one-half of the proportion expressing conditional intentions (that is, of those who said that they might buy) is added in both years.

SOURCE: Nationwide sample interview surveys conducted by the Survey Research Center. (These surveys represent the source of all charts in this chapter.)

quickly change and the buying they pretend to foreshadow will never develop. Consumer surveys will be proved misleading.

The findings were published and attracted little attention. Production was indeed curtailed and unemployment did grow that spring—but consumer purchases did not fall off. Sales of automobiles and of other consumer durables kept on rising in 1949.

In July, 1949, a further survey was conducted. The proportion of people reporting income declines was higher than in January and the proportion reporting income increases, lower. Yet consumer attitudes remained quite favorable. People expressed a great variety of desires for automobiles, household durable goods, and many other articles. They thought that buying conditions were good and that there would be no depression.

Consumer expenditures did not decline in 1949. In January, 1950, the Department of Commerce summarized the situation as follows: "The most important area of stability throughout 1949 was in the consumer sector of the economy." By the last quarter of 1949, recovery had begun, primarily as the result of large consumer purchases.

The experience of 1948–1949 taught some important lessons. Although the surveys of those years were not sufficiently complete to support definite conclusions, certain hypotheses seemed justified. These hypotheses served as guides for the study of consumer behavior in subsequent years:

1. It is possible for the consumer sector to exert a decisive influence on economic trends.

2. Expected price reductions may favorably influence consumer attitudes and may stimulate consumer buying.

3. Consumer attitudes and expectations need not follow the trend of incomes; they may develop contrary to the direction of income changes.

Korea

At the end of June, 1950, North Korean troops invaded South Korea. Within a few days the American people learned with satisfaction that a police action would restore order. Then came a most unusual and shocking experience, news of military setbacks. In the summer of 1950, the American people learned that their armies had been almost driven out of Korea. In the winter of 1950, after the intervention of the Chinese Communists, they learned that their armies had been driven back several hundred miles from the Yalu River.

Little information is available about the economic attitudes prevailing at those times. But a survey conducted in August, 1950, revealed that one person out of every four anticipated substantial price increases—increases of more than 10 per cent within a year. During previous inflationary periods, as they had occurred during and shortly after World War II, most expectations had envisaged small price increases.

Recollections of World War II were revived following the military setbacks, and people expected restrictions of civilian production and subsequent shortages. Business firms hoarded raw materials, and consumers embarked on waves of scare buying. Sales records of department stores indicate that the large buying waves coincided with the bad military news. While up to that time autumn had generally been the slow season for automobile sales, purchases of passenger cars, remembered as unavailable in time of war, soared in the second half of 1950. The increase in prices was the most rapid in our recent history. Between June, 1950, and early 1951 the price index for basic commodities, such as copper and rubber, most of which could be purchased speculatively and hoarded for long periods, rose by 50 per cent. The index of wholesale prices advanced by 16 per cent; and the index of consumer retail prices, popularly called cost-of-living index, which contains many slow-moving items such as rents and the cost of electricity, went up 8 per cent.

Total personal income increased very slowly during that period. Extensive rearmament and a corresponding increase in Federal expenditures were announced shortly after the outbreak of hostilities, but the amount of money actually spent on armament rose only very slightly in 1950. On the other hand, tax increases enacted by Congress had an immediate effect in siphoning away some consumer funds and increasing Federal revenues. In the second half of 1950 there was no cash deficit in the Federal budget.

There was fairly general agreement about the interpretation of these developments: the anticipation of huge deficits and of price increases and shortages had made business firms as well as consumers stock up, and the soaring demand had driven prices up. Many experts concluded, therefore, that further substantial inflation was ahead: if the mere expectation of government spending had had such great effects, how much worse would the situation be when people's purchasing power was actually increased by several billions of dollars! President Truman requested the reenactment of price controls and Congress speedily complied toward the end of January, 1951. Government expenditures and national income did rise substantially, as expected, in 1951. But other developments did not conform to the predictions made in the winter of 1950–1951. Raw material prices fell rapidly, wholesale prices declined moderately, and the cost-of-living index remained stable. Manufacturers' inventories rose and consumer demand fell, primarily because of a substantial decline in the rate of durable goods purchases. The American people decided to save money rather than buy goods. Statistical data may illustrate the dramatic change from the first to the second phase of the Korean War. Table 3 shows how extensively American consumers shifted from spending on durable goods to saving in 1951.

Why did this most unexpected reversal in people's behavior take place? A survey conducted as early as January and February, 1951, revealed increased pessimism and uncertainty. At that time the front in Korea was

TABLE 3. CHANGE IN SAVING AND IN SPENDING ON DURABLES DURING
TWO PHASES OF THE KOREAN WAR

	Nine months from July 1, 1950, to Mar. 31, 1951	Nine months from Apr. 1, 1951, to Dec. 31, 1951
Expenditures on consumer durables	$23.8 billion	$19.3 billion
Liquid saving*...........	3.5 billion	12.2 billion

* In currency, bank deposits, savings and loan shares, and securities.
SOURCES: U.S. Department of Commerce and Securities and Exchange Commission.

stabilized and the acute threat of military defeat had vanished, and with it the expectation of a third world war. Instead of expecting rapid price increases and shortages, people assumed that inflation would continue gradually—and they disliked this prospect. In Figure 2, therefore, the expectation of price increases is counted as a deterioration of attitudes, just as the opposite expectation was recorded in Figure 1 as indicating an improvement of attitudes. Figure 2 shows that many more people reported income increases in 1951 than in 1950, but because of rising prices, they did not feel better off.. They thought their incomes would continue to advance but would still not keep pace with prices, and ex-

Figure 2. Change in attitudes from early 1950 to early 1951

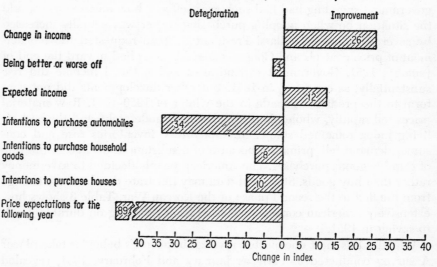

NOTE: For explanation of this and the following figures, see Figure 1.

pressed intentions to buy automobiles, houses, and household goods declined in frequency.

A survey conducted in June, 1951, revealed how fundamentally consumer thinking had changed from the previous year.[2] During the spring and the summer of 1951 newspapers and periodicals characterized the decline in consumer spending as a buying lull caused by overbuying during the preceding year. A lull, according to Webster, is a temporary cessation, but there was nothing temporary about people's opinions. It was not saturation as the result of having bought too much, but a shift in attitudes which had shaken consumer demand. The following findings of the June, 1951, survey indicate the nature of consumer sentiment at that time:

1. A new expression spread rapidly and was widely accepted: cold war. It meant for the American people long-lasting conflict and the disagreeable state of affairs of being dependent on what Moscow did. It meant a state of continuous anxiety, but no shooting war.

2. It was believed possible to produce guns for a cold war and butter, too. The expectation of shortages disappeared and resentment of inflation grew. Buying conditions were viewed most unfavorably: the majority of people said that high prices made it a bad time to buy automobiles or household goods.

3. Because of the price increases the number of people who felt they were worse off exceeded by far the number who felt better off. The most common response to questions about the respondent's financial prospects were expressions of uncertainty about the future.

4. Past and expected price increases did not shake people's trust in the value of the dollar. Government bonds and bank deposits remained the favorite forms of saving. In a time of rising prices and growing government deficits people used much of their income gains to add to their bond holdings and bank deposits.

The recovery from the sudden and sharp deterioration of consumer attitudes and the corresponding restraint in consumer spending was slow. The low point was reached in the fall of 1951 and was followed by a period of habituation. Slowly and gradually the American people got accustomed to the cold war and to the higher price levels. Early in 1952 the majority still thought it was "a bad time" to make large purchases. At that time survey findings were summarized as follows: "Consumers are planning to purchase durable goods in moderate volume in relation to income." By the summer of 1952 complaints about high prices declined

[2] A detailed analysis of changes in consumer attitudes during the Korean War has been presented in the monograph by G. Katona and E. Mueller, *Consumer Attitudes and Demand.*

in frequency and stable prices were expected. Somewhat more people felt better off and income expectations improved. A slow and gradual improvement occurred also in people's general economic outlook. There were no specific events to which this improvement could be attributed until the election of General Eisenhower to the Presidency in November, 1952. Then the proportion of people saying that times would improve rose, and people argued that it would be the business of the Republican administration to insure good times.

A series of surveys on consumer attitudes was conducted during the Korean War, but it is not easy to present their results systematically

Figure 3. Change in attitudes after the summer of 1951

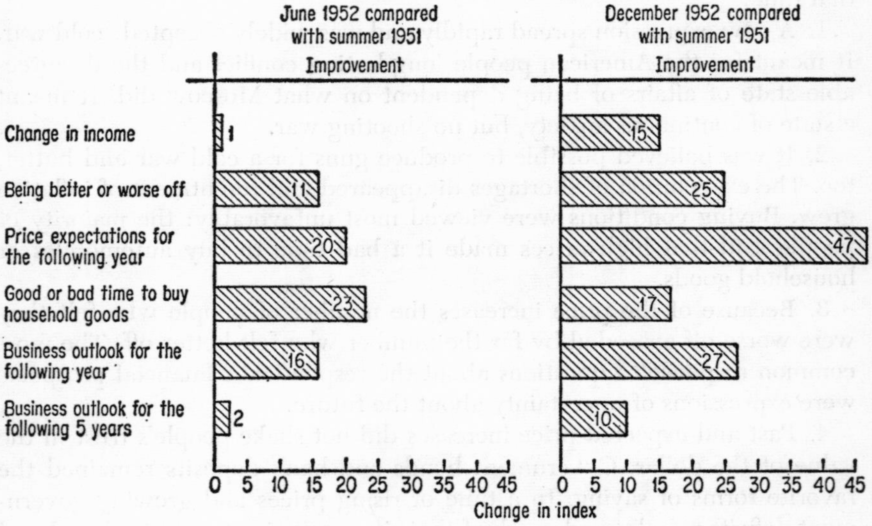

because experiments with new approaches to the measurement of attitudes were carried out at that time. Figure 3 presents, however, some indications of the recovery from the unfavorable sentiment registered in the summer of 1951.

The consumer surveys carried out during the Korean War were the first ones in which the relation of a variety of consumer attitudes to buying behavior was analyzed in detail. These studies revealed:

That total durable goods purchases had declined at times when the proportion of people thinking "This is a bad time to buy" had increased;

That fewer plans to purchase durable goods were made by people who felt it was a "bad time to buy" than by those who felt it was a "good time to buy"; and

That the main reason given for feeling that it was not a good time to buy was "Prices are too high."

Upturn in 1954 [3]

Consumer optimism reached a high point toward the end of 1952. At that time, in contrast to 1951, most people thought that the Korean War had had a favorable effect on the domestic economy. People had become accustomed to the price level, which had risen in 1950–1951. Also, as we said, there was widespread confidence that the newly elected Eisenhower administration would stimulate business. Therefore many more people than before expressed intentions to purchase automobiles and other durable goods.

The upswing did not last long. In the third quarter of 1953, following the truce in Korea, news about government economies led businessmen to reduce their inventories, resulting in some decline in production and an increase in unemployment.

That economic trends had taken a turn for the worse was widely known by the end of 1953. What was not known at that time was that the recession of 1953–1954 would be recorded in economic annals as one of the mildest ever experienced, rather than the initial phase of a severe depression. The noted Australian economist, Colin Clark, was in the forefront of those who held that this recession heralded the onset of the allegedly long-postponed postwar readjustment. Even many American experts who took issue with Clark were greatly concerned because they saw no new factor which might pull the economy out of its decline.

The new factor seems to have been in the minds of the consumers. True, they did react to news about production declines and to rumors about overproduction and an impending depression by restricting their rate of spending. A survey conducted by the Survey Research Center in October, 1953, showed that attitudes had worsened substantially as compared to the high point reached in December, 1952, but that they were no worse than they had been in June, 1952 (see Figure 4). In the fall of 1953 people who said their incomes had declined exceeded in number those who said they felt they were worse off. Consumers were satisfied with stable prices. Those whose incomes increased together with those whose incomes were stable constituted the majority, and they were also satisfied with their personal financial progress despite what they read in the papers and heard over the radio and television.

Toward the end of 1953 it became clear that people are not easily swayed by hearsay regarding vital matters about which they have some

[3] For a detailed discussion of the developments related in this section, see the monograph *Consumer Expectations, 1953–1956,* by G. Katona and E. Mueller.

personal experience. In June, 1954, when the next survey was conducted, it became clear that consumer attitudes may change autonomously (i.e., in a way not related to changes in their incomes) and may determine consumer expenditures as well as business trends. National income was stable at that time, and the traditional economic indicators did not signal an upturn. But consumer confidence and consumer inclinations to buy improved greatly. Figure 5 shows that reports on income received deteriorated further from October, 1953, to June, 1954. And yet more people said they were better off, and a variety of economic attitudes improved, with the greatest change for the better occurring in the evaluation of

Figure 4. Change in attitudes in 1953

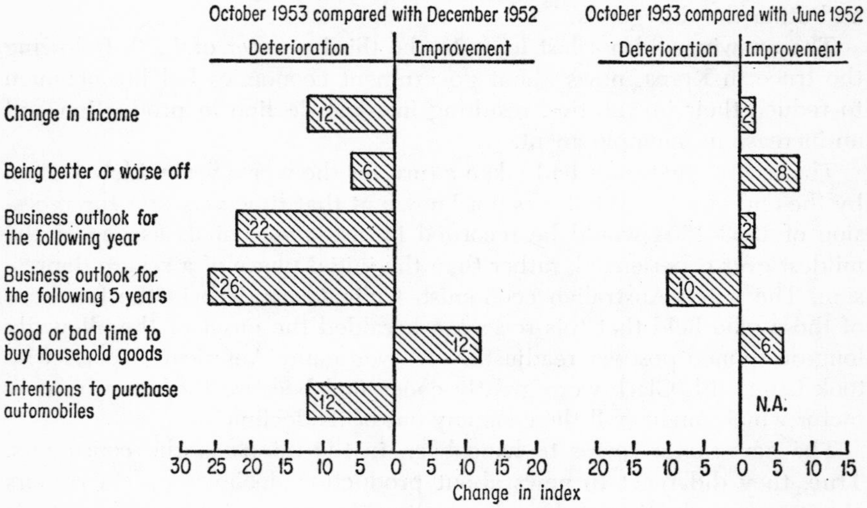

buying conditions for durable goods and in the frequency of expressed intentions to purchase automobiles and houses.[4]

How did this change come about? The surveys which provided the data presented in the charts did not remain satisfied with collecting such data alone. Following each question the respondents were asked for reasons for their attitudes or expectations. The answers received revealed two basic aspects of the thinking and feeling of the American people in the summer of 1954:

1. Underlying feelings of confidence were not destroyed by the recession in 1953. Some caution and hesitation were evident but relatively few people had actually been hurt. They had heard the dire predictions and had been agreeably "disappointed" when their incomes and their

[4] There were some tax reductions in 1954. It is not known whether and to what extent they contributed to the improvement in sentiment.

Figure 5. Change in attitudes in 1954 and 1955

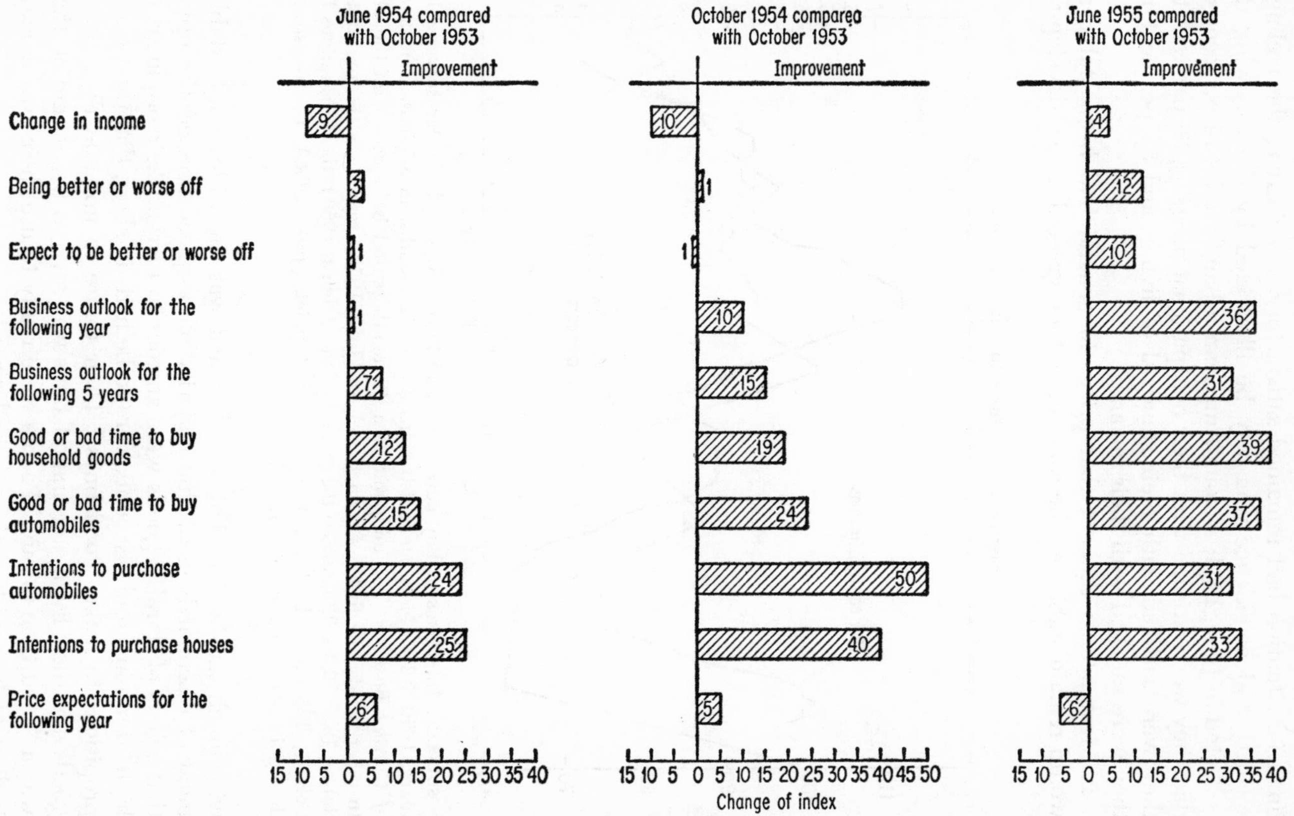

financial situation had remained satisfactory. How strong the feeling of
security and confidence was may be illustrated by the following data
collected in June, 1954: Among American urban families 74 per cent said
that they were satisfied with their occupational progress, 68 per cent that
they were satisfied with their standard of living, and 58 per cent that
they were satisfied with their income.

2. Most people thought that prices in general had been stable and
would remain stable. At the same time, they greeted a new development

Figure 6. Intentions to buy new cars

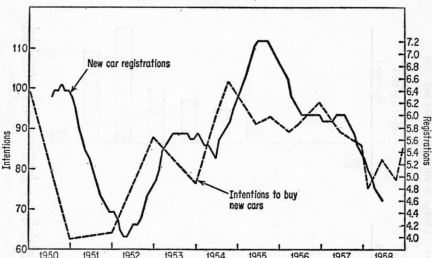

SOURCES: Intentions to buy new cars, from Survey Research Center surveys; February, 1950 = 100. New car registrations during 12 months, in millions, from *Survey
of Current Business*. The midpoint of a 12-month period is indicated on the chart.
In other words, the first point on the chart (July, 1950) represents the registrations
during 1950 (6.3 million cars); the second point (August, 1950), the registrations from
Feb. 1, 1950 to Feb. 1, 1951; and the last point (July, 1958), the registrations
during 1958 (4.6 million cars).

with much satisfaction. This development was the widespread establishment of discount houses. The majority of people expressed the opinion
that sellers of durable goods were anxious to market their products, that
high "trade-ins" and discounts were to be had—in short, that the time was
propitious to make "good buys." Their desire to upgrade their durable
goods and their living accommodations was revived by the notion that it
was a "good time to buy." People were ready to use their own money as
well as to borrow to satisfy their desires.

By October, 1954, these optimistic attitudes had grown still further

(Figure 5), and intentions to purchase a car during the succeeding twelve months reached an all-time high. Shortly thereafter the 1955 automobile models were introduced, and installment maturities were lengthened. By the summer of 1955, time payments extending over more than thirty months, often to thirty-six months, became the rule for buyers of new cars, as against less than twenty-four months a year earlier. Since many buyers look primarily at monthly charges, some people felt that the cost of buying a new car had declined. Many people who were traditionally used-car buyers and many people who had not yet reached the time at which they usually traded in their car, purchased the 1955 models, which were generally called different from and more attractive than the previous models. Figure 6 indicates the increase in automobile sales in 1955 as well as the close correspondence with which expressed buying intentions had anticipated the upturn.

On a High Level

By June, 1955, consumer optimism had increased sharply beyond the 1954 levels. While in 1954 many people acknowledged that business conditions were worse than a year earlier and nevertheless expected an upturn, in 1955 practically everybody knew that business had improved and expected the improvement to continue. Many more people reported income increases than income declines in 1955, and the subjective evaluations of the personal financial situations improved even more than the income reports.

The overall findings of the June, 1955, survey, as well as of the surveys conducted later in that year and in 1956, were of little interest to some members of the community of economic analysts and forecasters. While in 1954 some students disregarded the surveys because they found their results unbelievable, during the next two years they condemned the surveys as yielding nothing but well-known information. By that time the boom, especially in consumer durable goods, was an accepted fact. Consumer income was rising and consumer spending, out of income as well as through installment buying, proceeded at an accelerated rate. Under these circumstances, the reports about optimistic attitudes contained nothing new. It appears then that under certain conditions changes in income represent an influential factor in spurring changes in attitudes. It does not follow, however, that attitude surveys are superfluous when they indicate a continuation of prevailing trends. In 1955 and 1956, the finding that attitudes had improved in line with the improvement in incomes served to convey the reassurance that an extrapolation of past trends was justified.

There was also some new information that could be derived from con-

sumer surveys in those years. Intentions to purchase homes and to make
additions and repairs to homes increased substantially in 1955 despite
the fact that the rate of marriages and of household formation had
declined steadily since 1949. Net family formation fell from approximately
1.2 million in the first few postwar years to about 800,000 in 1954. Pessimistic predictions about housing needs were therefore very common. Studies
of the feelings of the people stood out in contradiction to the widespread
pessimism. Surveys conducted in 1954, as well as during the following
two years, warranted the conclusion, later confirmed by the facts, that
the trend toward suburbs was as strong as ever, or perhaps even stronger
than before.[5]

By 1955 the overwhelming proportion of major durable goods bought—
autos, refrigerators, washing machines, television sets, etc.—were replacements. Most American families already owned these articles, and very
many of them were relatively new and in good condition. If people purchased new durables only after the old ones became worn out, consumer
purchases would have slumped. Yet these purchases remained high—
automobile sales were somewhat lower in 1956 than in the record year of
1955 but still remained very satisfactory—because optimistic and confident
people hastened to upgrade their possessions.

The first phase of the boom, from the fall of 1954 until the fall of 1955,
was of the consumers' making. In that period practically the entire increase
in Gross National Product was due to increased spending on consumer
durables and residential construction. Capital expenditures by business
firms did not increase at that time. Consumer expenditures on nondurables
and on services, which often follow income trends, began to advance in
1955. The year 1956, on the other hand, was primarily a year of business
investment. The building of new factories and the reequipment of old
ones were undertaken on a very large scale after sales to the ultimate
consumer had advanced and profits had risen. The boom received new
stimulation from business activity, and consumers, impressed by the
trend of their own incomes and the general business news, remained very
optimistic.

The extent of optimism may be gauged by answers received to the
following survey question which was formulated deliberately to induce
people to express misgivings: Do you happen to know about any unfavorable developments which may make the country's business situation worse?
In 1955–1956 more than two-thirds of all respondents replied in the
negative. A further question What do you have in mind? addressed to
the minority who had answered affirmatively, yielded references to the
international situation and the President's illness. Only relatively few

[5] The residential mobility of the American people and its underlying motivational
forces will be analyzed in Chapter 8.

people mentioned economic factors as, for instance, the large consumer debt, low farm incomes, and inflation.

Many indicators remained most favorable even as the year 1956 ended. But by that time some signs pointed toward a cautious appraisal of prospects. Fewer people than at earlier times said, "Business is better than a year ago," and more said, "Business is just as good as a year ago." Whether this change should be viewed as a correct factual appraisal or as an indication of lesser optimism was not known at that time. That intentions to buy new cars had declined and intentions to buy used cars had increased was likewise hard to interpret. One thing was clear, however, in the second half of 1956: people were aware of rising prices and expected further price increases. Complaints about inflation and the expression of worries about how to make ends meet became more frequent. That times were opportune for buying durable goods because "good buys" were available was stated with lesser frequency. New incentives for buying were not available, and as early as in October, 1956, *Business Week* magazine summarized the findings of the Survey Research Center by speaking of the zestless consumer. In December, 1956, the results of a nationwide survey were summarized by the Survey Research Center in the following cautious terms: "While the December survey does not point to a buyers' strike in 1957, neither does it show any new strength or impetus in the consumer sector to pick up slack if it develops in the economy." [6]

Downturn in 1957

According to the traditional economic indicators, most of the year 1957 was prosperous. National income, and consumer expenditures as well, reached their highest levels as late as the third quarter of 1957. Yet the increases over 1956 in these as well as in several other business indicators were small and were due, partly at least, to higher prices. Inflation accelerated in 1957 when food prices, which had been responsible for the stability of the cost of living in some preceding years, joined in the upward trend.

The Survey Research Center conducted one of its periodic surveys of consumer attitudes in June, 1957. All the indicators pointed downward (Figure 7, first column). The deterioration was rather small in evaluations of personal financial welfare, although the proportion of people expressing worries had risen substantially. People's opinions about general economic trends had worsened to a much greater extent. Also, people knew that prices had risen and almost without exception called this an

[6] Quoted from a press release issued by the center following the December, 1956, Periodic Survey.

unfavorable development. Many fewer said in June, 1957, than six or twelve months earlier, "This is a good time to buy automobiles and durable goods." Still optimists outnumbered the pessimists. The title of the survey report issued early in July, 1957, was "Consumer Optimism Weakening." [7]

How did people explain their opinions in the summer of 1957? We find, first, that new incentives were entirely lacking. It became evident at that time that consumers constantly need new support for the main-

Figure 7. Change in attitudes in 1957

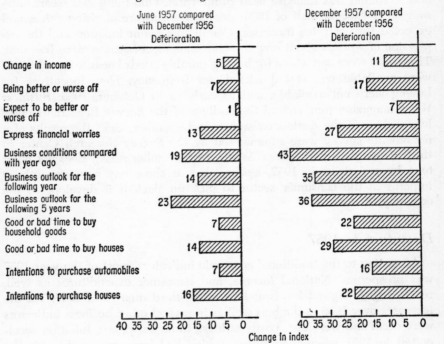

tenance of optimistic attitudes. A much larger proportion of people knew in June, 1957, than in 1956 that business was leveling off rather than continuing its advance. This was interpreted as a sign for caution. Second, there were some soft spots in the economy—mostly of local character as, for instance, shorter working hours in one or the other factory—which attracted a great deal of attention. It appears that, following several good years, people tend to notice and discuss even occasional and slight bad news. Third, there was concern with rising prices,

[7] The report was issued by the Foundation for Research in Human Behavior.

which created dissatisfaction and made for uneasiness. Finally, there is evidence that a very substantial proportion of the people were aware of rising interest rates—about three-fourths of those with an annual income of $7,500 and over reported this correct information—and interpreted it as a bad sign. Not only were conditions for buying houses judged to be much less favorable than before, but the news that it was harder to get credit contributed to dampening optimistic views about business prospects in general. We quoted before that in 1955–1956 relatively few people acknowledged having heard unfavorable business news. In June, 1957, close to 25 per cent, compared to less than 5 per cent in May, 1956, said that they had heard of declining business activity or even of layoffs of workers.

In the fall of 1957 there was some good news as, for instance, the record personal incomes mentioned before. There was also a great deal of bad news about cutbacks in government spending, in residential construction, and in plans for business expenditures on new factories and machinery. Surveys showed that for consumers the unfavorable news was salient. By December, 1957, a substantial proportion of consumers thought that a recession had already developed. Though many of these people admitted that they, themselves, were well off, they expressed worries about their jobs and incomes. Concern with inflation had grown and there was a sharp increase in the proportion of people who felt that these were bad times to buy automobiles and other durable goods.

The sputniks also contributed to the deterioration of confidence. For most Americans, Communist achievements, the armament race, and international conflict have unfavorable connotations which are carried over into other areas. Instead of thinking that the sputniks would stimulate the American missile program and thereby make our production go up, the unexpected news that the Russians had put a satellite into orbit brought concern and dismay. Close to one-third of the American people reacted by saying that war had become much more likely. And among those who felt that war was more likely, only 46 per cent said in December, 1957, that business conditions would remain "good"; among those who felt that war was less likely, 67 per cent said so!

The deterioration in consumer attitudes was substantial by December, 1957 (Figure 7, second column). Expressed intentions to buy automobiles had also dropped sharply. Intentions to buy new cars were heard less frequently at the end of 1957 than at any time since 1953 (Figure 6).

In order to appreciate the significance of the great deterioration of sentiment toward automobile buying, we must be aware of the fact that toward the end of 1957 there were good arguments supporting the opinion that 1958 would be a good automobile year. The best of all auto years was, of course, 1955, and only relatively few of the 7¼ million people who had purchased a new car in 1955 had traded in their cars in 1956 and 1957. Therefore, early in 1958 less than 19 per cent of American families owned "late-model cars," that is, cars of 1958, 1957, and 1956 vintage; early in 1957, when the 1955 models still fell in the "late-model car" category, the percentage was 23. Furthermore, the consumer debt situation was bound to be better in 1958 than in the preceding years. After its very sharp increase in 1955, consumer installment debt rose only moderately while incomes rose substantially. In addition, it could be reliably calculated that a substantial number of families would become debt-free in 1958.

Despite these objectively favorable factors, automobile sales slumped in 1958. People decided not to trade in their cars for new ones. The situation at that time can best be illustrated by contrasting it with that of 1954–1955. At the end of 1954 widespread knowledge about high trade-in values and discounts had had a most favorable impact on auto buying. By the end of 1957, however, most informed people thought that automobile prices had gone up and would go up further. They were dissatisfied with the price situation and the majority said that the succeding twelve months would be a bad time to buy cars. In 1954–1955 installment maturities had been lengthened; in 1957–1958 they were kept unchanged. In the fall of 1954 new auto models had been thought to incorporate great improvements and had been most favorably received, while in 1957 only 20 per cent said that the 1958 models differed markedly from the previous year's models (a year earlier this proportion had been 38 per cent). Even though the criticism of long, low, and ostentatious cars, which became widespread in press reports published later in 1958, may have been exaggerated—we shall come back to this point in Chapter 10—there can be no doubt that in 1958 there was practically nothing to stimulate auto purchases. No wonder then that the automobile industry bore the brunt of the worsening consumer sentiment and growing uneasiness.

The American people's *ability* to buy remained high during the first half of 1958. The decline in national income was insignificant because some people were still receiving wage increases and others, unemployment compensation. On food and on necessities consumers as a whole spent substantially the same amounts of money as a year earlier. But the index of industrial production fell from the fall of 1957 to the spring of 1958 from 145 to 126, and unemployment rose from 2.5 to 5.2 million. The steepness of the decline, the sharpest since 1937, was due to the curtailment of business investment and of consumer investment at the same time.[8]

[8] Further data about the recession of 1958 and data about the subsequent recovery will be presented in Chapter 13.

Index of Consumer Attitudes

In our discussion of the developments between 1945 and 1958, we reported changes in a variety of consumer attitudes. Although reliance was placed on the consistency of change in different attitudinal indicators, it was pointed out that the reasons for strengthened or weakened confidence differed from time to time; at certain times price developments were placed in the foreground, and at other times business news or personal financial attitudes. Such a procedure has its merits because no two periods are alike in all respects. On the other hand, uniform methods in summarizing changes in sentiment may be called for so as to add to the objectivity of analysis and simplify the use of attitudinal data. At an early stage of its research work the Survey Research Center therefore prepared, on an experimental basis, a composite index of consumer attitudes.

The index is available since 1952. It comprises the answers to eight questions, two of which inquire about personal financial attitudes, two about attitudes toward business conditions, two about attitudes toward market conditions, and two about buying intentions. The answers given by the respondents are grouped into three categories: (1) up, better, or good; (2) same, no change, or uncertain; (3) down, worse, or bad.[9]

Figure 8 presents the fluctuations of the index of consumer attitudes from the end of 1952 to October, 1958. The figure also indicates changes in sales of durable goods and in personal disposable incomes, as computed by the Commerce Department. Sales of durables and income are adjusted for seasonal variations but not for changes in prices. In other words, the rise in income and in sales, especially during the years 1956 and 1957, is partly due to inflation rather than to a real growth in economic activity. Yet for our purposes a correction for inflationary effects is not necessary. The figure shows clearly that the substantial fluctuations in the sales of durable goods cannot be explained by income developments alone (although the fact that the level of durable sales has risen is related to rising incomes). Consumer attitudes, however, do provide an explanation for the direction of fluctuations in durable goods sales.

The figure shows that in 1954 the index of consumer attitudes advanced earlier than sales of durable goods: attitudes led demand. In 1955 and

[9] The index is constructed by deducting the proportion of responses of the third type from the proportion of responses of the first type. Problems connected with the construction of the index, as well as a special treatment of buying intentions and price expectations, are described in the monograph *Consumer Expectations* by G. Katona and E. Mueller. The justification for treating the expectation of small price increases as unfavorable for spending will be given in Chapter 12.

1956 the direction of changes in the index appears to parallel that of sales fluctuations, though the extent of the decline in sales, caused by lower automobile sales in 1956 than in 1955, is not fully reflected in the index. In 1957, when again there was a crucial turning point, attitudes declined long before demand fell.

This simple graphical analysis confirms our earlier argument: Sometimes attitudes change autonomously and indicate changes in demand

Figure 8. Index of consumer attitudes and sales of durable goods
(in current dollars)

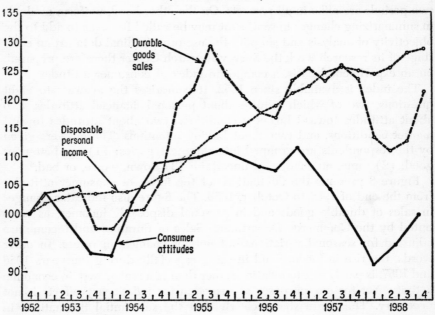

SOURCES: Durable goods sales and disposable income are based on U.S. Department of Commerce quarterly data, seasonally adjusted; last quarter, 1952 = 100. Consumer attitudes are Survey Research Center data; November-December, 1952 = 100.

for consumer durables which cannot be explained by changes in income or other traditional financial data; sometimes attitudes are influenced by past developments in incomes, production, sales, and the like, and do not contribute significant new information. It seems probable that the former is the case when the impending changes in economic trends are substantial.

It is always possible to translate a graphical presentation of correspondence or lack of correspondence between sets of data, as presented in Figure 8, into an algebraic equation. Thereby a measure of the degree of correspondence is obtained. Yet such a measure will reflect average correspondence without differentiating between what have been called crucial times (1954 and 1957, for instance) and other times. In our case the exact mathematical procedure has an additional drawback: the number of available observations is small; the chart contains attitudinal data obtained in sixteen successive surveys only. Nevertheless, it may be reported that a substantial proportion of the fluctuations in expenditures on durables is explained by the fluctuations in the index of consumer attitudes. The contribution of changes in the income level to the explanation of fluctuations in sales is very much smaller.[10]

Thus, on the basis of six years of study of changes in consumer attitudes this conclusion emerges: Changes in consumer attitudes are advance indications of changes in consumer spending on durable goods and make a net contribution to the prediction of such spending after the influence of income has been taken into account.

[10] The calculations have been carried out by E. Mueller in "Consumer Attitudes: Their Influence and Forecasting Value" and showed a highly significant influence of attitudes on durable-goods expenditures in the two quarters following each survey.

CHAPTER 4

The Nature of Attitudes and Expectations

In order to understand the effects which attitudes and expectations have on economic action, we must get acquainted with certain psychological considerations regarding the function of attitudes.

I turn a switch and the light goes on. In this case a mechanism reacts in the same way over and over again. For centuries many thinkers conceived of human behavior as if it were analogous with that of machines. They postulated that the same stimulus always brings forth the same reaction and proposed a mechanistic theory of human behavior, characterized by order and simplicity. They believed that to give up such principles would be to abandon all hope of understanding human behavior. Modern psychology does believe in determinism, law, and order in human behavior. Yet it does not conceive of people as automata and does not posit a fixed, one-to-one relation between stimuli and responses.

Stimuli elicit responses; they present occasions for responses rather than fully determining them. It is not possible to predict the response by knowing the stimulus alone. Two persons may react differently to the same stimulus, and the same person may react differently to it on successive occasions. Human beings are capable of learning. Mechanistic or quasi-automatic reaction determined by immediate stimuli alone is extremely rare in the case of what psychologists call the higher mental processes, which include most of economic behavior.

Intervening Variables

The psychological field contains intervening variables. Between the stimuli and the responses is the organism. As the result of past experience there exist habits, attitudes, and motives which intervene by influencing how stimuli are perceived and how the organism reacts to them. The response then is a function of both the environment and the person.

Turning to economic behavior, level of income and financial assets function either as enabling conditions (if they are ample) or as constraints (if they are insufficient). Things that happen to the decision

54

maker are precipitating circumstances or stimuli. A change in salary or the breakdown of one's car may serve as examples. News and information which reach the organism are a very important category of stimuli. Economic behavior in particular is most commonly stimulated by information received by consumers and businessmen.

Yet the same level of income or the same new information may be viewed differently by different people or by the same person at different times. Information transmitted is not identical with information received and with information which becomes salient. How we perceive changes in the environment depends to some extent on us, that is, on subjective or intervening variables. The most important function of intervening variables is to organize. What fits in or what is consistent with our predispositions has the best chance of influencing us. All intervening variables are learned through experience but some are relatively permanent as, for instance, sociocultural norms, well-ingrained motives, and personality traits acquired early in childhood. Stability over fairly long periods also characterizes a variety of habits developed and sustained over many years. Other motives and attitudes change much more easily under the impact of situational factors and nevertheless influence our perceptions of the environment.

One important aspect of our behavioral environment is group belonging. It is the individual who feels, thinks, and acts. But how he feels, thinks, and acts is influenced by the group to which he belongs. Most of the time each of us is a member of a group, sometimes a member of several groups, and at different times of different groups. Some groups are very powerful; then it appears justifiable to speak of group motives or group attitudes. One of the most powerful groups to which practically all of us belong is the family. What happens to other members of our family affects us and we act in behalf of our family. But a person may shift from being a family member and acting as one to being a member of a business firm. What happens to the firm concerns him then and he acts in the name of the firm. Or a person may identify himself with a social group or with a political or national group. Submerging of the ego in a group—as in the case of soldiers on patrol, members of a basketball team in action, or people in a mob—is one, but not the only, form of group influence. Weaker influences are much more common, as well as conflicts from belonging to several groups. One major principle applies to all these cases: swimming with the current is much easier than swimming against the current. What news and information reach us is at least colored by our group belonging; so is our interpretation of the news; and the principle of social facilitation says that action similar to the action of other members of our group is easy, while contrary action is difficult. We often act as we believe others act, who are either members of our group or of reference groups which we set as standards without really belonging to them.

Attitudes are generalized viewpoints with an affective connotation. The usual sharp distinction between cognition and affect or emotion must be abandoned when we turn to the sets or frames of mind which influence our perceptions and behavior. We are for or against innumerable things. Sometimes we may be able to give clear reasons why we favor or oppose an idea or development. But the underlying set of liking or disliking is not the same as the reasons occasionally presented. Attitudes, that is, emotionally colored points of view, may influence behavior irrespective of whether they are based on rational arguments or held without clear awareness of their reasons.

Expectations are a subgroup of attitudes. They, too, are intervening variables which influence behavior. They are those attitudes which represent an extension of the time perspective into the future. Expectations are, then, subjective notions of things to come colored by affect, approval or disapproval, satisfaction or dissatisfaction. Expectations—expressed intentions to act in a certain way as well as notions about what will happen to the person holding the expectations, or to the society or the economy—are current data which represent attitudes held at the time they are expressed. To what extent expectations can be viewed as predispositions to future action and have a predictive value will be discussed later.

Enduring and Variable Attitudes

Frequently in the past, general and specific attitudes have been distinguished from each other. Optimism, irrespective of its specific content, would then represent a different kind of attitude from optimism regarding one's own immediate income prospects, for instance. This, however, is not a fundamental distinction but rather a matter of the degree of generalization. There exists a tendency toward generalization and toward consistency in attitudes. But consistency is not always achieved and often specific attitudes conflict with more deep-seated general attitudes. Thus it is possible for a person with optimistic personality traits to expect unfavorable economic conditions to prevail at a given time, as well as for a pessimist to expect business recovery. The basic distinction between different kinds of attitudes and expectations is that between stable and enduring attitudes on the one hand and variable attitudes on the other.

Some attitudes are acquired very early in life and may be viewed as permanent personality traits. Others depend on new experiences and information and may change in the short run. More correctly, all attitudes have situational determinants as well as a personality basis. In the case of some attitudes, however, either the situational or the personality aspect predominates. All attitudes tend to become habitual, reinforced by repeated action or reiteration. Yet some become deeply ingrained habits while others, held for a short time, may be changed easily. Honesty, punctuality, or conservatism, for instance, are personality traits which give rise to attitudes in the former category. No doubt, such attitudes may be influenced by changing conditions or new experiences, but to a much smaller extent than other attitudes.

It has been demonstrated that some attitudes relevant, for instance, to political behavior and voting—such as conservatism or liberalism, favoring the Republican or Democratic party—are acquired early in life and may remain in force during an entire lifetime. But obviously, with some people at least, the events that occur before an election or the personality of a candidate also give rise to attitudes which may influence their action.

In studying business behavior, enduring attitudes are found which have become part of the psychological make-up of practically all businessmen at a given time and country (honesty or concern with profits, for instance). Other attitudes differ from person to person—as, for instance, attitudes toward risk taking and speculation—though they, too, may be acquired in childhood or during early business experiences and may endure over long periods of time. Finally, there are attitudes which vary from time to time and develop in response to changes in environment.

Our concern is with attitudes which are variable because they are influenced by economic developments—both on a personal and on a national level—and which in turn influence our reactions to these developments. Expecting or not expecting inflation or recession belong in this category, even though they are associated with more enduring attitudes as well as such personality traits as being of a basically optimistic or pessimistic disposition.

The differentiation between relatively stable and relatively variable attitudes is a question for empirical research. To be sure, attitudes that are, in principle, variable may remain unchanged over several years, provided nothing important happens during those years to make for changes. Yet if the measurement of a variety of attitudes is repeated at times when the economic climate has undergone substantial changes, we should expect to find great differences in the degree of stability of different attitudes among a large number of people.

Such a study of the degree of stability in economic attitudes was carried out recently.[1] Over a period of three years (1954–1957) the same attitudinal questions were addressed to the same representative sample of the urban population three times. The statistical measures developed for

[1] See G. Katona, "Repetitiousness and Variability of Consumer Behavior."

the measurement of the extent of homogeneity or repetitiousness in attitudes showed great differences. At the one extreme were the answers received when people were asked whether in their opinion their personal financial situation would be better or worse a few years from the time of questioning. Close to one-half of the sample gave identical answers three times in three consecutive years and most others gave the same answer twice and slightly different answers once (for instance, they said "same" rather than "better" but only a handful shifted from "better" to "worse"). Similarly, questions about satisfaction with standard of living or with amounts saved resulted in a relatively low degree of variability.

On the other hand, expectations about how business conditions or prices would change "during the next year" showed great variability. Only one out of every five people gave the same answer three times when asked about their price expectations and most of these were people with little education who said three times, "There will be no change." The proportion of people who shifted from "Prices will go down" to "Prices will go up" was much higher than the proportion with stable attitudes.

These studies did not show that there existed two classes of attitudes, entirely independent of each other. They did show, however, that it is possible to designate the relatively variable attitudes. Thus it was possible to select the most promising candidates for studies of the relation between changes in attitudes and changes in consumer expenditures as reported in Chapter 3.

Selectivity and Organization

We may recall the previous references to the substantial role of habits in economic behavior as well as to genuine decision making which commonly takes the form of deviating from habitual behavior. Situationally determined opinions, attitudes, and expectations are of primary relevance when habitual behavior is *not* followed. When no problem is seen and the stimuli elicit almost automatically the usual, oft-repeated responses, expectations are not aroused and do not intervene. But when the decision maker finds himself in a crossroad situation in which he is aware of different possibilities of action, attitudes and expectations serve the function of steering the decision in a certain direction. Expectations do not play a role in each and every form of economic behavior, and businessmen and consumers do not have expectations about each and every aspect of the future. But under certain circumstances expectations are of crucial importance.

Learned behavior is highly selective. In any given situation only certain aspects of the past and certain notions about the future become salient. Problem solving obtains direction through suppressing certain notions and being preoccupied with others which appear to fit. The organization of information according to affective predispositions helps in solving the problem—though of course not necessarily in attaining the best solution.

Evidence supporting these statements will be presented later when we shall show that at certain times, in the face of diverse news, the information of which people were aware remained highly consistent. In times of unfavorable attitudes and expectations, good business news frequently did not become salient; at other times good news only could make itself heard.

Further, in analyzing the expectations of managers of different kinds of business firms, a definite structuring of attitudes appeared.[2] Some business leaders, for example, were found to be preoccupied with marketing problems and to view all kinds of news and information exclusively from the point of view of the possible impact on their sales and sales prospects. With managers in other branches of industry, excess capacity or the problem of automation were so predominant that their thinking and their expectations revolved almost exclusively about those issues. In other industries or at other times, cost of production or, specifically, wage increases so dominated businessmen's thinking that all expectations were colored by it.

Organization of attitudes not only makes problem solving manageable but also serves to reduce uncertainty. Logically the problem of uncertainty may be formulated thus: The future is uncertain because such a multitude of factors may influence it that it becomes impossible to obtain a clear picture of each. When, however, only a few developments are viewed as relevant, or when the trend of business is seen as going on as it has been going except for one or two crucial question marks, businessmen and consumers may focus their attention on those few questions and arrive at a solution. This explanation is supported by the finding that for most people the term uncertainty does not have the meaning of simply not knowing what will happen in the future. Uncertainty has definite unfavorable connotations; it implies fear of adverse developments because the feeling of uncertainty arises only when problem solving has been attempted but has not been successful.

The Representation of the Future

Certain aspects of the future do, of course, appear fairly certain. Such aspects have been ruled out of our definition of expectations, which are conceived as representing subjective notions of things to come.

[2] These studies have been described in the author's "Business Expectations in the Framework of Psychological Economics." Many other references to business expectations, made later in this chapter, are taken from the same essay. An earlier formulation of the theory of expectations is found in the author's article "Expectations and Decisions in Economic Behavior."

In the field of business it is fairly simple to distinguish between information about the future which is held with some certainty and the subjective notions about the future. Business data regarding future developments—which economists call "ex ante data"—may be classified into four categories, the first three of which are not included in our definition of expectations. They represent information which is customarily written into or available from business records in the same manner as such ex post data as past sales or profits.

1. *Contracts.* Contracts entered into represent the first category of ex ante data. Records of contracts already awarded represent information about future activity, information which is widely used for predictive purposes. To be sure, contracts may be canceled, but this is a relatively rare occurrence except under catastrophic circumstances. New orders received by manufacturers and unfilled orders of manufacturers are further examples of this category of ex ante data which are found in business records and which represent information about the future.

2. *Budgets.* Corporation budgets prepared by business executives and approved by the board of directors are part of business records and yet reflect future activity. (The same is true, of course, of government budgets.) Budgets, in contrast to contracts, can be changed unilaterally. Budgets are often revised and represent a guide for future behavior rather than rigorous standards.

3. *Estimates.* Various departments of business firms prepare a variety of estimates and forecasts of things to come. These estimates, usually recorded in business memoranda, serve as information for business management and may influence its decisions, but rarely determine them.

4. *Opinions, notions, intentions, and guesses of executives.* This final category of ex ante data, in contrast to the preceding categories, is hardly ever recorded on paper and may nonetheless influence the firm's behavior. Information about such opinions can become available to the researcher through skillful personal interviewing. It is this category alone which we shall designate by the term expectations.

Many of the business anticipations data regularly collected by various government and private agencies during the last few years fall into other categories. Thus the Securities and Exchange Commission and the Commerce Department conduct mail surveys to collect information on business capital expenditures to be undertaken during the next quarter or year. Much of the information they collect represents contracts awarded or budgets approved. Information on sales expectations, collected for instance by Dun & Bradstreet, may often be classified as estimates (category 3), but sometimes also as opinions or guesses (category 4).

Turning to consumers, we may obtain some information on the contractual obligations of all consumers—for instance, on prospective repayments of mortgage and installment debt—from business records. We may also study the distribution of contractual obligations and of numerous other commitments through personal interviews with a representative sample of households. Consumer plans for the future fall overwhelmingly into the fourth category of ex ante data, and can be studied only through personal interviews. The sample survey alone can yield information on plans or intentions to buy houses, automobiles, and other goods, as well as on a variety of other expectations. At any given time only a very small proportion of people have already contracted to buy a house or a car, or made a definite decision within their family about a future purchase. The difference between people who are committed to buy a car and people who have a notion that they might buy a car in a few months is related to differences in the degree of confidence attached to expectations. No doubt, the subjective probability attached to expectations varies greatly. But, as we shall see, it would be a great mistake to restrict the study of expectations to those which are held with a high degree of confidence.

Expectations may refer both to matters on which the person who expresses the expectation may take action and to matters on which he has no influence whatsoever. In the field of business, expectations have sometimes been divided into those concerning (1) the firm of which the person expressing an opinion is an executive, (2) the industry to which the firm belongs, and (3) the economy as a whole. The assumption was that opinions about future developments should be most reliable in the first and least reliable in the third category. It was assumed, for example, that an executive would know most about the future sales of his firm, somewhat less about the future sales of his industry, and least about the future Gross National Product representing the total of sales in the economy. When, however, executives were questioned about all three areas, it frequently appeared that the subjective degree of certainty of expectations did not correspond with this assumption. Often very confident judgments were made about next year's GNP or next year's trend of the cost-of-living index, while conditional answers were given about next year's sales of the executive's own firm or even about the prices to be charged by his firm. These differences could be attributed partly to the detailed knowledge available to the executive about his own business. He might be aware, for instance, of the great extent to which pending negotiations with one large customer could influence the firm's next year's sales. Furthermore, it was found that general expectations obtain much more frequent external confirmation than expectations regarding one's own activities. Reports and conversations often result in an executive's forming fairly definite opinions about the economy as a whole, but not about his own business. Finally, some people believe that the multitude of influences to which the entire economy is subject make for fairly small changes so that the total result is more easily foreseeable, while the single case, what happens to the individual, is subject to much uncertainty.

The same holds true of the public at large. People often have definite notions about the prospects of war or peace, prosperity or depression, inflation or deflation, while they are highly uncertain about what will happen to their own jobs or incomes. That the opposite may also occur is of no concern here. Our present concern is to refute the notion that the researcher should be concerned only with expectations held with great confidence, or with expectations about developments which the subject can influence.

How do a person's expectations about things that may happen to him compare with expectations of things he may do? In comparing income expectations, for instance, with expectations of spending on durable goods, we found a variety of situations. Sometimes income expectations are very definite and held with great certitude, while intentions as to savings or purchases are most indefinite. Sometimes just the opposite is true. Among business expectations it is quite difficult to find any which may be classified as referring exclusively to the executive's or firm's own decisions. Prices set by manufacturers on their products, or wages paid to their employees, are often felt by business executives to depend on circumstances over which they have no control. The extent of felt discretion in action varies greatly. Again the conclusion emerges: We would not be justified in refraining from inquiring about any kinds of expectations on the basis that they are uncertain or that they are irrelevant or outside the scope of the subject's possible knowledge. A person's opinions may be just as strong —or sometimes even stronger—in areas beyond his control as in areas determined by his own action. For a complete evaluation of the relationship between consumer expectations and the economy we must, therefore, collect information on the respondent's expectations, whether they be firmly or lightly held, about his own actions, about things which may happen to him, about things which may happen to groups to which he belongs (family, neighbors, people with the same occupation, or the industry), as well as about developments in the entire economy or society.

The questions should refer to the near as well as the more distant future. Even though few people have given thought to the business outlook during the next five years, their answers to such a question reflect their underlying sentiments. The questions about expectations must be supplemented by questions about the past and the present so as to determine the degree of satisfaction with what has been achieved.

Every question intended to elicit an attitude or an expectation is followed by a question about underlying reasons. We always ask, Why do you think so? This serves, first, the elementary purpose of eliminating some reporting and recording errors. Then, an expectation for which a person has no explanation may not be held very firmly. This deduction is, however, open to doubt because of interpersonal differences in abilities to verbalize thoughts and opinions. The major value of the "why" question may be in its enabling us to differentiate between periods in which different reasons are given for the same expectation. For example, it is most useful to note that at one time when the majority opinion is that "prices will go up," the most common reason given for the belief is that "the government is spending lots of money," while at another time the same majority opinion is most commonly explained by "I don't know, but everybody says that prices will be higher next year than they are now." Changes in the frequency with which different kinds of reasons are mentioned give us significant clues for understanding changes in people's sentiments.

Expressed Intentions to Buy

Is there really anything to be gained by studying such a great variety of attitudes and expectations? Even if they were to influence action, why should the student of economic trends be concerned with them? Being interested in predicting prospective purchases of consumer durable goods, should he not leave the resolution of the various motives, attitudes, and expectations to the consumers themselves and simply ask them about their purchase plans? Is not each consumer himself in the best position to resolve the various influences to which he is subjected and come up with the most reliable prediction of his future actions? [3]

Studies of consumer buying intentions were, in fact, begun by the Survey Research Center and its predecessor organization somewhat earlier than studies of other expectations. The studies of buying plans did provide very useful information concerning purchases which are commonly planned ahead for a considerable length of time. But they provided no substitute for the study of other expectations. Buying intentions simply represent one of several ways in which attitudes may express themselves.

When we measure buying intentions, we intercept the decision-making process at a rather late stage, when the underlying sentiment has already become somewhat crystallized. Reliance on buying intentions alone, in place of studies of expectations about income and the trend of business does not suffice because changes in incipient, underlying tendencies are of paramount interest. The emphasis placed on studies of buying plans represents but another instance of some students' desire to neglect the less certain aspects of behavior in favor of supposedly definite aspects. Yet

[3] Among others, Okun expressed the opinion that much greater reliance should be placed on buying intentions than on other expectations (see "The Value of Anticipations Data").

even buying plans are far from definite in the sense of ruling out the impact of the uncertainty of the future.

Like all other expectations, consumer buying intentions are attitudes held at a given time and not definite predictions of things to come. As said before, the proportion of consumers who at any given time have made definite decisions to purchase durable goods is quite small. When people are asked whether they expect to buy a car or a television set during the following six months or twelve months, they most commonly express their attitudes toward such a purchase rather than a definite plan. Vague opinions and guesses, or even indefinite statements, such as that the car is fairly old and it might be a good idea to replace it, may be put into definite categories by the researcher, who obtains a measure of change by using the same principles of classification in successive studies. But the researcher in doing so should not assume that the respondent has already resolved his conflicts and has made a final decision.

The planning period varies greatly for different goods. Certain inexpensive durable goods are often bought after consideration for a few days or a few weeks. Even automobiles and houses are sometimes bought without advance planning; sometimes, however, after many years of planning. In classifying answers to questions about buying plans as expressed attitudes, the researcher may disregard differences among individuals in the definiteness of plans and in the length of planning periods. His interest lies in finding out whether buying intentions are more or less frequently expressed in one survey than in the preceding one. His findings will then represent indications that consumer inclinations to buy have increased or decreased, rather than represent predictions of things to come.

Expectations and Prediction

What is the relationship between changes in consumer attitudes and forecasts of economic trends? Can studies of attitude change serve to forecast forthcoming developments? This crucial question has been variously answered in the past. The first two answers, listed for the sake of completeness, are of course unacceptable since they contradict the psychological considerations presented in this chapter.

1. There are those who hold that attitudes and expectations originate in emotional or impulsive factors. Therefore they are not understandable and are so unstable that they can have no predictive value.

2. Some others contend that expectations are the results rather than the causes of economic and financial developments. Therefore they do not influence behavior, and information about them cannot add significantly to our knowledge.

3. Still others hold similarly that expectations originate in past develop-

ments but concede that they, in turn, influence behavior. People expect those things to happen which have happened in the past. An upward movement of prices or profits gives rise to the expectation of a continued upward movement; generally prosperous economic conditions arouse the expectation of continued prosperity; prevailing unemployment, the expectation of further unemployment; etc. Therefore, even though expectations may influence behavior, it would be much simpler to measure the specific factors which generate the expectations and thus arrive at equally valid predictions.[4] As we have already seen in the last chapter, our surveys have revealed that occasionally, under certain circumstances, expectations may originate in past trends and indicate a continuation of those trends. But this is not generally true.

4. The experience provided by fifteen years of survey research supports a fourth position which holds that a direct study of changes in expectations is scientifically feasible and can be used in forecasting economic trends. Expectations originate in a variety of economic, political, social, or personal developments. The manner in which they are formed is a very complicated process. A study of the multitude of environmental "facts" would not suffice to show in advance how these facts are perceived and what expectations they will produce. Therefore we have no recourse but to measure directly the prevailing expectations which help to shape business and consumer action.

Attitudes and expectations influence demand for certain goods at the time they are held. Information on changes in attitudes and expectations helps to explain changes in demand. The primary function of a study of attitudes and expectations is diagnostic. Good diagnosis of prevailing trends and their causes, of course, helps in making predictions. But forecasting remains a separate step, additional to the measurement of prevailing expectations.

Any forecast derived from attitudinal measurements obviously postulates endurance of the attitudes. Suppose we find in June that people are more optimistic than they were earlier in the year. In order to make any statement about consumer behavior in the third and fourth quarter of the year we must assume that new measurements in, say, July or October, would not contradict the findings of June. It is possible that expectations might undergo a change even shortly after their measurement. But attitudes and expectations of broad groups of people (not necessarily of each individual) hardly ever change abruptly except under the impact of major events. That major events would abruptly change attitudes is easily understood. If a war should break out unexpectedly soon after a study of attitudes was completed, one would hardly attribute any predictive value

[4] Some writers speak of "proxy variables" when they substitute past changes in prices or incomes for price or income expectations.

to the attitudes. Which events, of much lesser importance than war, may constitute unexpected major events is a question for empirical studies.

We must not forget, of course, that changes in consumer attitudes, and in consumer demand as well, do not depend on the consumers alone but are subject to influence by business and government action. Assume, for instance, that consumer surveys disclose a substantial trend toward a pessimistic and uncertain evaluation of the future; thereupon business or government or both introduce such new measures as price reductions, lowering of interest rates or of taxes. If then the prediction derived from the attitudinal measurements—that consumer demand for durable goods will decline—does not come true, should we assume that attitudes have no predictive value? Would it not be justified to contend that attitudinal measurements had been most useful and fulfilled their ultimate function? In either case, government or business action would no doubt constitute major, unexpected events which obviate the predictive value of the attitudes as they were originally determined.

Data on expectations are not forecasts but ingredients of forecasts. Major new developments which take place after the measurement of expectations are further ingredients which eventually will be known to the forecaster. He may also be aided by the fact that survey research can usually determine whether or not the people have anticipated the subsequent developments.

In the absence of major events, substantial changes in the attitudes of masses of people will not occur without casting shadows ahead. In other words, a reversal of observed attitudes is much less probable than a further accentuation of a trend. This is true, at least, for the period immediately following the determination of attitudes. No general rule can be made about the length of that period, but empirical studies, reported in the previous chapter, disclosed that most commonly the anticipatory value of attitudinal data extended over a period from six to nine months.

In summary, attitude change has both an explanatory and a predictive function. Attitude change is defined as a finding that at a given time a significantly higher or lower proportion of the population holds certain attitudes than at an earlier time. To explain the double function of such a finding let us say, for example, that at time point 3 a significantly higher proportion of a representative sample is found to be optimistic, confident, and secure than at a preceding time point 2 and a still earlier time point 1. Under such circumstances we would expect to find that more people had bought durable goods during the period between time points 2 and 3 than between time points 1 and 2. Therefore we would conclude that the change in attitudes had contributed to our understanding of the increase in demand. Secondly, we would expect the demand for durable goods to rise after time point 3, which means that we assign predictive value to the change in attitudes.

Both the explanatory and the predictive function of attitude change has then been related to a change in the *direction* of demand for durable goods. How about the *magnitude* of the change in demand? In a certain sense the two questions are closely related. If attitudes remain unchanged —in other words, if differences between two successive measurements are not significant—we conclude that demand will either increase or decrease slightly but will not change greatly. If the attitude change is substantial, not only are we more confident that demand will change but we shall expect the change to be of significant magnitude in the direction indicated by the attitudes. Nevertheless, there is a great difference between predicting direction and predicting magnitude of a forthcoming change. Although it is possible to devise a scale for measuring attitudes, it is hardly possible to correlate attitude measurements with such others as dollar sales of durable goods and thus to say, for example, that a "10 per cent improvement" in attitudes would indicate a 10 per cent increase in sales. There exists a second reason why this kind of prediction of the magnitude of change is not justified: the magnitude of consumer demand is much more susceptible to the influence of external developments than is the direction of demand. The latter, as we said, is subject to change only as the result of major new events. The former, on the other hand, is influenced by a variety of less important developments and therefore may change more frequently. Furthermore, there exist "feedback" effects which may in turn serve to cause still more change in magnitude—but not direction—of demand. To illustrate, an increase in demand for durable goods, initiated by an improvement in attitudes, may serve to spur consumer confidence and thus result in still further increases in consumer demand.

That studies of consumer attitudes serve primarily to enable us to understand and predict the direction, rather than the magnitude, of changes in demand does not detract greatly from the value of such studies. It is indeed the question of what direction the economy will take that is of prime importance to students of business cycles and to policy makers both in business and in government. Will the prevailing trend continue, or will there be a change? If there is a change, will it be upward or downward? These are the questions of primary interest and precisely the ones which studies of changes in attitudes help to answer.

CHAPTER 5

On the Origin of Changes in Attitudes

One of the most challenging questions in the field of psychological economics is that of the origin of changes in attitudes and expectations. Substantial changes in consumer sentiment were observed at certain times, notably in 1954 and 1957. The presence of such changes was determined by asking the same attitudinal questions from different representative samples of the population several times in succession. The changes were explained in Chapter 3 by studying the reasons people gave for their attitudes and finding out how those reasons changed from time to time. The question we raise now is whether it is possible to go further and to study directly the dynamics of the process of change. Since it is the attitudes and expectations of individuals which change, the question is whether it is possible to study why individual people feel and think differently at one time from how they have felt and thought at an earlier time. A method different from the one used before must then be applied: the same individuals must be interviewed twice, or even several times, in succession so as to determine what has happened to those who changed their expectations in comparison with those who did not.

A word of caution is necessary. We speak of individual people, but we are not interested in a particular individual or family who has become more or less optimistic or who bought or did not buy durable goods. We wish to make average judgments about groups of individuals, since we are concerned with the characteristics, experiences, and behavior of the changers as compared with the nonchangers. In more general terms: our aim is to contribute to an explanation of changes in mass attitudes, that is, to obtain macroeconomic insights. Yet macroeconomic or aggregative developments result from microeconomic processes which occur in a significant number of individuals or in homogeneous subgroups of the population. The relation of micro to macro changes is in the center of our interest.

We shall compare situations in which attitudes changed substantially with situations in which they did not change to any appreciable degree. Our studies fortunately covered periods in which each situation prevailed

—substantial change in 1954 and 1957, and over-all stability in the second half of 1955 and in 1956. Furthermore, even in periods in which there were great changes, changes did not take place in all kinds of attitudes, or in all individuals. Therefore, it is possible to analyze the differences between presence and absence of substantial change in attitudes with the aim of finding out how a change in attitudes comes about.

Instability of Response and Acquisition of Information

We begin with a discussion of the situation in which attitudes remained fairly stable. Suppose that in each of two surveys, taken six months apart, 60 per cent of a sample were found optimistic and 40 per cent pessimistic. The simplest way of explaining such a finding is to attribute absence of aggregate change to absence of change on the part of individual people. We assume then that everybody, or practically everybody, feels and thinks the same way at one time as he did at the previous time because— and this is a further assumption—nothing new has happened. In other words, we assume that the same stimuli affected people at both times and brought forth the same responses.

This is not a very plausible assumption. It is improbable that the same things should influence all people on two successive occasions several months apart. This may be true, of course, for some people. But there always will be others who had different personal experiences in the period between the two interviews, even though general economic conditions remained unchanged and could conceivably influence all alike. Sickness or recovery from sickness, progress in one's career or disappointment about one's progress, increase or decrease in income—to mention just a few major factors—are never absent in our society and vary greatly among individual people. Therefore when two successive measurements of expectations yield the same aggregate distributions, we should expect to find that some or even many individuals have changed in one direction and a similar number of others in the opposite direction. Two consecutive relatively stable distributions of attitudes would then be explained by the presence of real changes in both directions which cancel one another.

What follows then for the other situation, more pertinent to our interest, in which aggregate measurements indicate a substantial change in mass attitudes? Suppose we find 40 per cent optimists and 60 per cent pessimists in the first survey, and 60 per cent optimists and 40 per cent pessimists in the second survey. (Shifts of that magnitude were observed, for instance, between the spring and the fall of 1954.) Naturally, in this instance many more individuals must have shifted from pessimism to optimism (P-O) than from optimism to pessimism (O-P).[1] Simple arithmetic indicates that actual findings about individuals must fall between the following two limits, the first of which represents the absence of any cross-shifts and the second the largest possible number of individual variation.

Limiting conditions	Frequency of			
	P-O	O-P	O-O	P-P
I. Absence of cross-shifts..............	20%	0%	40%	40%
II. Maximum possible number of cross-shifts	60	40	0	0

Will actual findings be closer to the first or to the second limiting condition? Or more precisely, under what circumstances will actual findings resemble the first and under what other circumstances the second limiting condition?

The difference between the two conditions may become clearer if we introduce two concepts. The first is *instability of response*. Suppose we determine the short-term business expectations of a representative sample in April and again in October and our findings resemble Condition II. We may then report that in October there were many more optimists than in April, but we shall also have to report that the responses were highly unstable, or that there were crosscurrents of influences. If cross-shifts are found to be frequent not only in the entire population but also in its major subgroups—say, among people in low-income as well as in high-income brackets—we may have reason to believe that the measurements represent nothing more than guesses or opinions made up on the spur of the moment. Probably many people vacillated between optimistic and pessimistic replies in both tests. Instability of response would greatly detract from the reliance to be put on data about changes in aggregate distributions.

The second concept, which characterizes findings resembling Limiting Condition I, is that of the *acquisition of information*. Unidirectional changes and an absence of cross-shifts occur typically in successful learning. Suppose we ask a class of pupils who have never heard of square roots, What is the square root of 81?, let them choose between two given alternatives—say, 9 and 11—and record the answers. Suppose we test them again a few months later, after they have learned about square roots.

[1] This form of designation will be used in the entire chapter. The capital letter O stands for people giving optimistic responses (better, up, favorable, etc.), the capital letter P for people giving pessimistic responses (worse, down, unfavorable, etc.). The sequence of the letters indicates the responses in successive surveys; for instance, O-P the people who gave optimistic responses in the first and pessimitic responses in the second survey, P-P the people who gave pessimistic responses in both surveys, etc.

Ignoring misclassifications, we shall find some individuals who have shifted their answers from 11 to 9, some who have given the answer 9 both times (the first time, to be sure, as a lucky guess), perhaps some who have given the answer 11 both times (they did not learn)—but practically none who have shifted from 9 to 11.

The question then is, Can an absence of cross-shifts of attitudes and expectations result from masses of people acquiring the same information at the same time? Is it possible that a current of opinion may develop which may influence practically all the people so that they may find it very difficult to swim against the current, even if their own personal experiences are not in accord with the information? (Since personal experiences, such as illness and the like, always change in both directions, there must be some people in such a conflict situation!)

Should changes in mass attitudes reflect instability of attitudes, we may assume that people vacillate or express guesses and are easy subjects of propaganda and rumors. If, however, changes in mass attitudes result from acquisition of information, these conclusions are not warranted. To be sure, contrary information may be acquired subsequently, but in its absence the newly acquired attitudes will be relatively stable and permanent.

A simple example of acquisition of uniform information by masses can be given from opinion research, that is, from inquiries about people's information rather than their expectations. A representative sample was asked the following question: What has happened to the prices of things you buy during the last twelve months; have they stayed about the same, gone up, or gone down? This question was asked the first time in a period of price stability (1954–1955) and a second time after prices had gone up substantially and the inflationary trend had been widely discussed (end of 1956). Then, many individuals were found to have shifted from "Prices have been stable" to "Prices have gone up" and hardly any in the other direction. There were practically no cross-shifts.

If the acquisition of information may result in unidirectional change and the absence of cross-shifts in the realm of reports on facts, does the same hold true in the realm of expectations, and especially of optimism and pessimism regarding fluctuations in the economy? Approximately 800 families, representing a random sample of all urban families in the continental United States, were interviewed five times between the summer of 1954 and the spring of 1957 in order to collect data on the turnover of expectations by individuals in relation to changes in aggregate distributions.[2]

[2] This chapter is based on these studies, carried out by the author and published under the title "Attitude Change: Instability of Response and Acquisition of Experience." For detailed information on the methods used and the statistical formulae

We shall not attempt to explain here how an index of unnecessary turnover, that is, a measure of changes in attitudes by individuals which were contrary to the observed direction of changes in aggregate distributions, was constructed. Suffice it to say that the conclusions were drawn from calculations based on approximately forty attitudinal measurements repeated twice in succession with the identical 800 people. Since we

TABLE 4. AGGREGATE CHANGE AND TURNOVER BY INDIVIDUALS

Forms of successive response	Personal financial expectations 1954–1955	General economic outlook 1954–1955
Improvement (P-O)	19.5%	34%
Deterioration (O-P)	18.5	4
Unchanged, favorable (O-O)	20.5	50
Unchanged, not favorable (P-P)...............	41.5	12
Total....................................	100%	100%
Aggregate change:		
O in first measurement.......................	39%	54%
O in second measurement.....................	40	84
Difference................................	1%	30%

THE QUESTIONS WERE: Do you think that a year from now you people will be better off financially, or worse off, or just about the same as now? Do you think that during the next twelve months we'll have good times financially, or bad times, or what?

NOTES: Approximately 800 people, representative of the urban population in the United States, were asked the two questions once in 1954 and once in 1955. Though a greater variety of answers were recorded, for the sake of simplicity in this table the answers are classified in two groups, namely, such optimistic answers as "better" or "favorable" (O) and all other answers (P).

SOURCE: 1954–1957 panel study of the Survey Research Center, as reported in G. Katona, "Attitude Change."

shall not here repeat those calculations, we shall at least present a few examples which may convey an understanding of the conclusions.

Table 4 contains a greatly simplified presentation of findings as obtained with two different questions. When the sample was queried about personal financial expectations (first column), practically identical aggregate distributions were obtained in 1954 and in 1955. Both times the proportion that said they would be better off in twelve months and that said they did not expect any change in their situation remained substan-

developed, the reader is referred to that publication. The 1954–1957 panel study was made possible by a grant from the Ford Foundation.

tially the same. (Both times only a small proportion expected to be worse off.) Yet this absence of any change in mass attitudes was not brought about by most people expressing the same opinion both times. Close to two out of every five people changed their minds, half of them by becoming more optimistic and half by becoming more pessimistic; the individual changes canceled out.

A different picture emerged with respect to expectations as to general business conditions (second column). At the time of the first measurement in 1954, about one-half of the sample expected an improvement in national business conditions; in 1955, however, more than 80 per cent did so. This substantial improvement in the aggregate distribution was brought about by more than half of the sample giving the same answer both times, a substantial group (34 per cent) becoming more optimistic, and only a very small group (4 per cent) becoming more pessimistic. The extent of unnecessary turnover was small. Instead of individual changes averaging out, the direction of change was overwhelmingly uniform.

In most cases of substantial aggregate change the unnecessary turnover was found to be small. The result of the statistical studies was to show that the larger the change in aggregate distribution, the smaller the index of unnecessary turnover.

We may then draw the following conclusions from the studies just illustrated:

When two successive attitudinal measurements yield similar aggregate distributions, it is not probable that most individuals maintained their previous attitudes and expectations. On the contrary, it is likely that many individuals changed their attitudes in one and many others in another direction.[3]

When two successive attitudinal measurements yield substantial differences in aggregate distributions, it is likely that the changes will be predominantly in one direction. The population then tends to fall into two major groups, those who shifted in one direction and those who did not shift at all.

Social Learning

Successive interviews with identical people offer unique opportunities for studying the origin of change or lack of change in attitudes or overt

---

[3] This finding concerns what was called in Chapter 4 "situationally determined attitudes." When relatively deep-seated attitudes that are linked with personality traits were studied, small changes in aggregate distributions were observed to occur together with infrequent cross-shifts by individuals. The same result was obtained, of course, when simple factual questions, say about age or occupation, were asked twice of the same sample.

behavior. Two techniques are at the disposal of the researcher. First, on the basis of data obtained at the time of the first interview, he may group the respondents according to age, income, education, etc., and may then see whether those who have changed their attitudes or behavior at the time of the second interview and those who have not changed them fall into different groups. Alternatively, at the time of the second interview, the researcher may make inquiries about what has happened in the interim. He may study financial and other personal developments as well as the information acquired in the period between the two measurements, so as to find out whether such information or developments are related to the observed change or lack of change in attitudes or behavior. The major findings obtained in applying both research techniques to changes in personal financial expectations and in attitudes toward the general economic outlook (Table 4) will be reported here.

Beginning with *personal financial expectations,* we may study the people who have become more optimistic (P-O) in comparison with those who have not (P-P). At the time of the first interview their personal financial expectations were the same (P); yet more of those who have become more optimistic than of those who have not were found to be in upper-income groups, in younger age groups, to have had more education, and also to have been more optimistic in respects other than personal finances. In view of these differences it is possible that the first measurement P concealed certain significant differences in attitudes.

The two groups also had different personal experiences during the period between the two measurements. As compared with those who had remained pessimistic (P-P), the ones who had shifted to optimism (P-O) included many more whose income had increased and who said that conditions in the industry or trade in which they were working had improved.

As regards attitudes toward the *general economic outlook* the findings were quite different. The crucial large group registering an improvement (P-O) did not differ at all from those who remained unchanged (P-P) in regard to income, education, or age; the two groups also expressed very similar personal financial expectations at the time of the first interview. There were some differences between the two groups in personal financial experiences between the two interviews, but the really substantial differences were found elsewhere. Many more members of the Group P-O than of the Group P-P were aware of favorable developments in the American economy between the end of 1954 and the summer of 1955.

The information acquired about economic developments during the period between the two measurements was studied by handing a card to each member of the sample. The respondents were told: "This card contains some answers we received when we asked people about what had happened during the last twelve months in the American economy. Please check those items which you agree have happened." The card contained seven statements about developments that had allegedly taken place in the economy, and three columns entitled "Happened," "Did not happen," and "Don't know." Some of the statements were correct (e.g., "The cost of living was stable"), some were false (e.g., "Unemployment increased"). The check marks made by the respondents were scored for correctness of information and people who marked "Don't know" were taken as not having correct information. In fact, since the economy greatly improved in the twelve months between the two interviews, those people were correct who marked all favorable statements as "Happened" and all unfavorable statements as "Did not happen." It suffices to quote a few figures to indicate the results. Of those whose general economic outlook was unfavorable in both 1954 and 1955 (P-P), 63 per cent had hardly any correct (and therefore favorable) responses (0, 1 or 2 out of the 7) and 14 per cent had many (5, 6, or 7); in Group P-O only 27 per cent had hardly any correct and favorable responses and 35 per cent had many.[4] The two groups were similar in education (both groups contained slightly over 40 per cent with grade school, slightly over 40 per cent with high school, and 15 per cent with college education). Nevertheless, one group knew much more than the other about the economy, and their attitudes changed correspondingly.

One further item of some interest in this connection: When asked whether they had had any conversations with friends or colleagues about business conditions and economic developments, less than one-fourth of the sample answered in the affirmative and the number of conversations did not differ much from group to group. But in replies to a follow-up question about the content of the conversations, it appeared that people who were optimistic at the time of the second interview had had many more conversations relating to favorable developments; and those who were pessimistic, more conversations relating to unfavorable developments.

As said before, the studies just reported were carried out in a period in which business conditions improved greatly. The rate of industrial production, the size of national income, and the volume of retail sales all showed very substantial gains from 1954 to 1955, that is, in the time between the first and the second interview. During that time very many people were found to have acquired the same information about the economy. It may be said then that under such economic conditions the uniform acquisition of information on the part of masses of people is

[4] The O-O Group was also found to have much correct and favorable information. Possibly the general economic outlook of this group likewise improved. The crude measurements used made it impossible to find out.

possible. When significant new developments take place in the environment and information about them is widely transmitted, very many people
will comprehend the information in a similar manner. The information is
reinforced through personal contacts and discussions, and similar changes
in attitudes arise. Expectations of masses of people, that is, subjective
notions of things to come which have an affective connotation, are then
influenced by the information acquired. The influence is uniform, which
means that contrary changes in attitudes and therefore cross-shifts are
infrequent.

This last point requires further study. In personal financial expectations,
changes in which were related to instability of response and personal
experiences, cross-shifts were found to be frequent. In national business
expectations, changes in which were related to the acquisition of information about the environment, that is, to public rather than private events,
cross-shifts were found to be infrequent. How about the people who had
had unfavorable personal experiences and whose personal expectations
had deteriorated? Did they, too, acquire the favorable information about
the environment and express optimism about the general economic outlook? It appears that from 1954 to 1955 this was overwhelmingly the
case. In studying the people with unfavorable personal experiences between the two measurements—from the point of view of research it is
advantageous that even in times of growing prosperity there are some
people whose incomes decline, or who even lose their jobs!—we find that
about three-fourths became more optimistic or remained optimistic regarding business conditions. Thus there is evidence for a current which
overrides unfavorable experiences and affects very many people uniformly.

The finding that acquisition of information may result in change in
attitudes means that cognition may influence affective notions and preferences. There is nothing new in this statement, even though the process
has rarely been demonstrated, and the reverse process, affects influencing
cognition, has been given much more attention in recent psychological
research. The impact of cognition has here been demonstrated in a social
situation. There is every reason to believe that the similarity of the information acquired by members of the same group, or by people with
similar interests, is an essential feature of the learning process here
studied, and that the similarity of affective reactions is greatly promoted
by social interaction. It may therefore be justified to introduce the expression "social learning," which results in changes in mass attitudes as well
as in mass behavior. How the behavior of individuals is affected by a
change in their attitudes we shall discuss in the next chapter. Here it
suffices to recall what was related in Chapter 3. Following the improvement in mass attitudes in 1954 there was a substantial increase in demand
for consumer durable goods. Thus uniform acquisition of information—

social learning—had an impact on mass action and thereby on the economy.

Social learning did not take place in all areas of economic attitudes. For instance, in opinions about the economic effects of the cold war a fairly large number of cross-shifts were observed in 1955. The question in this instance was one about which uniform information was not transmitted. For some people cold war at that time meant rearmament and had the favorable connotation of growing production; for others, the majority, it meant the threat of war and heightened anxiety. Although shifts toward a pessimistic evaluation of the situation were more frequent than shifts toward an optimistic evaluation, both shifts occurred.

Studies of attitude change were carried out during 1956 along the same lines as the studies for 1954–1955. While in the first period the American economy improved substantially, in the second period the level of activity remained high with little further improvement. Some of the economic news of 1956 was favorable, for instance, that over-all industrial production had increased; some unfavorable, e.g., that auto sales had declined. Differences in the extent of correct information did not help to explain the presence or absence of change in attitudes. Even people who were well informed about economic developments were more effectively influenced by their personal experiences. Under these circumstances there were many cross-shifts of opinion—many people changed their expectations in one direction and many others in the opposite direction—and there was no indication of social learning.

We must conclude, therefore, that only under certain conditions does uniform learning take place and influence people's opinions and attitudes in the same direction. Under other conditions the information acquired is not uniform, and cross-shifts of attitudes result. The difference between the two conditions may be accounted for partly by the extent of changes in the economy (whether they are large or small) and partly by the uniformity of news about changes (whether most of it is or is not in the same direction). In the first instances, but not in the second, a positive relation could be established between information received and changes in attitudes.

In the summer and fall of 1957, in contrast to 1956, economic attitudes again changed substantially, this time by becoming much more pessimistic. The statistical data did not all show unfavorable trends at that time; for instance, it was widely reported that national income and retail sales had risen to their highest level in the third quarter of 1957. But questions about the economic information received by the respondents indicated that for most people the unfavorable news alone was salient. Great attention was paid to unfavorable news at that time, because it differed radically from the news to which people had become accustomed during the preceding years. These findings, like those of 1954, reveal a powerful tendency toward consistency in social cognition. There is a pressure to reduce dissonance arising from contradictory information, so that our comprehension and interpretation of news will be more consistent and more one-sided than an objective recording of the news warrants.[5] Without this tendency toward consistency of opinions, a current of opinion could hardly develop and attitudes would not spread by contagion. But there are limits to the power of the tendency toward consistency. Sometimes, as in 1956, we live with divergent trends, and uniform social learning does not take place.

These last remarks may help us to answer a question which may have come to the minds of some readers. We have explained certain substantial changes in attitudes through the uniform acquisition of information. Why then bother with attitudes? Why not just consider changes in economic behavior as resulting from objective events about which people have received information, and deduce what people will do from the nature of the economic information that has been disseminated? A closer look at the picture reveals that all we were able to do was to explain attitude change *post hoc*; after knowing how attitudes had changed, factors explaining the change could be found. The other way around this process is much more difficult and often not possible. Even complete knowledge of all events and developments would represent nothing more than a listing of possible stimuli. If such a listing were obtained, for instance, through content analysis of all news transmitted, we would still not know which items of the news were salient and how they were apprehended. This can be done only by starting with attitudes. Knowing the prevailing attitudes and changes in them, we may connect them with relevant events and developments because then we are in a position to select what has been salient. Therefore it is not possible to dispense with the study of attitudes and to study the economic or political developments which gave rise to them in their stead.

There may, of course, be certain events from which one might conceivably deduce how they would influence people's attitudes and actions. Developments of overwhelming significance, especially of a catastrophic nature, may belong in this category. But with the possible exception of those rare events which we know for sure will be salient (e.g., Pearl Harbor, the outbreak of the Korean War), it appears to be most difficult to deduce from observed events their probable effect on attitudes.

Conclusions

We may summarize what we have learned about the origin of changes in expectations in a few fairly definite statements. But the language used

[5] Cf. the studies of L. Festinger in his *Theory of Cognitive Dissonance*.

should not imply that the conclusions are definitely established. Further research will no doubt amplify and modify the statements presented.

1. Change in expectations is due either to the acquisition of widely transmitted public information (a), or to personal experiences (b).

2. At any given time there will be individuals who are influenced by personal experiences (b) in one direction, and individuals who are influenced in the opposite direction. On the other hand, most commonly, public information (a) is either noninfluential or operates in the same direction with very many people.

3. If variable a is not influential, aggregate changes in consumer expectations will usually be small because the changes in individual expectations cancel out. Observing on successive occasions substantially unchanged distributions, the researcher cannot assume that most individuals have maintained their previous expectations; on the contrary, it is probable that among individuals there have been frequent changes in both directions (due to different personal experiences or to vacillation on the part of many people).

4. If variable a is effective and important, the aggregate changes in expectations will tend to be substantial. In this case it is likely that contrary effects of personal experiences will be suppressed or lessened. Substantial aggregate changes in expectations may therefore be attributed to public information. There is little reason to doubt the significance of survey findings about substantial changes in expectations, because they tend to occur without the presence of numerous cross-shifts in attitudes.

5. Whether or not information is acquired in a uniform manner depends primarily on the kind of news about which information is transmitted. Social learning will occur when masses of people become convinced that something which they consider important has happened. Widely anticipated, gradual, and small changes in the environment, or events about which controversial information is transmitted, usually do not result in substantial changes in the attitudes of the masses. But there is no easy way to predict the impact of news on attitudes; direct measurement of attitudes remains indispensable.

CHAPTER 6

Attitudes and Behavior of Individuals

The relation of attitudes to action was studied in Chapter 3 in terms of aggregate behavior: When successive measurements disclosed that the proportion of optimists or pessimists in the American population had changed substantially, a corresponding change in demand for durable goods was demonstrated. Is there no simpler and more direct way of testing the basic assumptions of psychological economics? Growing or declining optimism could hardly influence demand if it were not true that optimists—people who regard the present and the future with confidence and expect good times and an improvement in their financial situation—buy more durable goods than pessimists. A direct test of the relation between attitudes and action would then consist of comparing two groups of people, one optimistic and the other pessimistic, but similar in other respects (e.g., in income and age), and studying their subsequent purchases. Should such a test fail, then, so it has been argued, differences in aggregate purchases in periods following greater or lesser optimism would be hard to understand and might even be viewed as not conclusive or as accidental.[1]

The argument just presented is deceptive. Although the premises are correct, the conclusion is not justified. The explanation of why this is so involves problems of measurement. Since these problems are technical, they are discussed in the Appendix to this book, in the section on Difficulties in Measurement (pages 254–256).

[1] The Consultant Committee on Consumer Survey Statistics, set up by the Federal Reserve Board, wrote in 1955: "The only satisfactory way to test relevance and predictive value of attitudes, expectations, and intentions is to find out how differences in attitudes of individuals influence the subsequent action of these same individuals." The author replied to this contention in his article, "Federal Reserve Committee Reports." The problem was again taken up in the papers presented at the Conference on the Quality and Economic Significance of Anticipations Data. The papers by Okun (followed by replies by Katona and Mueller) and by Mueller contain an extensive discussion of the value and limitations of research with individuals. See also J. Tobin, "On the Predictive Value of Consumer Intentions and Attitudes."

Fulfillment of Expressed Intentions

In spite of great difficulties in measurement, several studies have been carried out in which actions of small groups of individuals who had expressed different attitudes and expectations were compared. Before reporting on the differences in purchases by optimists and by pessimists, we shall analyze the correlation between expressed intentions to buy and the subsequent purchases of the same people. The problems confronting measurement are much smaller in the case of buying intentions. For instance, in measuring the fulfillment of expressed intentions the problem of timing (point 4) does not arise at all and interpersonal comparisons

Figure 9. Comparison of intentions to buy cars during the next twelve months with subsequent purchases on the part of the same people

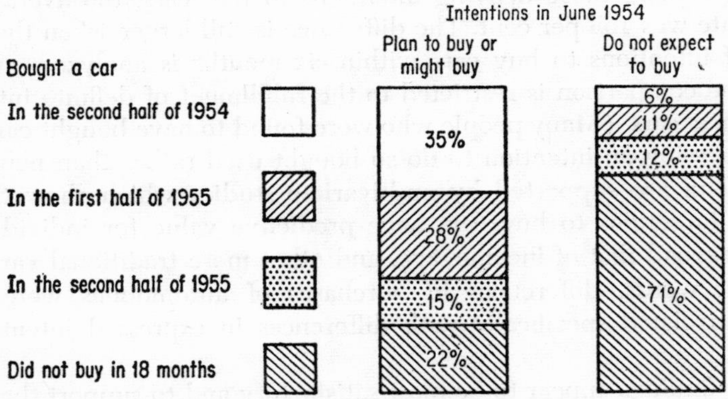

SOURCE: C. Lininger, E. Mueller, and H. Wyss, "Some Uses of Panel Studies in Forecasting the Automobile Market."

(point 1) are much more valid (reference is made here to points discussed in the Appendix). In order to study the fulfillment of buying intentions, once again the methods described in Chapter 5 were used: the same sample was interviewed at least twice in succession, once to determine the intentions to buy and once to determine the purchases in the subsequent period.

A representative sample of urban families was asked in June, 1954, Do you people expect to buy a car during the next twelve months or so? In Figure 9 the sample is divided into two groups, those who said No and all others. (Definite buying plans and conditional answers are therefore combined.) The entire sample was reinterviewed several times later and it was determined when, if at all, during the following eighteen months members of the two groups had bought a car.

Close to two out of three families who in June, 1954, expressed a definite or conditional intention to buy a car did so in the following twelve months. It is hardly surprising that some families did not carry out their intentions. Adverse developments making it impossible or inadvisable to carry out our plans do occur. The purchase rate of 63 per cent is much higher than that of 17 per cent on the part of those who did not express an intention to buy. The difference is most pronounced during the six-month period immediately following the expression of intentions (35 and 6 per cent) and less pronounced during the period six to twelve months distant (28 and 11 per cent). The purchase rates of the two groups during the second half of 1955 are similar; this is a period beyond the one about which intentions have been ascertained.

Similar measurements were made in four additional reinterview studies, carried out between 1948 and 1956. The average fulfillment rate in the five studies was 60 per cent for intentions to buy cars within twelve months. Among those denying intentions to buy cars, the average purchase rate was 16½ per cent. The difference is still larger when the fulfillment of intentions to buy cars within six months is analyzed, and also when the comparison is restricted to the fulfillment of definite intentions to buy *new* cars. (Many people who were found to have bought cars without expressing an intention to do so bought used rather than new cars.) These data are supported by multivariate studies which show that expressed intentions to buy cars have predictive value for individual behavior beyond that of income, age, and other more traditional variables.[2] In other words, differences in purchases of automobiles were found to be correlated specifically with differences in expressed intentions to buy.[3]

These findings appear to be most satisfactory and to support the aggregative test of car-buying intentions as presented graphically in Figure 6 of Chapter 3. The fact remains, however, that what has been shown is no more than could be expressed by the following little-surprising analogy: If a salesman first ascertains which families expect to buy a car and then concentrates his sales efforts on those families, he will save himself a lot of effort; those who express intentions to buy are much better prospects than those who do not.

A further finding detracts from the significance of the results: Usually of five people queried, one expressed an intention to buy a car within twelve months and four did not. Suppose we have one hundred randomly

[2] See the studies by Klein and Lansing; de Janosi; Okun.

[3] Studies relating to the fulfillment of intentions to purchase large household appliances yielded similar results, although the rate of fulfillment was lower (approximately 45 rather than 60 per cent in twelve months), and a larger proportion of total purchases of household goods was not reflected in buying intentions (that is, was found not to have been planned several months in advance).

selected people. Among them twenty express an intention to buy and twelve of the twenty actually buy within twelve months (60 per cent of the twenty). Among the eighty who say that they do not expect to buy a car, thirteen actually buy a car (16 per cent of the eighty). In other words, we designate in advance only one-half of the twenty-five actual car purchasers.

Several studies were undertaken to find an explanation for the numerous purchases on the part of people who expressed no intention to buy. One major result of these studies is particularly interesting: Among those who had bought a car, although they had said earlier that they did not expect to do so, unexpected favorable developments—as, for instance, unexpected income increases—were more frequent than among the others. This finding and a variety of others—occasional short planning periods, suddenly arising needs, etc.—indicate that in retrospect it is usually possible to find an explanation for the behavior of individual families. But for predicting individual rather than aggregate purchasing behavior, the simple method of asking for buying intentions does not suffice.

The findings with respect to consumers' expressed intentions to purchase durable goods are analogous to the findings of the Securities and Exchange Commission and the Commerce Department with respect to capital expenditure plans of business firms. The surveys carried out by these agencies have a good record in predicting annual changes in aggregate business investments. Yet when those plans were compared with the actual expenditures of the identical corporations (determined a year later), substantial deviations were found in the majority of the cases.[4] The deviations in both directions cancelled out and left a high degree of accuracy in the aggregate figures. If such two-directional changes from original plans occurred among corporations, when many of the plans represented actual commitments, it is certainly to be expected that similar changes would also occur among consumers, whose expressed intentions usually represent subjective notions and attitudes.

Purchases of Optimists and Pessimists

Consumers' expressed buying intentions were tested by assessing their predictive value. The relation of consumer attitudes and expectations toward personal financial and business conditions to spending behavior must be studied in a broader context. In addition to asking whether consumer attitudes are useful for *predicting* the prospective durable goods purchases of those who have expressed the attitudes, we must also find out whether these attitudes *influenced* at all the purchases of individ-

[4] See I. Friend and J. Bronfenbrenner, "Business Investment Programs and Their Realization."

ual consumers. In attempting to answer the question about predictive value, only information can be taken into account which was available before the period in which the purchases were made. To answer the broader question about influence, information about changes in attitudes during the purchase period is also relevant. Since there are more frequent fluctuations in individual than in aggregate attitudes, an analysis of the effects of improvement or deterioration of individual attitudes may yield new insights despite the prevailing difficulties in measurement.

Studies carried out by Eva Mueller on the influence of attitudes were based on the index of consumer attitudes, exclusive of buying intentions. On the basis of the index the consumers were divided into three groups characterized as "optimists," "medium," and "pessimists." The number of major durable goods purchased (automobiles, major household goods, power lawn mowers, speedboats and the like, as well as major repairs and improvements to homes) was determined for each family in a sample representative of the urban population. The number of purchases rather than the dollar amounts spent was compared, first, to simplify the analysis and second, because changes in consumer sentiment may well influence the decision as to whether or not to make a purchase more decisively than the decision as to the amount spent on each purchase.[5]

The number of purchases increases, of course, with income (the correlation is even stronger in the case of amounts of money spent). Appropriate statistical methods were used, therefore, to exclude the effects of income. In the process a variety of other effects, notably those of education and age, were simultaneously reduced, if not eliminated. The data presented in Table 5 represent index-values computed as the ratio of the number of actual purchases to the number of purchases which would have been expected on the basis of the income distribution of families falling into the various attitudinal groups. The differences between the index-values represent, then, the influence of attitudinal differences on the number of purchases.

We shall look first at durable-goods purchases during the twelve months between June, 1954, and June, 1955, that is, in a period in which the economy as well as consumer attitudes improved considerably. (Consumer attitudes had begun to improve even before June, 1954.) Separate data were collected for purchases made during the second half of 1954 and the first half of 1955. Attitudinal data were determined at the beginning and at the end of the twelve-month period. Attitudes in June, 1954, will be called *initial attitudes,* and those in June, 1955, *final attitudes.* In addition to studying the purchase rates of people classified according to either their initial or their final attitudes, it was possible to group the

[5] See E. Mueller, "Effects of Consumer Attitudes on Purchases." The index has been described in Chapter 3 of this book.

families into three new classifications: those whose attitudes *improved,* remained the *same,* and *deteriorated* from June, 1954, to June, 1955. The problem posed in analyzing the influence of attitude change on purchases resembles the problem investigated before on the aggregate level. For the study of business cycles our concern has been with the relationship between changes in attitudes (increased or decreased proportion of optimists) and changes in the rate of spending (larger or smaller expenditures on automobiles and other durable goods in the United States).

TABLE 5. COMPARISON OF PURCHASE RATES OF FAMILIES WITH DIFFERENT ATTITUDINAL CLASSIFICATIONS

(June, 1954–June, 1955)

Grouping of families	Index-value of number of durable goods purchases * by		
	Optimists	Medium	Pessimists
By initial or final attitudes:			
Initial attitudes, purchases in first 6 months	1.15	0.95	0.88
Initial attitudes, purchases in 12 months...	1.07	1.02	0.86
Final attitudes, purchases in 12 months...	1.06	0.99	0.78
	Improved attitudes	Unchanged attitudes	Deteriorated attitudes
By change in attitudes:			
Purchases in first 6 months..............	1.04	0.99	0.95
Purchases in last 6 months..............	1.11	0.95	0.87

* Income held constant.
SOURCE: E. Mueller, "Effects of Consumer Attitudes on Purchases."

We see in Table 5 that the index-value of purchases by optimists is higher than that of people with medium attitudes, which in turn is higher than that of the pessimists. The same relationship exists among those whose attitudes improved, remained the same, and deteriorated, respectively. Initial attitudes appear to influence the purchases during the first six months somewhat more strongly than during the entire twelve-month period. In fact, and this is not shown in the table, the predictive value of initial attitudes for purchases made during the period six to twelve months after the measurement is negligible. This is not surprising since very many people changed their attitudes between June, 1954, and June, 1955, and attitude change is related to purchases. It is seen from the table that the influence of attitude change was more pronounced in the first half of 1955 than in the second half of 1954. We do not know when people changed their attitudes during the twelve-month period, but there can be no doubt that the number of changers must have increased as time went by after the initial measurement.

Certain cautions must be borne in mind in evaluating the data in Table 5. First, the differences among the attitudinal groups are small, in some cases not statistically significant. Second, in studying the predictive value of attitudes, when initial attitudes alone must be considered, the differential effect of attitudes on subsequent purchases was found to be much smaller than the income effect or the predictive value of expressed buying intentions. Third, repetition of the same studies during other periods did not fully confirm the findings obtained in 1954–1955. Durable-goods purchases made in the second half of 1955 were not influenced much by attitudes expressed in June, 1955. In the first half of 1956 again some influence, albeit a smaller one than in 1954, was apparent. The purchase rate of those who were classified as optimists in December, 1955, was 1.14 in the first half of 1956 as compared to a purchase rate of 0.91 by others.

The differences in findings obtained in different periods are in accord with our position that attitudes are not always influential. During the second half of 1955, for instance, attitudes changed very little and our previous explanation of cyclical behavior (Chapter 3) was entirely in terms of ability to buy, rather than in terms of changes in willingness to buy. The former was also the major factor in determining durable-goods sales in 1956. It is reassuring that a study of the purchases of individuals at that time could still show some differential effect of attitudes.

The relatively small size of the observed differences between the purchase rates of families grouped according to their attitudes may be attributed to the difficulties in measurement, as described in the Appendix. Because of these difficulties, attitudes are correlated with spending behavior much more strongly on the aggregate than on the individual level. There is nothing in the findings which would cast doubt on the high correlations obtained in aggregative tests.

Achievement Orientation versus Security Orientation

Up to now we have discussed the impact of what have been called situationally determined attitudes, which alone are relevant for the understanding of cyclical fluctuations. Yet we also have postulated the existence of more enduring attitudes related to personality traits and have spoken of the possible impact of such attitudes on long-range economic developments. In this area the usual aggregative tests would be meaningless; the respective frequencies of different personality-related attitudes could not be expected to vary during cyclical upswings or downswings. Data on the distribution of such attitudes during the prosperous fifties as compared with the depressed thirties would be most valuable from the point of view of understanding long-range trends, but, unfortunately, there are no such data for the thirties. Lack of data also prevents us from making intercultural comparisons, say, between the United States and European or underdeveloped countries. Yet we do assume that the American economy in the fifties has been influenced by a relatively high proportion of people holding certain fairly stable attitudes conducive to prosperity. Support for this assumption may be derived from performing a test similar to the one made with cyclical attitudes. If it is found to be true that individuals holding certain prosperity-related attitudes differ in their spending and saving behavior from individuals holding opposite attitudes, our conclusions about the significance of these long-term attitudes would be greatly strengthened.

Which attitude of this nature should be studied? The foremost candidate among psychological factors related to progress and growth in the economy is achievement orientation.[6] There can be no doubt that entrepreneurs with achievement motivation and rising levels of aspiration contribute to economic advancement. Consumers' drives toward accomplishment, higher incomes, and better jobs and positions, as well as their striving for improved standards of living and the ownership of more and better consumer goods, are likewise closely related to prosperity and progress, and may be grounded in underlying motives and attitudes. The extent of achievement motivation among individuals could best be determined through indirect psychological tests in which reactions to pictures and stories would be evaluated. Since, however, the time available in the course of the interviews was not sufficient to permit the administration of such psychological tests, a simple method was devised which was deemed sufficient to separate people with pronounced achievement orientation from those with pronounced security orientation. It was assumed that striving for achievement includes not only upward mobility but also the acceptance, or at least the tolerance, of some risks. By contrast, security-oriented people were defined as those concerned primarily with maintaining and holding what they had and having a closed image of the future.

We do not presume to report how many people in America are achievement-oriented and how many security-oriented. We know simply what proportions were found through a specific method of measurement. Had we used a different method, no doubt different absolute frequencies

---

[6] Long-range income expectations were not considered in this connection. Answers to a question about one's probable income trend over several years seem to represent an intermediate category of attitudes, being influenced strongly by situational as well as personality factors. We shall discuss such expectations in Chapter 9.

would have been obtained. In our studies in 1954, in which husband and wife were interviewed alternately, a sample representative of all urban people was given a card which read as follows: "Would you please look at this card and tell me which thing on this list about a job (occupation) you would most prefer (would want most for your husband); which comes next, which third, and so forth."

	Rank from 1 (*most preferred*)
An occupation or job in which:	to 6 (*least preferred*)
A. Income is steady	. . . .
B. Income is high	. . . .
C. There's no danger of being fired or unemployed	. . . .
D. Working hours are short, lots of free time	. . . .
E. Chances for advancement are good	. . . .
F. The work is important, gives a feeling of accomplishment	. . . .

In analyzing the responses, all those who numbered both A and C as 1, 2, or 3, or who ranked both A and C higher than E and F, were classified as security-oriented. All those who numbered both E and F as 1, 2, or 3, or who ranked both E and F higher than A and C, were classified as achievement-oriented. All other combinations were treated as unclassifiable. Although these criteria set for classifying people as either achievement- or security-oriented are fairly rigorous, over 80 per cent of the sample qualified as belonging in one of the two groups. The following division of urban people was obtained:

Achievement-oriented	28%
Security-oriented	54
Not classifiable	18
	100%

No doubt, there were errors of measurement and misclassifications. Yet repetition of the same series of questions in 1958 with a different representative sample yielded substantially the same division of the urban population. Also, the classifications were confirmed through a variety of cross-tabulations with demographic variables. We would expect, for instance, to find a relatively high proportion of business managers and professional people in the achievement group and a low proportion in the security group. These expectations were confirmed. Orientation was also found to be related to income. Within the lower- and middle-income groups the proportions of achievers and securers did not differ much, while in the higher-income groups a disproportionately greater number of people were achievement-oriented. The relationship to age was not very pronounced, although among the security-minded there was a somewhat larger number of people forty-five to sixty-four years of age and among achievers somewhat more younger people. People of security orientation more frequently had had one job for over ten years, while those of achievement orientation had changed their jobs more often. Residence in suburbs was relatively frequent among the latter as compared to the former.

Although each of the demographic variables served to lend confirmation to the validity of our method of classifying attitudes, no one of the variables—and no combination thereof—bore a sufficiently strong correlation with our achievement-security measurements to warrant substituting the former for the latter. It should also be noted that achievement and security orientation are not synonymous with short-term optimism and pessimism. Yet, as expected, among those in the former group there were somewhat more optimists and in the latter group somewhat more pessimists—using the terms optimist and pessimist in the sense of expecting personal financial advancement in the short run and good times for the economy in the near future.

Further studies by Elise Boulding resulted in findings which were not anticipated.[7] The proportion of homeowners, of owners of two cars, and of newer, not yet commonly owned household durables, as well as of fair-sized liquid reserves was higher among the achievement-minded than among the security-minded. Thus it did not appear to be true that the ownership of many goods and assets makes people anxious to hold and maintain what they have rather than strive for more. Nor can it be concluded that the have-nots are characterized by frequent desires and thus become achievement-oriented. These findings underline still more significant relationships that were revealed.

Achievement mindedness was defined in terms of orientation toward the future. How was it found to relate to satisfaction and dissatisfaction with past progress and present conditions? Among those who were satisfied with their current income and current standard of living, there were more achievement-oriented people, and among the dissatisfied more security-oriented people. Thus it is not dissatisfaction which creates striving for achievement and upward mobility, and it is not saturation which results in attitudes laying stress on maintenance and security. These findings deserve somewhat closer scrutiny.

In 1954 in the entire urban sample 58 per cent said they were satisfied with their income or, more precisely, that their income at that time was what they thought they ought to be getting; the others thought that they ought to be earning more. In the same sample 68 per cent said that they were satisfied with their standard of living, and the rest that their stand-

[7] E. Boulding, "Achievement and Security Orientation and Consumer Behavior." The studies described on the following pages are tentative and require repetition on a broader scale. Nevertheless, the highly suggestive findings of these studies are worth reporting.

ard of living was not as good as they would like.[8] Altogether there were 45 per cent who professed to be satisfied both with their income and their standard of living. Among the achievement-oriented, two-thirds were satisfied both with income and standard of living; among the security-oriented, only 40 per cent.

Questions were also asked about satisfaction with past occupational progress and it was found that in 1955, a prosperous year, the great majority of the achievers expressed such satisfaction. The security group, on the other hand, consisted of three subgroups. One of these was satisfied with their past progress as well as their current situation; another reported good past occupational progress but dissatisfaction with the current situation. The third subgroup, the smallest of three, reported unsatisfactory occupational progress and dissatisfaction with their current situation. It appears, then, that dissatisfaction and "bad breaks" are much more frequently associated with security than with achievement orientation. Nevertheless, security orientation also arises under different circumstances.

In the two years following the classification of people according to their orientation, data were collected on the economic behavior of the two groups. We shall report, as in the previous section, the number of durable-goods purchases by each group, after eliminating income effects. In addition, we shall eliminate differences in satisfaction with the past and present economic situation by restricting the comparison to satisfied achievers and satisfied securers.

The differences shown in Table 6 are not substantial, but consistent in both years. Similar differences were found between the two groups after age, stage in the life cycle, and recent income changes were taken into account. It is hardly surprising that the differences in the rate of spending of the two groups were not larger since obviously many other factors were also operative. It is rather highly suggestive that some marginal effects of long-range orientation were found, even though long-range orientation was defined neither in terms of optimism or pessimism, nor in terms of striving or not striving for a higher standard of living. People who placed a high value on having an important job in which the chances for advancement were good purchased somewhat more durable goods then people who were interested in a steady and secure job. This relationship between upward job mobility and speedier acquisition of relatively permanent consumer goods is hardly an inevitable one, but it did prevail in the United States in the fifties and seems to have been related to prosperous economic conditions.

Studies of discretionary saving—adding to bank deposits and purchasing government bonds and other securities—likewise yielded differences

[8] Further data on consumer satisfaction are presented in Chapter 11, where the questions used are quoted verbatim.

TABLE 6. COMPARISON OF PURCHASE RATES OF FAMILIES WITH
DIFFERENT ORIENTATIONS

Year	Index-value of number of durable goods purchases *	
	Achievement group	Security group
1955.....................	1.11	0.90
1956.....................	1.14	0.95

* Income held constant; dissatisfied families are eliminated.

SOURCE: E. Boulding, "Achievement and Security Orientation and Consumer Behavior."

between the achievement and security groups. In each of the three years 1954, 1955, and 1956 a somewhat higher proportion of middle-income achievement-oriented people engaged in discretionary saving than of middle-income security-oriented people. This finding may be considered surprising since saving is generally viewed as contributing to security. The finding contradicts the widespread notion that mobile people spend and nonmobile people save. It suggests that adding to liquid reserves is a dynamic form of behavior which represents the achievement of highly valued goals.

The achievement group was found to be engaged more frequently both in spending on durables and in discretionary saving than the security group. What did the latter do with their income? They must have spent a larger proportion of their income on nondurables and services than the former. We shall come back to this point in the next chapter and conclude here simply that achievers are more concerned than securers with those forms of economic behavior which are oriented toward the future: accumulating durable goods as well as money.

CHAPTER 7

Stability of Consumer Saving

Traditionally, economists have laid great emphasis on the variability of consumer saving. In contrast, we have stressed the fluctuations of consumer expenditures on durable goods. A study of savings practices and motives is therefore in order.

The theoretical propositions about the dependence of the state of the economy on variations in the amounts saved may be simply stated. If all consumers spent all their incomes, all business firms spent all their receipts, and government budgets were always balanced, money would circulate in the economy without any additions or diminutions. If, further, the velocity of money were constant, for instance, because everybody paid out promptly everything he received, a static equilibrium would prevail. Saving constitutes an interruption of the money flow. Consumers as well as business firms, through not spending some of their income, may retard economic activity. The use of accumulated savings, on the other hand, may serve to inject new money into the economy. Thus, retarding forces are set into motion when the rate of saving is increased, and accelerating forces are released when the rate of saving is reduced. It is thus to saving that a major role in determining economic fluctuations is attributed.[1]

In discussing consumer saving we must first of all make clear that saving, that is, income not spent,[2] is an accounting rather than a behavioral concept. It consists of at least two fundamentally different components: contractual and noncontractual saving. Contractual saving includes repayment of mortgages and of installment debt, as well as payments into retirement funds and of life insurance premiums, which, as we have said in Chapter 2, are carried out in a routine manner except under catastrophic circumstances. Previous commitments also determine some other forms of saving. Some people, for instance, make arrangements with

---

[1] The argument, as presented, overstates the role traditionally assigned to consumers. Consumer savings are used primarily for business investments, and the volume of savings is thought to be determined by the volume of investment.

[2] By definition, as textbooks of economics put it, Y (income) = C (consumption) + S (saving) and therefore S = Y − C.

their employers for the purchase of government savings bonds through payroll deductions. Certain other savings as, for instance, regular additions to savings accounts, are habitual and to this extent resemble contractual savings even though they may be discontinued or stepped up more easily. These forms of savings, then, cannot be of great importance in a study of economic fluctuations.

Borrowing is negative saving; amounts borrowed are deducted from amounts saved in calculating net savings. But borrowing is dependent on those activities which make people borrow money. In most cases buying a house is the reason for incurring mortgage debt, buying automobiles and other goods the reason for incurring installment debt, and adversity (decline in income, illness, etc.) the reason for borrowing cash. In attributing to the purchases of consumer durables and houses a major importance in economic fluctuations, we have already considered this aspect of saving. We must therefore focus our attention on a third and and last form of saving, which we call discretionary saving.

Discretionary saving consists of additions to liquid assets (bank deposits and the like) and to security holdings. According to the usual classifications entrepreneurial saving, that is, profits plowed back by owners of unincorporated businesses and by farm operators into their enterprises, falls into the same category. Reduction of liquid-asset holdings and sale of securities may enable people to increase their expenditures and represent, then, dissaving of a discretionary nature. To understand stability or variability of discretionary saving and dissaving we must first know what the underlying motivational forces are.

Motives for Saving

Why do people save? The prevailing reasons for saving have been studied repeatedly over the last few years by asking representative samples of the American people the following question: Different families have different reasons for wanting to save; in your family, what are the main purposes of saving? Anything else? [3] The findings that resulted from asking this question, both shortly after World War II and more recently, may be summarized as follows: [4]

1. The question is clearly understood by people with low as well as high incomes. Practically everyone tells of at least one, more often of two,

---

[3] To what extent such simple inquiries can legitimately be used for the purpose of analyzing motives will be discussed in Chapter 8.

[4] We summarize here results of repeated surveys by the Survey Research Center; see G. Katona, "Attitudes toward Saving and Borrowing." We speak here only of saving in times of peace. During World War II some additional savings motives were found to prevail and made for unusually large savings.

and sometimes even of several reasons for saving. In 1956, for instance, only 2 per cent of family heads replied that they had no reason for saving; and 4 per cent, mostly with low incomes, appeared not to have understood the question or said they did not know.

2. Two potentially important reasons for saving—saving so that heirs may inherit and that one may earn interest—are mentioned by only a very small proportion of people, although both reasons have been given much weight in economic literature. Today in America the conscious wish to build up a family fortune in order to transmit it to one's children appears to be the exception rather than the rule. To be sure, as will be shown shortly, most people are concerned with the possibility of unexpected misfortune and so buy life insurance and save money in many ways to provide for their wives and children, if, unexpectedly, they should suffer an early death. Most people also want to start their children out well in life and to give them the best possible education. What is denied here is the prevalence of a motive of accumulating capital in order to leave it to one's children.

Similarly, relatively few people are motivated to save so as to earn income from savings. Possibly many years of low interest rates after World War II influenced people's notions, or possibly the image of the rentier and the capitalist cutting coupons became unpopular even earlier. Today in America relatively few people restrain themselves from spending in order to accumulate capital which would supply them with supplementary income in the form of interest or dividends. This appears to be the case even though thousands and thousands of families have such receipts year after year. In Chapter 13 we shall also show that small increases in interest rates have little influence on amounts saved by consumers.

That these two motives are not popular today may be significant in an attempt to understand the differences between different historical periods. In studying short-run cyclical fluctuations they may clearly be disregarded.

3. Entrepreneurs tend to save on the average a larger proportion of their incomes than other people with similar incomes and have a unique and apparently powerful motive to save.[5] Many unincorporated businesses are chronically short of funds and often do not have ready and easy access to the capital market. Ownership of small business is also commonly associated with the desire to be independent and to be one's own boss. Paying off partners and creditors, who may restrict the independence of the owner, then becomes a strongly felt need. The owner may therefore reduce his personal expenditures for the purpose of plow-

[5] See L. R. Klein and J. Margolis, "Statistical Studies of Unincorporated Business," and J. N. Morgan, "The Structure of Aggregate Personal Saving."

ing back more money into his firm. Still more important may be the fact that profits are often not available in the form of additional cash funds for personal expenditures of business owners; profits may be used for business purposes together with other business funds. Farm operators are likewise entrepreneurs in a certain sense. In addition, their love of their land often makes them wish to own it unencumbered. Therefore repaying the mortgage debt on the farm is often a highly desired goal of many farmers.

These motives to save again have long-run rather than short-run impacts on the economy. In comparing two societies in one of which there are many and in the other few business owners, one may expect to find different rates of saving. But changes in the proportion of business owners occur very slowly and cannot serve as explanations of business fluctuations.

4. There are only two motives to save which today are widely held by masses of the American population. They want to save, first, in order to accumulate a reserve fund against unforeseen contingencies, and second, in order to spend the money later for specific purposes. (Many people, of course, have both goals in mind.) There are great differences in how people express their aims and desires, but the variety of ex-, pressions recorded in interview surveys all seem to belong in one or the other of these two categories.

Most people hold that the future is uncertain; they speak of possible emergencies such as accidents, illness, unemployment, or bad times as their reasons for accumulating reserve funds. Reference to rainy days occurs most commonly. The frequency with which such reasons are mentioned does not differ much with differences in income.

The specific forms of the second major motive underlying saving, for future spending, are manifold. A substantial proportion of the people, primarily those between forty-five and sixty-five years of age, speak of saving for retirement or old age. A fair proportion save or desire to save for the education of their children and related family needs. Two other quite common goals behind savings are to make a down payment on a house and to buy a business. A variety of other large prospective expenditures is in the hearts and minds of different people as they save money. Some plan additions and improvements they would like to make to their homes, others speak of European or other long trips they would like to take, of summer homes, hobbies, and other plans for the future. Saving is motivated by desires and longings which differ from individual to individual but have in common that they represent unusual expenditures, require funds which constitute a fair proportion of annual earnings, and must be saved over more than one year.

Interestingly enough, neither household appliances—television sets, refrigerators, washing machines, and the like—nor automobiles are among the specific needs commonly considered as valid goals of saving. They are usually viewed as expenditures which should be paid for out of income rather than savings. Buying on installment is the accepted method of paying for them. This is not a new development. Even in interviews conducted during World War II, when saving was very widespread and automobiles were greatly desired, few people said that they were saving for the purpose of buying a car after the war.

The percentage of people who desire to save for specific purposes increases with income. Among those with lower incomes the only oft-repeated goal of saving was to provide for old age or retirement. It was found that the higher the income, the greater the number of motives for saving.

TABLE 7. SATISFACTION WITH LIQUID RESERVES

Attitude	Families with an annual income of			All
	Under $3,000	$3,000 to $6,000	$6,000 and over	
Satisfied	47%	34%	51%	42%
Unclassifiable	4	6	4	5
Dissatisfied	49	60	45	53
	100%	100%	100%	100%

NOTE: The question, addressed in a nationwide survey conducted in June, 1954, to families who had some liquid reserves, was, How do you feel about the amount of money you now have saved up—is it far too little, fairly satisfactory, fully adequate, or what? Why do you feel that way? Very similar results were also obtained in 1952 and 1955.

SOURCE: Periodic Surveys, Survey Research Center.

The degree of satisfaction with the size of reserve funds already accumulated does not differ greatly in the various income groups. As may be seen in Table 7, fairly similar substantial proportions of people in the high- as well as low-income brackets profess to be dissatisfied with the amounts of their liquid reserves. It appears that low-income families desire to save because they have no reserve funds or very small ones; middle-income families because their somewhat larger reserve funds are viewed as unsatisfactory in comparison with the needs they foresee; and those with high incomes because they feel the need for the largest amounts of reserve funds to maintain their standard of living and are aware of the difference between what they have and what they would like to have to cope with contingencies.

Thus it is not the have-nots who have the greatest desire to save, and the desire to save is not easily satiated. These psychological findings are no doubt related to a well-known fact: on the average, upper-income people have much greater savings than lower-income people; yet many more of the former save money, and they save a larger proportion of their income than the latter. Therefore saving is highly concentrated. A very substantial share of all personal saving is carried out by a relatively small proportion of American families. A society with relatively few high-income people will have many fewer savers than a society with a relatively broad upper-income group. Age distribution may also have a differential effect because of the powerful motive to save for retirement on the part of people some ten to twenty years under retirement age. A society with relatively many family heads in the forty-five- to sixty-five-year age group will save more than a society with fewer such families.

Are we justified in assigning a decisive role in cyclical fluctuations to changes in discretionary saving by consumers? This would seem highly questionable if we consider the two major reasons why people save. The desire to build up emergency reserves should certainly prevail in good times as well as bad. Felt need may be stronger in bad than in good times, but ability to save may be more pronounced in good than in bad times. Of course, if during good times and high incomes a depression is confidently anticipated, or during a depression an upswing seems assured, the motives to save may be strong in the former period and weak in the latter. But these are no doubt exceptional circumstances. Should they actually occur, we should have to look elsewhere for an explanation of such countercyclical expectations rather than consider the fluctuations in saving as the primary explanation of the reversal in the cycle.

No more definite are the cyclical effects on the economy of savings accumulated for the purpose of later spending. The usual theory is, of course, that in a recession people save because they postpone spending, and during prosperous times spend rather than save. But the motive to save for later spending should be strong in prosperous times as well, because widespread desires to acquire goods, both immediately and later on, characterize good times, and long-range planning is particularly frequent during prosperity.

Has the Desire to Save Declined in Recent Years?

Some students of the American scene believe, or did believe during the prosperous years 1955–1956, that the will of the American people to save has greatly weakened during the last decade. William H. Whyte, Jr., in a provocative article in *Fortune* magazine of May, 1956, asked: "Is thrift un-American?" and answered his question in the affirmative:

"As a normal part of life, thrift now is un-American." He went on to say that people "no longer identify saving with morality"; "they save little because they do not really believe in saving."

Similar notions, though usually in less extreme form, could be found in numerous articles dealing with economic developments in 1955 and 1956. The two events of those years which apparently impressed economic analysts most were a substantial increase in short-term consumer indebtedness and the shortage of capital resulting in higher interest rates. In order to explain these developments, several analysts assumed that something had happened to the psychological make-up of the American people. It was said that people had become interested in things rather than in money, or that their will to save had been paralyzed by the habit of installment buying. The will to save allegedly declined also because of inflation and the influence of collective security plans.

Let us look first at the argument that social security and private pension and retirement plans make it less necessary now to save for old age than even a few years ago.[6] More than three-quarters of heads of families now have social security coverage, and over one-third participate in pension or retirement plans; both proportions are much higher than ten years ago. But do *collective security plans* actually obviate the need for independent saving? We must remember that in former generations financial protection for old age was not generally achieved by individual savings efforts. In many socioeconomic groups this type of aid was provided by relatives, particularly grown children. Also, at the present time and probably for years to come, there is a considerable gap between the standard of living to which an employed family is accustomed and the standard of living provided by social security benefits and private pension plans. It is conceivable, therefore, that the minimal protection afforded by collective insurance plans may even stimulate people to save in order to achieve more adequate protection. Without these plans economic insecurity would be inescapable for many lower- and middle-income families. With these plans people may feel closer to their goal and highly motivated to attain it.

People who participate in collective retirement systems may be compared to people who provide for old age through individually purchased life insurance. It was actually quite difficult to make such a comparison in surveys, because families not covered differ greatly from those covered by social security as to both occupation and income. Nevertheless, it was possible to contradict the contention that families covered by social security put a smaller proportion of their income into private life insur-

[6] Cf. for instance, the following statement by Milton Friedman: "The availability of assistance from the state would clearly tend to reduce the need for private reserves and so to reduce planned saving." (*Theory of the Consumption Function,* p. 123.)

ance than those not covered, other things being equal. Comparison of families participating and not participating in private pension plans appears even to indicate that life insurance holdings and new purchases of private life insurance policies are larger among participating than nonparticipating families.[7] Collective insurance may, then, serve as a stimulus to additional saving. Although this conclusion has not been definitely established, it is fairly clear that collective insurance is not viewed at present as a substitute for private saving and has not impaired the will to save.

What then of the impact of *inflation* on the will to save? Has that will been impaired in those who have experienced a depreciation in the value of money and expect a further depreciation? Numerous data will be presented in Chapter 12 which contradict this assumption. For the moment, it may suffice to state that it is true that most people are aware of the substantial past price increases that have made today's dollar worth much less than the dollar of ten or twenty years ago. It is also true that most of the time in the recent past the majority of people have expected prices to rise further (though slowly rather than rapidly). Despite all this, however, the majority of people not only spoke highly of the value of saving but also asserted that putting money into savings accounts, depositing it with savings and loan associations, and buying government savings bonds represented the best ways of saving.

Should we conclude that people are irrational? Ample evidence will be presented later to indicate the common sense and even high intelligence of the average consumer. Here we shall restrict ourselves to indicating the resolution of the apparent contradiction on the part of many people. First, though many people do expect a continuation of inflationary price increases, they do not feel sure that their expectation is correct; on the other hand, they feel very sure that they need savings and reserve funds because the future is uncertain. In what form should they then save? Most people do not see any alternatives to saving in funds which are subject to depreciation in the case of inflation. Buying common stock and real estate appeals to some people but is considered risky and speculative by many more who say that one has to have expert knowledge before one puts one's savings into such investments.

Secondly, many people do not feel that they have fared badly with their past savings. They may admit that their savings bonds are worth

[7] A nationwide survey conducted by the Survey Research Center with a sample of 4,000 families revealed that among blue-collar workers who belonged to a private pension plan 76 per cent carried individual life insurance (group life insurance was excluded) and among such workers with no pension plan, only 61 per cent. The ownership of sizable amounts of insurance was likewise larger in the first than in the second group. See further data, also about social security, in Institute of Life Insurance, *The Life Insurance Public,* 1957.

what less than ten years ago, but they argue as follows: If ten
s ago we had not put $75 in savings bonds we would have spent that
ney on many small and unimportant things and today would have
nothing; having $100 today is much better than not having anything.

Finally, what of the effect of *installment buying* on American thrift?
It has been said that the ease of such buying has removed any reason
to save for the purpose of acquiring cars, large household goods, and
many other things. We do indeed find that saving to buy durable goods
does not rank among the important reasons for saving. But the same was
found to be true ten or fifteen years ago, and probably even much
earlier. Most people have viewed, and still view, the acquisition of
durable goods as expenditures which ought to be paid out of income,
either in cash or in the form of time payments.

Buying on installment is popular—but far less popular than saving.
Many more people do not believe in going into debt than do not believe
in saving. This is indicated by the answers to a simple question Do
you think it is a good idea or a bad idea to buy things on the installment
plan? We find, first, that practically everybody has an answer to the question. Buying on installment is generally known, and most people have
either a positive or a negative attitude toward it. In 1956, approximately
half the people held that buying on installment was "good," while one
out of every three thought that it was "bad" (the rest thought that installment buying had both good and bad aspects).

People with very low and very high incomes have the least favorable
opinions about installment buying. The middle- and upper-middle-income
groups thinks most favorably of it. As is well known, installment buying
is practiced most frequently by the latter two groups. The finding was
hardly surprising that opposition to installment buying was by far most
frequent among those people who themselves had no debt. Conceivably,
their adverse attitudes influenced their behavior. Equally conceivably,
however, their unfavorable opinions about installment buying were linked
with their having no need for it or no use of it.

Practically everyone asked to expand on their belief that installment
buying was either good or bad did so in great detail. There was one overwhelmingly frequent argument in favor of installment buying: it would
be impossible to buy many important things without it. Some people
added that it was a good thing to use the goods while paying for them.
Among the other favorable arguments, one mentioned by a small proportion of the people, that installment buying helps one to save, is of
particular interest to us. Many people who have sufficient bank deposits
to pay cash still buy on the installment plan. Some of them argue that they
do not want to touch their reserve funds; if they paid cash they would
not add regularly to their depleted bank deposits, but after buying on

installment they are compelled to repay the debt and to budget carefully.

Of the 33 per cent of the people who argue that installment buying is a bad idea, about one-third do not believe in debt; "one should never borrow" is an expression which they frequently use. Others, 16 per cent of the total population, complain about the cost of installment buying, while still others believe that installment facilities induce some people to buy too much. Finally, a substantial number of people qualify their opinions; installment buying is good only provided necessities are brought or the amount borrowed is not too high.

A few additional findings may serve to round out the picture of the importance the American people attach to saving. When asked whether they expect to save any money during the next year, year after year many more say that they definitely will save than actually do so. This is in contrast to the relationship between saying and doing as regards buying durable goods; in that case the proportion of actual purchases exceeds the proportion of expected purchases. The great frequency of savings plans can only be explained by the widespread desire to save. Furthermore, we find that many more families have savings or reserve funds (liquid assets, securities, and the like) than actually add to them in any given year. Correspondingly, more than half the people say that their current savings are not as large as they were at some time in the past. It follows that years in which people draw on their savings and years in which savings remain unchanged alternate with years of adding to them. The widely cited statistical data which show that during each of the last few years only a few billion dollars, representing a very small proportion of national income, have been added to liquid savings cast no reflection on the importance of motives to save. It must be remembered that the amounts saved, as published, represent the excess of amounts saved by savers over the amounts dissaved by dissavers.

The following definition of saving is widely accepted among economists: "Saving consists in the negative act of refraining from spending the whole current income." [8] Accurate as this may technically be, we can only conclude from our studies that the definition in no way reflects the manner in which the people themselves view saving. For most people saving is something positive. Subjectively it is not merely a consequence of not spending, but rather the result of substantial pressures directed toward achieving highly valued goals of life. Saving is considered most important and its absence is greatly regretted. In all these respects the acquisition of money and wealth resembles the acquisition of goods of permanent value, such as homes and durables. And in all these respects there has been no change in recent years. In spite of social security, inflation, and the

[8] J. M. Keynes, *Treatise on Money*, Vol. I, p. 172.

popularity of installment buying, most people still greatly desire to save. Their actual savings performance may, of course, remain much below the desired level. Conflict among different uses of money exists, and has always existed. Some people are aware of the great difficulties which confront them when they try to save as much as they would like to. Therefore they introduce constraints on their behavior through budgeting devices and saving for specific purposes, through payroll deduction arrangements, and even through buying on installment, because repaying debt appears easier than adding to bank accounts.

Dissaving

If these things are true of saving, what can be said of the reverse process, dissaving? Dissaving consists either of borrowing or of the reduction of assets. We may increase our expenditures beyond our income by buying on installment or obtaining a cash loan, or, alternatively, by reducing our bank balances or selling securities.[9]

It was once fairly generally assumed that dissaving was the function of poverty or distress and, therefore, occurred essentially during periods of depression. Poor people cannot make ends meet, it was argued, and so go into debt; unemployment likewise induces people to borrow or to draw on previously accumulated assets. Without denying that all this does happen, the generalized theory has nonetheless been disproved by recent findings. In the United States during the last ten or twenty years, rather than being a result of poverty and distress, dissaving has primarily been a sign of prosperity and has contributed to prosperity.

Three major circumstances were found to result in dissaving: inability to meet necessary expenditures out of income, unwillingness to keep habitual expenditures at the level of income, and willingness to make unusual expenditures beyond the level of income. The first of these circumstances is what those who associate dissaving with poverty and distress have in mind. It is no doubt true that the unemployed will draw on their savings. Nevertheless, the relationship between bad times and dissaving should not be overestimated. For the most part low-income people have no assets on which to draw and no credit on which to borrow. Illness, accidents, and the like, represent occasions for dissaving primarily by middle- and high-income people—and this is so equally in times of prosperity and of recession. Dissaving to pay living expenses during retirement naturally occurs regardless of the economic climate.

Unwillingness to keep usual expenditures at the level of income does,

---

[9] Arranging for a mortgage loan is omitted here because it is done almost exclusively in connection with buying a house, which in economic statistics is not considered an expenditure but a form of saving.

of course, occur during recessions, and especially during short and mild recessions. The interesting finding of our studies was that it also occurs, and often to a very large extent, during periods of prosperity. It is associated with what the author has called "temporary income reduction." [10] If a person's income has gone down but he believes that it will go up again relatively soon, there is a tendency to supplement income through dissaving rather than to adjust to the lower level. This is a fairly frequent occurrence in prosperous times. If on the other hand, income declines during a depression, expectations will hardly be optimistic and the person may try to adjust his expenditures to the changed circumstances as fast as possible. Then, too, in good times some of the most ambitious and optimistic young people voluntarily change their jobs and start anew at lower income levels because of better prospects for advancement. Even if the reduction in income is involuntary, satisfactory general conditions help to evoke the belief that the old income and job will soon be regained. Under such circumstances the traditional living standard to which people are emotionally and habitually attached will not be given up and income will be supplemented through borrowing or drawing on assets.

The most frequent cause for dissaving was found to be people's willingness to make unusual expenditures. The purchase of automobiles and large household goods, additions and repairs to the home, as well as the variety of expenditures mentioned above as goals of saving, were all reported as reasons for dissaving. When the purchase is made for cash, assets are reduced; when it is made on time payments, borrowing occurs. Such purchases are, of course, much more frequent in good times than in bad times.

It is then not surprising that dissaving is not a function of income. The belief that the lower the income, the more frequent is dissaving has been contradicted through Survey Research Center studies in each of the last ten years in the United States.[11] True, families in the highest-income groups do not dissave very frequently, nor do those in the lowest-income groups. Dissaving is most frequent among middle- and upper-middle-income families.

Dissaving, especially in the form of installment buying, is closely correlated with the life-cycle stage. It is most frequent among young married couples with children. Household formation and equipping a home, which usually take place during the first five or ten years of marriage, are the

---

[10] See G. Katona, "Effects of Income Changes on the Rate of Saving," and G. Katona, "Analysis of Dissaving."

[11] At the same time, it has been true that the proportion of savers increases with income. The apparent contradiction between the two findings is resolved by the fact that the lower the income the greater the proportion of people who break even, neither saving nor dissaving.

periods in which many people buy on installment. By contrast, saving, as we reported before, is most common between the ages of forty-five and sixty-five.

Dissaving is also related to income changes and income expectations. People with stable incomes dissave least frequently. On the other hand, temporary declines in income have already been mentioned as providing occasions for dissaving. The term "temporary," of course, implies optimistic income expectations. Such expectations affect installment buying and drawing on assets even without prior reductions in income. People experiencing rising incomes embark on unusual expenditures more frequently than those with stable or declining incomes. People who confidently expect their income to increase often adjust their expenditure level and satisfy their needs for durable goods even before the expected increase takes place. We shall refer to this finding in later chapters.

Young people, soon after their marriage, are commonly in the stage of their career in which incomes rise and are expected to rise. Upward mobility and striving for upward mobility are associated with the relatively frequent incidence of dissaving. It is then difficult to tell whether it is age and stage of the life cycle or expected improvements in income to which dissaving should be attributed.

Variability of Saving among Individual Families

In most families periods of saving and dissaving alternate. Of course, there will be some who save year after year and others who dissave several years in succession. How many they are and what kinds of families behave in these ways can be found out when representative samples of the population are followed over many years. The only such longitudinal study undertaken was spread over three years.[12] This may not be enough to draw definite conclusions but the results of the study are revealing.

Variability of individual behavior was, of course, not studied regarding "total personal saving," the accounting concept used in Federal statistics and defined as income minus expenditures. Contractual saving is highly repetitive. It was found that most people year after year put the same or similar amounts into life insurance, retirement funds, and the repayment of mortgage debt; repayment of installment debt also often continues over two or three years. Such contractual saving was therefore excluded and the following three variable activities were considered:

1. Borrowing or incurring debt—in connection with installment buying as well as cash borrowing from banks, loan and finance companies, and

[12] This was the 1954–1957 panel study, data from which were used in Chapters 5 and 6.

credit unions. Incurring mortgage indebtedness was excluded since it is usually connected with the unique and rare transaction of purchasing a house.

2. Additions to bank deposits, savings and loan shares, and securities (government savings bonds, common stock, etc.) which we call discretionary saving.

3. Reductions of deposits and securities which we call discretionary dissaving.

Data were collected about each of these transactions separately for the years 1954, 1955, and 1956. A sample representative of all urban people

TABLE 8. REPETITION OF SAVING BEHAVIOR OVER THREE YEARS

Form of discretionary behavior in 1954, 1955, and 1956	Frequency of occurrence	
	Per cent in one of the three years	Per cent in each of the three years
Borrowing:		
All urban families	65	13
Low-income families	54	10
Upper-income families.............	69	14
Discretionary saving:		
All urban families	60	11
Low-income families	38	3
Upper-income families.............	79	23
Discretionary dissaving:		
All urban families	41	2
Low-income families	40	2
Upper-income families.............	38	1

NOTE: Low-income families, annual income under $4,000; upper-income families, annual income over $6,000. Self-employed are excluded.

SOURCE: G. Katona, "Repetitiousness and Variability of Consumer Behavior."

in the United States was drawn. Self-employed people (owners of unincorporated businesses and self-employed professionals) were excluded because survey data about their savings are relatively unreliable and are often confused with their business savings. The findings obtained are presented in a simplified form in Table 8.

We see from the table that 65 per cent of urban families borrowed money either in 1954 or in 1955 or in 1956, but only 13 per cent in each of those three years; 60 per cent saved in discretionary form in one of the three years, but only 11 per cent in each of the three years, etc. Thus a rather substantial proportion of the population occasionally engaged in each of the three forms of behavior. But only relatively few did so in each

of three successive years. Continuous borrowing and continuous saving—
the latter especially among upper-income families—were more frequent
than continuous drawing on assets. Statistical calculations, presented in
the paper from which Table 8 was taken, indicate that all three forms of
behavior are somewhat more repetitive or homogeneous than could be
expected by chance and that saving is significantly more repetitive than
dissaving.

Why should some people repeat their behavior in two or even three
consecutive years? The studies do not provide much support for the
assumption that repeat behavior is the result of personality traits, such as
differences between thrifty people and spendthrifts. More probably,
similar circumstances or stimuli arise again and again and bring forth
similar behavior. Young married couples with children have a variety of
needs for household goods and often borrow year after year—or borrow
promptly after repaying a previously incurred debt—so as to satisfy their
needs for one item of equipment after another. By the same token, the
motivation to save continues to be strong year after year among people
in the age ranges of forty-five to sixty-five.

Yet in saving as well as dissaving, repeat behavior is much less frequent than changing behavior. Suppose we observe a family to have saved
in two consecutive years; what should we expect it to do in the third year?
The studies indicate that the best prediction we can make is that the
family will dissave—borrow or draw on assets—during the third year. The
chances that it will do so are much higher than the chances that it will
save again.

Sequences of, say, SSDSSD (each letter denoting one year's performance of either Saving or Dissaving) appear to be more common than
sequences of the type of SSS or SDSD or SDDSDD. During the past few
years with the great majority of American families, the pattern has been
one of an occasional year of dissaving interrupting years of saving.[13] The
year of dissaving varies from family to family. It will occur frequently
in good times if people dissave to purchase commodities, and in bad
times if people dissave because of a decline in income.

Optimism or Pessimism and Saving

The contention that curtailment in business activity is associated with,
or even brought forth by, an increase in amounts saved has been commonly explained as follows: Since expenditures on durable goods are
reduced during a recession, and money not spent is saved, amounts saved
must increase when times are bad. To pursue the logic still further: it is

[13] We disregard here the fact that many families, especially low-income families,
neither save nor dissave but just break even.

a major thesis of this book that the willingness to purchase durable goods may decline at a time of relatively high and stable incomes and may usher in a recession. If this premise is accepted and if money not spent on durables is saved, would it not then follow that increased saving would be one of the precipitating causes of recessions?

The fallacy is, of course, that it is possible that income not spent on durable goods is not saved but rather spent on food, services, and innumerable other small nondurable items. From the point of view of individual families this often means that the money is frittered away. People often do not know where it has gone. After either spending on durables or saving, something tangible remains, in articles to be used for many years to come or in the form of higher bank balances and securities. When more food and more convenience goods are purchased, permanent possessions do not grow. From the point of view of the economy, the consequences may likewise be substantial: the acceleration effect of durable goods spending, resulting from the fact that the production of durable goods requires many parts and machine tools, is reduced when the spending is for food and convenience goods.

Making discretionary purchases and adding to discretionary savings are not necessarily alternatives. Some people do both during the same year. They buy durable goods so as to improve their standard of living immediately and they also save so as to be in a position to improve their standard of living still further later. Ability to do both in the same year increases, of course, when incomes go up, and willingness to do both is promoted when optimistic and confident attitudes prevail. By contrast, a decline in income and a pessimistic and anxious frame of mind may result, not in saving rather than spending, but in doing neither.

Statistical data are available on the frequencies of different combinations of spending and saving. These data were collected for the year 1955, a good year in which both income and optimism were on the rise. Families constituting a representative sample of the urban population were divided into four groups: (1) those who purchased durable goods and did not save any money, (2) those who saved money (discretionary saving) and did not buy any durables, (3) those who did both, and (4) those who did neither. We are concerned with the last two groups. As expected, we found that substantial proportions of families in the upper-income brackets did both and substantial proportions in the lower-income brackets did neither. The data presented in Table 9 are therefore restricted to the middle-income groups (defined here as families with an income of between $4,000 and $7,500 in 1955).

We find that buying durables *and* adding to liquid savings during the same year were more frequent among those who felt better off and were optimistic than among those who felt worse off and were pessimistic. A

TABLE 9. JOINT OCCURRENCE AND ABSENCE OF DISCRETIONARY SPENDING AND DISCRETIONARY SAVING

Attitudes about the personal financial situation	(1) Bought durables and did not save money	(2) Saved money and did not buy durables	(3) Bought durables and saved money	(4) Neither bought durables nor saved money
	Percentage of middle-income families in 1955			
Better off	40	17	31	12 = 100%
Worse off	48	11	10	31 = 100
Expected to be better off	41	13	31	15 = 100
Expected to be worse off	45	14	18	23 = 100

NOTE: The significant differences between the attitudinal groups are found in columns 3 and 4.

SOURCE: G. Katona, "Attitudes toward Saving and Borrowing."

greater proportion of the latter than of the former engaged neither in discretionary spending nor in discretionary saving. Acquisition of durable goods and acquisition of reserve funds are not found to be mutually exclusive. Both represent positive goals which people want to attain. The accumulation of both durable goods and of money are activities oriented toward the future. It is not correct to assume that accumulators of products and savers represent two distinct basic types with little in common.

The data presented suggest these conclusions rather than prove their validity, since they are based on studies carried out in a single year and are derived from not-too-extensive differences between fairly small groups. Yet significantly enough the findings were confirmed by consumer surveys carried out in Great Britain. Again on the basis of data from a single year (1954), and from a small number of cases, Peter Vendome reported: "We find that those classified favorable put a larger proportion of their income into savings and durables than those unfavorably placed." [14] Optimism was associated both with purchases of durables and with saving in Great Britain as well as in the United States.

These findings are also confirmed by data obtained by Elise Boulding in the studies reported in the preceding chapter. More achievement- than security-oriented people were found to have purchased durables and also to have saved in discretionary ways; the latter had spent a larger proportion of their income on nondurables. Not only optimism and confidence, but also upward mobility appears to be associated both with discretionary spending and with discretionary saving.

Stability of Aggregate Consumption during a Recession

Does it follow then, contrary to usual thinking, that discretionary saving will be higher in good times (when the proportion of optimists is high) than in bad times (when the proportion of pessimists is high)? Not necessarily. The effects of the one factor singled out for consideration—optimism or pessimism—may be counterbalanced by the effects of other factors: In good times purchases of durable goods are extensive

[14] P. Vandome, "Aspects of the Dynamics of Consumer Behavior," p. 97. Income changes, feeling better or worse off, expecting income changes, and expecting to be better or worse off were determined. People who gave favorable reports on at least one of these four variables and not one unfavorable report were classified "favorable"; people who gave at least one unfavorable report and not one favorable report were classified "unfavorable." The average percentage of net income saved was 2.8 per cent among the "favorables" and −1.9 per cent among the "unfavorables"; the average percentage of net income spent on durables was 6.0 and 3.6 per cent, respectively. These data are taken from surveys conducted in Great Britain by the Oxford Institute of Statistics, which are similar to the Survey Research Center's Surveys of Consumer Finances and were initiated with the technical assistance of the center.

and are partly financed from liquid assets. In hard times some people .
who are unwilling to spend add to their liquid reserves.

How did discretionary saving actually vary during the postwar years?
This is not a simple question to answer because available statistics on
personal savings are inadequate. The Department of Commerce pub-
lishes quarterly data on aggregate personal savings, but these include
contractual saving and represent rough estimates derived from deducting
consumer expenditures from total income. The liquid savings series
prepared by the Securities and Exchange Commission is more appropriate
for our purposes because it permits the exclusion of contractual saving
and is computed from changes in total bank deposits, security holdings,
and the like. Yet this series includes entrepreneurial savings (unspent
profits of unincorporated business) as well as savings by trust funds and
nonprofit institutions, in addition to consumer saving. Nevertheless, it is
worth reporting that the SEC savings data provide no support for the
notion that personal liquid savings vary systematically with cyclical
fluctuations.

In 1950–1951, to be sure, expenditures on durable goods and amounts
saved were competitive: when the rate of purchases of durables rose,
additions to liquid savings were small; and when the rate of those purchases declined, the additions to liquid savings were substantial (see
Table 3 in Chapter 3). Yet the second half of 1950 was a period in which
shortages were expected, and 1951 was a year of rising incomes in which
most consumers, nevertheless, considered the time inopportune for
expenditures on durables. More relevant is the experience of the years
1954 through 1958 and especially the experience during the recession of
1958.

In 1955, which was the first boom year following a recession in 1953–
1954, net borrowing was increased by the unprecedentedly large amount
of $5 billion. At the same time, however, bank deposits, savings and
loan shares, and security holdings likewise increased much more than in
1954: according to the SEC the increase was close to $15 billion as against
$9½ billion in 1954. In both 1956 and 1957, that is, in good years in which
installment debt rose further by small amounts, aggregate liquid saving
was at least as high as in 1955.

Large-scale spending on consumer goods ended sometime late in 1957,
and the first half of 1958 was characterized by the worst recession since
the end of World War II. This was the period in which automobile sales
slumped and short-term consumer indebtedness was substantially reduced.
Yet there is no evidence of a corresponding increase in consumer saving.
True, savings deposits rose somewhat more than usual, but that increase
was balanced by a decline in demand deposits and money saved in securities. According to the computations of the SEC the increase in currency,

bank deposits, savings and loan shares, and securities amounted to $2.7 billion in the first quarter and $2.1 billion in the second quarter of 1958, against $3.5 billion and $3.3 billion in the same quarters of 1957.

Survey data confirm the conclusion that the onset of the recession was not a period in which masses of people turned to saving. Measurements of amounts of discretionary saving through interviews are difficult and the results are not fully reliable. Yet it is relatively simple to find out whether people themselves believe that they have saved. Representative samples were asked in repeated surveys, Would you say you people saved money during the last twelve months, or did you decrease your savings, or did you just break even? People who said they had saved were asked, In what form do you keep these additional savings? It appears that what people subjectively consider saving consists almost exclusively of additions to bank deposits (including deposits with savings and loan associations) and purchases of securities. When, in certain surveys, specific questions were asked about amounts saved in these forms, the results corresponded closely with the data obtained through the simple questions quoted above. (The differences between the two methods consisted primarily in that people often said that they had broken even when specific questions revealed that their bank accounts had changed by small amounts one way or the other.) Life insurance premiums, contributions to retirement funds, and repayment of mortgage or installment debt were rarely considered as "saving money." [15]

Even though the absolute number of people who said they had saved may have little significance, and even though amounts saved were not considered in these inquiries, a comparison of the results obtained from successive representative samples is of interest. At the end of 1955 about one-third of all urban families reported that they had saved money during the preceding twelve months—significantly more than in 1954; the proportion was slightly higher still in 1956 when incomes were higher. By June, 1958, however, the proportion had fallen to approximately 25 per cent. Thus we find a somewhat larger proportion of savers in prosperous than in depressed times.

No doubt, changes in the number of savers and in aggregate amounts saved during a recession are influenced by a variety of factors. Unemployed persons and others with greatly reduced income will stop saving and may dissave; people with satisfactory income trends, on the other hand, may increase their savings. The available statistical data do not permit us to separate the different factors. Yet the data contradict the widely prevailing notion that a major persistent difference between pros-

[15] People's subjective notions about having or not having saved are discussed in G. Katona and E. Mueller, *Consumer Attitudes and Demand*, and in G. Katona, "Attitudes toward Saving and Borrowing."

perous and depressed times is that in the former consumers spend and so stimulate the economy, while in the latter they save and so retard economic activity. This may happen but need not happen. The recession of 1958 was characterized by stability of consumer saving and therefore, necessarily, by stability of total consumer spending. The money not spent on consumer durables was used to pay for nondurables and services, rather than saved. How this could happen at a time of substantial unemployment, we shall discuss in Chapter 13.

At this point it suffices to say that the analysis of variations in liquid saving over time is in accord with the conclusions derived from our studies of consumer motives to save: Discretionary saving is not the consumer activity to which we should look for the major difference between prosperous years and recessions. It is the extent of discretionary spending by consumers rather than of savings which differs greatly between good and bad years; and it is variations in such spending, strongly influenced by changes in attitudes, which may bring forth an upturn or a downturn in the economy.

PART THREE

Psychological Findings

CHAPTER 8

Motives and Levels of Aspiration

What contributions can an analysis of the motives, habits, attitudes, and expectations of consumers make to an understanding of diverse forms of economic behavior? In our search for the answer to this question we shall relate psychological findings to different economic activities—in this chapter to the purchase of life insurance, one-family houses, and household appliances, as well as to the accumulation of liquid assets. The first concept to be studied, as it pertains to various economic activities, is that of motives. We are concerned with differences in behavior—among groups of people at the same time, as well as among all consumers at different times—and want to know whether or not such differences are related to differences in motives.

Whatever definition of motives is accepted, one major, undisputed characteristic of motives is that they are elusive. The direct question Why? put to a person who has acted in a certain way, will hardly ever yield information about all relevant motivational forces and may yield answers which are false in the sense of assigning reasons which were not the effective ones. Nevertheless, we shall turn first to motivational studies which make use of fairly simple methods. The direct question Why? was asked in these studies, but not in the sense of uncritically accepting the answers and relying on them. The answers given by respondents provided but the starting point of analysis. In addition to the direct question, the presence or absence of association between certain forms of behavior and certain responses reflecting opinions, information, or attitudes was relied upon to provide clues to the effective motivational forces. The discussion of hidden motives will be continued in the Appendix on Survey Research, where we shall refer to means of studying motivational factors which are not susceptible to analysis through the more traditional methods.

Multiplicity of Motives

Classical economic theory postulates a single comprehensive motive—maximization of utilities or profits. In a formal sense, this type of theorizing resembles other theories postulating a single drive of overwhelming importance, be it reduction of tension and anxiety or, as in psychoanalytic thinking, libido. In contrast, modern psychology postulates that behavior is multimotivated. The motives of different individuals making the same decision need not be the same; the motives of the same individual who is in the same external situation at different times may likewise differ. In studying a single decision or action, most commonly we find interaction among and influence of several motivational forces. Several forces play a role at the same time, some reinforcing others and some conflicting with others. Action is facilitated if all or most motives operate in the same direction and is impeded when they conflict.

The two views—the one emphasizing the unitary nature of all motivation and the other the multiplicity of motivational forces—are not necessarily in conflict. It is possible to assume that the multitude of forces represents description rather than systematization, the different forces described being ultimately reducible to one basic motive. If that single motive is made comprehensive enough, it can, of course, be said to encompass all the diverse forces which empirical studies have revealed. Then it would obviously be impossible to contradict the single motive theory. The argument against it is not that it is incorrect. The valid argument says that we lose information by adhering to such a theory. The study of differential effects of different motivational forces as well as the study of change in motives are ruled out if we concentrate on one alleged common core of all motives.

Numerous older as well as more recent students of the economic scene, dissatisfied with the concept of profit maximization as the only aim of business, have prepared lengthy lists of other economic motives. Pecuniary motives other than profit maximization, striving for power and for approbation by others (prestige), as well as security motives have been cited. But the mere listing of goals is of little value. Scientific progress is achieved only if the conditions are specified under which certain motives—or patterns of motives—are prevalent and if, in addition, it can be demonstrated that they produce different behavioral effects.

One of the simplest derivations from the assumption of the multiplicity of motives says that several mutually reinforcing motives influence behavior more strongly than one motive. Some early empirical studies in economic psychology, concerned with the purchase of war bonds during World War II, served to support this assumption. They helped to explain crucial differences between purchasers of war bonds, differences not explained by the income or occupation of the buyers. These studies have been described often and will be referred to here very briefly.[1] There were people who, in spite of intensive questioning, mentioned only one

[1] See D. Cartwright, "Some Principles of Mass Persuasion"; R. Likert, "The Sample Interview Survey"; and G. Katona, *Psychological Analysis of Economic Behavior*.

reason for their buying war bonds, namely, the patriotic reason "to help win the war." The purchases of these people were smaller in each income or occupational group than the purchases of other people who gave several reasons, for instance, not only patriotic ones but also personal financial reasons, such as wanting to use the money later to buy a house or a business. When, in addition, the hypothesis was tested that solicitation, especially personal solicitation, was effective in increasing war bond sales, this fact was confirmed even though the people themselves did not mention solicitation among the reasons for their buying bonds and seemed unaware of the great influence exerted by solicitation. People who were aware of several reasons for buying bonds and who were also solicited to buy were found to be the largest buyers. The more numerous the forces that drive a person in the same direction, the greater is his action. The practical applications of these findings consisted, of course, in advertising several reasons for buying bonds and in introducing personal solicitation.

More recently the effectiveness of several mutually reinforcing motives, as well as the different consequences of different motives, was demonstrated in studying *life insurance* ownership and purchases.[2] The following simple question was used in several personal interview surveys: One of the things we want to find out is how people like yourself feel about life insurance; what would you say are the major reasons for carrying life insurance? Anything else? Most people answered in terms of support for dependents; lower-income people also referred to burial and final medical expenses. In addition, some people mentioned a variety of other reasons, for instance, that life insurance may provide retirement income or funds for the education of children, that it may help in repaying mortgage debt, that it makes it possible to borrow money in case of need, and above all, that life insurance is a good way to save. A comparison between the amounts of insurance held by people who mentioned one reason and the amounts held by people who mentioned two or more reasons for having life insurance revealed substantial differences (after eliminating income and age effects). The people naming multiple reasons owned larger policies more frequently than the people naming one reason; the latter more frequently owned small policies (less than $1,000 face value) or none at all.

A variety of objections may be raised to this finding. It might be argued, for example, that we were testing ability to verbalize rather than motives. Suffice it to say that the same results were obtained when people were not asked to give reasons which spontaneously came to their

[2] See Survey Research Center data in the monograph *The Life Insurance Public,* issued by the Institute of Life Insurance, and in *Life Insurance Ownership among American Families, 1957,* by J. L. Miner.

minds, but were shown a card containing seven reasons and were asked to rate each of these according to its importance to them. Many more people acknowledged, then, the importance of saving and retirement considerations than had done so spontaneously. Yet the differences in insurance ownership persisted between those who said that several reasons had great importance to them and those who acknowledged few reasons for buying life insurance.

Mention of certain reasons was found to be associated with ownership of more life insurance than mention of other reasons. Most people view life insurance as a necessary expenditure: an outlay of money intended for the protection of dependents in case of unexpected tragedy. But, as we have said, some people also view life insurance as a good way of saving, or as serving needs during retirement, or as helping with education or business expenses. Separating the two groups—those who do and those who do not acknowledge savings reasons for life insurance—we find great differences in life insurance ownership. To illustrate: in 1956 in the income group from $5,000 to $7,500, people with savings reasons spent $270 on life insurance premiums on the average and people without savings reasons $155; in the income group $7,500 to $10,000 the respective premium payments were $320 and $215. Significant differences were also found in all other income as well as age groups.

Do these findings prove that awareness of savings reasons for carrying life insurance leads to higher coverage? It is possible to argue that the causation runs from amount of insurance owned to purpose of insurance, that is, that people who carry little insurance are aware only of the purpose which their small insurance may fulfill, while those who carry large amounts of insurance know much more about it. Yet studies of purchases rather than ownership of life insurance cast doubt on this possibility. People who had savings reasons were found to have bought larger amounts of insurance than people who knew only of the protective function of insurance. These findings again are not fully conclusive because it cannot be proved that people were aware of the reasons before buying the new policies. A variety of different circumstances may have prevailed in individual instances. Yet it is implausible that, on the average, people whose financial condition permits them to choose between higher and lower coverage and who have similar education and occupations would not be influenced by the purposes they believe life insurance serves.

Are acknowledged purposes or reasons for owning insurance motivational forces? No doubt, they are not the only relevant ones. If our purpose were to find out why two people—of the same age, income, occupation, and marital status and both in good health—carry greatly different amounts of insurance, we would have to consider many other variables, as, for example, relationship to life insurance agents, experience with deceased father's insurance, experience with and attitudes toward other forms of saving, to mention but a few. Our argument is not that we have determined all the motives for buying life insurance. But we have uncovered a motivational factor which makes a difference in the behavior of broad groups of people. Whether or not a person views life insurance as a good method of saving money is an intervening variable between the situation and the action, which reflects the contribution of the person rather than of the external environment. It is acquired through past experience and probably reinforced through contact with others who think and act in a similar manner. Usually people are not clearly aware that they carry relatively large amounts of insurance because they acknowledge its saving function; hardly ever are they conscious that they carry relatively little life insurance because they do not recognize this function. Yet such a relationship, being of both theoretical and practical significance, could be established through the use of fairly simple methods of research.

When a person buys a sizable life insurance policy because he is interested in saving in this way, and when another person buys a small insurance policy for the sake of protecting his family in case of untimely death, both persons act according to what they see best. In other words, both persons maximize their satisfactions or utilities. Similarly, to mention another example of different motivational forces disclosed by survey research, irrespective of whether one person buys a car because his old car broke down and another because his income went up and he feels optimistic, each does what is best for him according to his own judgment. Thus the one-motive theory is not contradicted. But it serves no useful purpose. Maximization of utilities has been called a tautology. Whatever a person does, the principle holds; it is impossible to contradict it. This is the case because the maximization theory explicitly assumes that there is a variable left outside of the system, the taste of consumers. Even if the same person chooses to save an increment to his income today and to spend a second increment tomorrow, the principle is not contradicted because the person's taste may have changed in the meantime. If we rest satisfied with one motive for all behavior, we abandon the possibility of utilizing motives to explain changes in behavior or different behavior by different people.

It may suffice to mention briefly that the same argument applies to the attribution of all business behavior to the single motive of profit maximization. Those who hold this theory include under profits subjective satisfactions (prestige, power, security, which are often called psychic profits) and do not differentiate between short-range and long-range pecuniary motives. Progress in analyzing business behavior may again be achieved only when different forms of behavior can be attributed to different motivational forces. For instance, this author presented some evidence about an association of favorable economic conditions with long time perspective and long-range planning and nonpecuniary motives; alternatively, unfavorable conditions seem to restrict the time perspective of business managers, make such pecuniary motives as short-range profits salient, and consequently lead to different behavior.[3] Even among pecuniary motives, a distinction could be made between striving for profits and striving for increased sales (larger share in the business) and for growth, and could be related to differences in business behavior. Finally, in studying profit motives alone—which remain very powerful even if nonpecuniary and growth motives are given their due—maximization has been distinguished from striving for subjectively satisfactory profits or "satisfyzing" (as Herbert Simon has put it), again with the purpose of relating different forms of behavior to differences in motives.[4]

Dissatisfactions and Attractions

Traditional economic theory, in postulating that economic behavior is motivated by the maximization of utilities, recognizes a *positive* motivational force. The most usual physiological and psychological theories, on the other hand, explain behavior in terms of *negative* motives, such as reduction of tension or avoidance of disturbance or disequilibrium. We are driven to act because something is disturbing us or is missing rather than because we are attracted toward something. This theory, derived from biological motives (hunger and thirst, for example, imply deprivation), if applied to economic behavior would make dissatisfaction with our income, assets, or savings the mainspring of action. If disequilibrium is conceived as absence of gratification, then gratification—whether it be eating or buying life insurance—can be regarded as restoring equilibrium and resulting in the elimination of the motive or at least the reduction of motive strength.

There can be no doubt that deprivation, disturbance, and dissatisfaction are powerful motives of behavior. Sometimes it is merely a verbal matter whether one speaks of dissatisfactions or of attractions by positive goals. But sometimes there may be a real difference. Our studies, guided by the assumption that both positive and negative motives prevail, arrived

[3] *Psychological Analysis of Economic Behavior,* Chapter 9.

[4] See H. A. Simon, *Models of Men;* G. Katona, *Psychological Analysis of Economic Behavior.* Recently an alternative to maximizing has been developed under the name of minimax strategy. Minimizing regrets is a highly conservative strategy which implies sacrificing chances for large gains in order to avoid the possibility of small losses. No evidence is as yet available as to the usefulness of this conceptual development for an understanding of the forms of consumer behavior studied in this book.

at the following conclusions as to economic behavior: First, the presence of positive motives in addition to negative ones strengthens motivation. Second, highly motivated behavior may arise even without dissatisfaction. Third, gratification of needs does not necessarily result in saturation.

Our analysis of achievement-oriented people in Chapter 6 may be recalled here. That analysis was related to studies of achievement motivation carried out by psychologists who, like the author, were dissatisfied with the deprivation theory of motivation.[5] It disclosed that achievement-oriented people are usually satisfied with their past occupational progress as well as their present situation, and still strive for more. The upward mobility of these people appears to be derived from and reinforced by past accomplishments. Let us investigate the problem of positive motivation in a relatively simple situation.

Why do people buy houses? The *purchase of a one-family house* for owner occupancy is one of the most important decisions a family ever makes. Decisions to buy houses are also very important for the economy since residential construction gives employment to many people, contributes to long-range economic growth, and by changing from time to time promotes cyclical fluctuations. Traditionally, changes in the rate of residential building have been explained in terms of very few variables. Outside of income and cost of money (interest rates), the rate of household formation has been considered to be the one relevant factor determining fluctuations in residential building and has been thought to suffice for the prediction of future trends. Since the average life of dwelling units is very long—sometimes set at 100 years—and even substandard houses remain inhabited for a long time, it has been believed that replacement demand, which is very important in automobiles of which several millions are scrapped every year, could be neglected. Thus the great upsurge in the construction of one-family houses shortly after the end of World War II was attributed to the coincidence of rising incomes and low interest rates with a very high frequency of marriages and with deferred demand. At the end of the war more than 3 million married couples were without their own households and started on a process for which the term "undoubling" was introduced.

By 1954 the prospects for residential construction appeared dim. At that time there were only 1½ million married couples without their own households. With lower marriage rates household formation had fallen from approximately 1.2 million in each of the first postwar years to about 800,000. Residential construction, relatively high and fairly stable in 1952 and 1953, was therefore expected to decline. In fact it increased sharply in 1954 and 1955.

[5] See the studies of McClelland and of Atkinson in the Bibliography.

The analysis of residential construction just described is, of course, an example of economics without psychology. It is assumed that there is a mechanistic connection between certain demographic and financial variables and mass action (in this case buying houses). The human factor is disregarded as if potential buyers had no discretion whatsoever. Yet ample evidence exists that the great postwar increase in home ownership and the trend to the suburbs was far from automatic; further, that the felt need for new housing was very strong, or even increased, at a time when household formation declined.

Our studies included the entire market for one-family houses rather than the market for newly built houses. There are some prospective house buyers who think exclusively of newly built houses and others who are interested solely in "old" houses. Recent studies indicate, however, that for the majority of people there exists but one market and the final decision—to buy a newly built or an older house—is determined by what is found to be available rather than by preconceived ideas. Extensive surveys were carried out with a sample representative of people who during the year prior to the interview had bought a house. In addition, in surveys representative of the entire population people were asked about their housing arrangements, possibilities of changing them, and reasons for planned or desired changes.

A few simple data may serve to place the study of motives in the proper perspective. First, some purchases of one-family houses, about 10 per cent of all purchases in the early fifties, serve the purpose of providing a place to live: Marriage, undoubling, eviction, and demolition of one's previous home may be viewed as such obvious reasons for purchases that further analysis of motives is hardly warranted. Household formation is much more frequent than buying a house by newly formed households; most newly formed families as well as those who undouble start out by renting an apartment. Second, one-fourth to one-fifth of home purchases occur when the buyer moves to a different, distant community (moving to suburbs is not included in this category). Again the number of movers is much higher than the number of purchasers because many movers rent apartments. We neglect the interesting problem of decision making—whether to rent or to buy—so as to focus our attention on the third group of home purchasers: those who have a place to live and have not moved to a different community but have still decided to buy a house. They comprise two-thirds of all home buyers and consist of a smaller group who had owned a house and a larger group who had rented before they purchased a house. They were all asked the following questions which referred both to dissatisfaction and to desire for improvement: What was it that made you think of moving from there? Was there anything (else) about your housing arrangements before you moved that was not satisfactory or that you wanted to improve upon? What was that? [6]

In addition, people other than recent home buyers who expressed intentions to buy or build a home were asked, What would you say are the main reasons why you plan to buy or build a new home? The answers to both inquiries were quite similar and will be discussed together.

Some of the buyers and prospective buyers as well gave reasons which implied dissatisfaction and clearly fit the deprivation theory of motives. "Our home (or apartment) is (or was) too small," was a frequent answer. The increased number of children per family which has characterized the past fifteen years fully explains such answers. Similarly, we need not be concerned with those relatively few purchasers (about 3 per cent of all home buyers) who said "Our home is (or was) too large." These were older people whose children had married and moved away. Then we found others—about 10 per cent of home buyers—who seemed to conform to the concept of the economic man. They were those who argued that home ownership was cheaper than renting or explained that home ownership was a good investment, especially in times of inflation.

Yet the great majority of home buyers discussed their purchase in different terms. Most of them gave other reasons exclusively. Some of them gave other reasons together with financial considerations and/or dissatisfaction with the size of their former house or apartment. The reasons given may be grouped in three categories: desire to own, desire for a better neighborhood, desire for a better home.

These reasons were given with similar frequency, we may repeat, by people who had bought a house shortly before being interviewed and by people who explained why they planned to buy a home during the next year or two.

The first reason—desire to own—was given, of course, by renters only. Many of them argued that everyone should own his own home; home ownership enhances one's standing in the community. Great stress was put on the needs of children: One must have a backyard in which the children can play, many people said. This argument is connected with the second category—the desire for a better neighborhood. The wish to have "nice" neighbors was often expressed with reference to the company the children keep. "We moved to live far away from juvenile gangs" or "We moved to live in a neighborhood where everyone owns his home" seem to refer to similar considerations. Arguments about location and desire to own were expressed as frequently in lower-middle as in upper-middle income groups. When recent home buyers were asked about the features

[6] See G. Katona and E. Mueller, *Consumer Expectations;* also E. T. Paxton, *What People Want When They Buy a House.*

they had looked for first in searching for a house, location was mentioned most frequently. These studies carried out in the early fifties, clearly indicated that the trend toward the suburbs was grounded in strong emotional desires which for many people had not been satisfied at that time.

The desire to have a better home—a newer one or a more modern one—was expressed most frequently by former owners who had changed, or wanted to change, their houses. Sometimes financial considerations explained this desire: With the widespread income increases during and after World War II it frequently happened that a family lived in a house which corresponded to its income at the time the house was bought, but not with its income in the early fifties. With increased ability to pay for housing the old house became unsatisfactory and new housing needs arose. In other instances people spoke of their needs and desires for certain conveniences lacking in their old houses—particularly two or more bathrooms and one-story or ranch-style layouts. No doubt upgrading takes place not only in durable goods but also in housing. Innovations and technological changes represent attractions for purchasers in both fields.

Whether needs and desires are expressed in negative or positive terms, whether the dissatisfaction with existing conditions or the advantage of a desired condition is emphasized, the difference may be purely verbal. Nevertheless, it appears that the rate of home purchases increased with the frequency of mention of positive attractions. More important, in answer to direct questions a fairly large proportion of would-be purchasers said flatly that their then current housing arrangements were satisfactory. For instance, in 1954 among families who expressed a desire to change their housing arrangements, not less than one-half said that the home they were living in was satisfactory. These people wanted something better than what was fairly good. Let us recall that this finding was obtained at a time which followed widespread home purchases (and also at a time which preceded further widespread purchases, which of course was not known when the studies were made). What is the relation between past purchases and desires for housing?

In 1954 and in subsequent years the Survey Research Center repeatedly asked the following question of all people in representative samples who said that they did *not* expect to buy a house or to move within the next twelve months: If you were free to choose would you *like* to stay here in this house (apartment) or would you like to move from this place? On the basis of the answers to this question and answers expressing definite intentions to buy or to move, not less than 34 per cent of urban homeowners and 70 per cent of urban renters were classified as potentially mobile. This is a very high proportion in view of the fact that most American families had moved during the preceding ten years and in doing so had probably acquired more suitable housing accommodations than they had had earlier.[7]

Potentially mobile people were least frequent among those who had not moved during the preceding ten years, that is, since World War II. As Table 10 shows these were about one-third of the urban American families. Among the other two-thirds, and even among those who had lived less than 2½ years in the dwelling in which they were found in 1954,

TABLE 10. RELATIONSHIP BETWEEN PAST AND POTENTIAL RESIDENTIAL
MOBILITY OF URBAN POPULATION *

(June, 1954)

Past residential mobility	Homeowners		Renters		Both
	Proportion	Potentially mobile in each group	Proportion	Potentially mobile in each group	Proportion
Less than 2½ years in same dwelling	19%	39%	57%	73%	34%
3–9½ years in same dwelling ..	38	41	27	75	34
10–19½ years in same dwelling ..	22 ⎫	29	12 ⎫	62	18
20 years or more in same dwelling	21 ⎭		4 ⎭		14
All	100%	34%	100%	70%	100%

* The table should be read as follows: Among the 19 per cent of homeowners who were found to have lived less than 2½ years in the same dwelling, 39 per cent were classified as potentially mobile on the basis of the questions quoted in the text, etc.

SOURCE: Survey Research Center; see G. Katona and E. Mueller, *Consumer Expectations*, p. 88.

a somewhat larger proportion desired to change their housing accommodations.

It appears then that gratification of needs does not necessarily satiate people. New motives to move may arise even a short time after such a major step as buying a house. These new motives must consist primarily of positive attractions rather than deprivations. Such findings represented the starting point of our study of saturation and levels of aspiration, which

[7] Circumstances may have compelled some people to move into unsatisfactory quarters. But most home buyers, when interviewed shortly after they had moved into their new houses, said emphatically that they were fully satisfied with what they had bought.

will be discussed in the next section. Let us ask first, however, what the meaning of a question is which asks people whether they would like to move if they "were free to choose." The answers to such a question do not represent idle dreaming. The reasons given for wanting to move were all very familiar: the desire for a bigger house, a better house, a better location and neighborhood, and the desire to own. We found that potentially mobile people were equally frequent in different income groups, yet somewhat more frequent among younger than among older families. Most significantly, potentially mobile people were most frequent among those who thought that in several years they would have a better position and income. It appears that people do place limitations on the expression "free to choose." Our hopes and dreams are, to some extent at least, reality-oriented.

Naturally, many people who would like to have better housing will not have the money to afford it. Others will satisfy their desires by improving, modernizing, or enlarging the houses they have. Nevertheless, the findings about the widespread desires for better housing and the strong under-pinning of people's felt needs clearly indicate that housing demand is not a function of income, interest rates, and household formation alone.

In the field of *household appliances* we looked further into the matter of replacement demand. Refrigerators, television sets, kitchen ranges, and washing machines are now owned by 75 to 90 per cent of urban American families. Market researchers therefore speak of high saturation in these articles. Most of the sales are for replacement rather than for use by newly formed families buying for the first time. The proportion of replacement purchases is overwhelmingly high in the case of goods of which the family ordinarily uses only one, as for instance refrigerators. According to the disequilibrium theory of motivation a family should replace its refrigerator only when it is in bad condition, trouble and dissatisfaction being mainsprings of action. Survey findings contradict this notion as shown, for instance, in Table 11.

Surveys revealed, as expected, that very few people reported at any time that their refrigerator was in bad condition. The majority said without qualification that their refrigerator was in good condition, and most others that it was in fair or quite satisfactory condition. This was true both of those who in the following eighteen months replaced their refrigerator with a new one and of those who kept their old one. Among those who made a replacement purchase, close to one-half had owned a relatively new refrigerator (less than ten years old), of which the owner had said prior to the purchase period that it was in good condition. Quite similar data were obtained by asking people about the age and condition of their refrigerator at a time when they expressed the intention to replace it. In studying replacement demand for washing machines and television sets, again similar results were obtained, while kitchen ranges were replaced more often when they were said to be in not wholly satisfactory condition.

Why should owners of durable goods which in their opinion are in good condition replace them? One answer which comes to mind relates to action by others; reasons of prestige or imitation may have induced some

TABLE 11. CHARACTERIZATION OF REFRIGERATORS OWNED BY FAMILIES WHO LATER REPLACED THEM OR BY PEOPLE WHO PLANNED TO BUY

Age and condition of old refrigerator	Families who bought for replacement between June, 1954 and December, 1955 *		Families who expressed intention to buy—June, 1955 †	
5 years or less and in good condition...................	27%		19%	
5–10 years and in good condition	18		17	
Over 10 years and in good condition......................	16		13	
Total in good condition......		61		49
10 years or less and not in fully satisfactory condition	8		14	
Over 10 years old and not in fully satisfactory condition	30		29	
Total not in fully satisfactory condition		38		43
Age or condition not ascertained	1		8	
		100%		100%

* Age and opinion about condition of old refrigerator determined in June, 1954; whether or not purchased determined through reinterviewing the same sample in June, 1955, and in December, 1955.

† Age, opinion about condition of old refrigerator, and buying plans determined in June, 1955.

OWNERS OF REFRIGERATORS WERE ASKED: About how old is it? Is it in good condition, or only fair, or is it no longer satisfactory? All answers other than "good condition" were considered as "not in fully satisfactory condition."

SOURCE: E. Mueller, "The Desire for Innovations in Household Goods," p. 17.

replacement purchases. Studies of this kind of motivation were not very revealing. When people were asked about the articles their friends had been purchasing, only insignificant relations to their own buying intentions were indicated.

A different approach was more rewarding. People were asked, Are there any new features or improvements in the latest models that you would like to have on any of your household goods? Those who answered in the affirmative were asked to name the appliance and describe the desired features. Then in comparing the answers of those who later bought with those who did not buy certain items, or the answers of those who planned or did not plan to buy those items, substantial differences were found. Attraction of new features was especially frequent among prospective buyers of automobiles and refrigerators. For instance, considering owners of refrigerators five years old or less and in good condition, we find that among those interested in new features many more bought a refrigerator during the following year than among those not interested.[8] Sizable differences were found in other groups of owners with one exception: among owners of relatively old refrigerators not in good condition, interest in new features made no difference at all and did not contribute to an explanation of later buying behavior.

Interest in new features of household goods was equally frequent in all income groups above $3,000 annual income, over 40 per cent of them expressing such an interest in 1954 and 1955. (The new feature of refrigerators that was apparently most attractive was larger and better freezing compartments.)

Let us add briefly the results of similar studies concerning replacement purchases of automobiles. In the years between 1954 and 1956 about three out of every four automobile owners said that their car was in good condition, and one out of four that it was in fair or in unsatisfactory condition. Among those who in 1956 replaced their car close to 70 per cent, and among those who did not replace their car slightly over 80 per cent had said in 1955 that their car was in good condition. The difference is small; it is clear that the majority of cars traded in were, in the opinion of their previous owners, in good condition. Interest in new features was studied by asking people how in their opinion new models compared with the previous ones and whether the new models contained any new features which they would like to have on their car. Again it was found that among those who bought a new car during the following year a larger proportion had answered both questions in a way complimentary to new models than among those who did not buy a new car. Thus interest in new features was found to contribute to replacement demand.

The findings about interest in and attraction by new features may be summarized as follows:

1. Interest in new features is much more frequent than expression of buying plans or actual purchases during the following twelve months. In other words, interest in new features alone does not make people buy.

2. Some replacement purchases are made without interest in new

[8] See E. Mueller, "The Desire for Innovations in Household Goods."

features, primarily by owners of older articles or articles in unsatisfactory condition.

3. Among owners of relatively new articles which are said to be in good condition interest in new features is an important factor contributing to replacement purchases.

In our discussion of replacement purchases we have preferred to speak in terms of positive motivational forces, as indicated by such expressions as "desire for," "interest in," or "attraction by" one thing or another. It would, of course, be equally permissible to think in terms of psychological obsolescence and thus to say that attraction by newer and subjectively more desirable articles creates dissatisfaction with the articles owned, even though those articles are acknowledged to be in good condition. Then, of course, action would be attributed to the negative force of dissatisfaction. In either case the essential finding conflicts with the theory that need gratification results in saturation. We found people who, having gratified their desire by making a purchase—of a house, a car, a refrigerator, etc.—felt moved to make another purchase of the same article, rather than feeling contented and without further desires.

We are now in a position to understand certain recent findings about the distribution of needs and desires among the American people. It has been argued that poor people who have very few of the goods which are highly valued in our society need the most things. According to this theory, relatively few needs and desires would be attributed to the rich who own a great variety of things, all in good condition. But what do we find? The Survey Research Center asked the following question in repeated nationwide surveys: Are there any special expenditures you would really *like* to make this year or next year? (Probes were added, such as Anything else? and How about your wife?) In reply, most people promptly described not one but several expenditures they would like to make. In one study carried out in 1954 only 14 per cent answered in the negative. Absolute frequencies obtained depended on the method of questioning and are not important.[9] Relevant are the differences in the findings among different groups. About one-half of those who said that they had no desires explained that they could not afford to spend on anything. Among low-income people, under strained circumstances, even desires and wishes may be suppressed. The other half who said that they had no special desires because they were quite well supplied consisted predominantly of older people.

While negative answers were most frequent in the lowest-income group, among income groups with over $3,000 annual income practically the

[9] When fewer probes were used and the questioning was restricted to the purchase of goods rather than allowing the inclusion of expenditures for travel, vacations, education, etc., the proportion was as "high" as 25 per cent negative answers.

same proportion of each group ($3,000–$5,000, $5,000–$7,500, over $7,500) answered in the affirmative. There was a difference, however, in the number of desired expenditures; the higher the income, the more things did people mention that they would like to have. It is improbable that these differences reflect nothing more than greater verbal facility on the part of the rich (who are, on the whole, the better educated as well). Speaking of a better car or of a new roof, or of new living room furniture and the like, is within the capability of very many people. It appears here again that our desires are reality-tested, that is, not independent of our situation and ability to buy. It appears also that accomplishment does not necessarily create contentment, but may make for new aspirations.

Levels of Aspiration

Let us repeat: When they are hungry or thirsty, animals or men are highly motivated to find food or drink; after gratifying their needs, the motive weakens or even disappears. From a study of biological needs the generalization was derived that gratification of needs results in the reestablishment of equilibrium and in the reduction of motive strength. On this basis, as has already been pointed out in Chapter 2, prosperous times in which very many people gratify many of their needs should bring forth reduction of motive strength or even saturation, and thereby business recession.

An alternative theoretical approach has also been indicated briefly. Kurt Lewin and his co-workers proposed a theory of levels of aspiration and demonstrated its operation, primarily through experiments with intelligence tests and simple motor tasks. It may suffice here to formulate a few generalizations which have been established in numerous studies of goal-striving behavior: [10]

1. Aspirations are not static; they are not established once for all time.

2. Aspirations tend to grow with achievement and decline with failure.

3. Aspirations are influenced by the performance of other members of the group to which a person belongs and by that of reference groups.

4. Aspirations are reality-oriented; most commonly they are slightly higher or slightly lower than the level of accomplishment rather than greatly different from it.

In simplest terms, then, a beginner in golf sets his goal low; making a score of, say, 100 represents his highest aspiration. If he accomplishes his goal he sets his aspirations higher—not much higher but somewhat beyond the accomplishment level. The greater his success, the higher he aims, and this will be particularly true if his friends and colleagues are

[10] See K. Lewin, "Level of Aspiration"; G. Katona, "Rational Behavior and Economic Behavior."

ardent golf players. However, if repeated efforts to improve his score fail, our golfer will set his aspirations lower. Frustration may result in absence of further desires or in contentment, or, if the goal is highly valued in the group to which he belongs, in leaving the group (in this case, resigning from the golf club).

What has been said about golf applies to aspirations about jobs and income. A promotion or a raise for which we strive may appear to us as something which, if obtained, will bring forth satisfaction and contentment. But after the better position or the higher income has been achieved, our outlook may change. The new position may then be seen as a step toward further advancement: gratification may create new ambitions. The level of aspiration may be raised with accomplishment.

This type of sequence is in accord with our findings about upwardly mobile people, as reported in Chapter 6, and also with repeated observations indicating that aspiration for higher income is at least as frequent among upper-income people as among lower-income people.

Most important in this regard are our findings about shifts in motives. In studying individual families over several years during the fifties, numerous instances were found in which a desire for a new car—or a house, or new furniture—first dominated the family's thinking. Before the car was bought, the building of a porch or the purchase of a TV set did not appear very necessary. After the car was bought these needs assumed great importance. "The most basic consequence of satiation of any need is that this need is submerged and a new and higher need emerges"—this is how a psychologist has formulated this principle of motivation.[11] We have to add only that the new need is not necessarily a higher need.

We may illustrate this process further by describing how it operates in an individual case. A man and his family live in a small apartment in the center of the city. Even before they were married, he and his wife had talked of a house with a garden, in a quiet suburban neighborhood, which they would own themselves and so not be dependent on landlords. When they had children, the desire became more pressing. They saved systematically every month to be able to buy the house. Finally, they had enough for the down payment, the husband's salary went up enough to enable him to meet the monthly charges on the mortgage—and they bought their home. What happened then? Did the family save less after their goal had been achieved? Not necessarily. To be sure, they no longer saved with the purchase of a house in mind. Now they saved just as much as before, but for purposes which had until now been pushed into the background—for the education of the children, for the purchase of a business, or for an emergency fund for "rainy days." The fulfillment of one salient and urgent desire may thus lead to the emergence of new needs and desires.

[11] A. P. Maslow, *Motivation and Personality*, p. 108.

Studies of purchases of newer durable goods and desires for those goods gave evidence of the same process in operation. Who were the people who had recently bought or were considering buying newer appliances (such as clothes dryers, dishwashers, freezers, air conditioners, and garbage disposals) which at the time of the study, the early fifties, had a relatively low penetration rate? Just one answer to this question will be reported here: Buyers of new appliances were found to be particularly frequent among owners of "traditional" appliances (cooking ranges, refrigerators, washing machines, and television sets), that is, appliances with a high penetration rate.[12] The better supplied the family was, the more it aspired to have the more recently developed household goods. This was found to be true in all income and age groups. This finding again suggests that needs are abundant and that sights are raised following the satisfaction of the most pressing desires.

Let us look now in greater detail at the operation of rising levels of aspiration in one important area of economic activity—the *accumulation of liquid reserves,* or what we have called discretionary saving. In studying the relation of liquid-asset holdings of households to saving, we may understand how closely the principle of saturation, derived from a study of biological needs, is related to traditional economic thinking.

The principle of diminishing marginal utility was called a "fundamental tendency of human nature" by the great nineteenth-century economist, Alfred Marshall. This principle says that the more an individual has of some object, the less will his satisfaction increase by obtaining an additional unit. In terms of an old textbook example, one drink of water has tremendous value to a thirsty traveler in a desert; a second, third, or fourth drink may still have some value but less and less; an *nth* drink (which he is unable to carry along) has no value at all. A generalization derived from this example is that the more of a commodity (or money) a person has, the smaller are his needs for that commodity (or money), and the smaller his incentives to add to what he has.

This generalization is clearly relevant for an important problem of post–World War II economy. Before the war the American people (not counting business firms) owned about $45 billion in liquid assets (currency, bank deposits, government bonds) and these funds were highly concentrated among relatively few families; most individual families held no liquid assets at all (except for small amounts of currency). By the end of the year 1945, however, personal liquid-asset holdings had risen to about $145 billion, and four out of every five families had some bank deposits or war bonds. The big question was, What effect would this great change have on spending and saving?

It seemed to several economic theorists and business cycle analysts that

[12] See E. Mueller, "The Desire for Innovations."

the question could be answered without empirical studies. Obviously, they wrote, the larger the assets, the smaller the need for saving. Or: the rate of saving is a diminishing function of the assets an individual holds. Alternatively: money burns holes in people's pockets. Clearly, cash, bank deposits, and liquid assets in general can be used only for two purposes: they can be spent or invested; and some people at least will be stimulated by their liquid assets to raise their expenditures. The broad generalization follows that spending is not a function of income alone; it depends on income and assets (wealth); the greater the assets, the greater the rate of expenditures. In other words, a society with large amounts of liquid assets is more prone to inflation than a society with small amounts of liquid assets.[13]

Obviously, actual conditions are much too complicated to permit of any pure test of the theory of saturation and of diminishing utilities. Spending depends both on ability to buy and on willingness to buy. The principle of saturation maintains that large amounts of liquid assets will cause a change in willingness to buy (having a lot of money in the bank, people have less desire to acquire more). But those same assets also provide a change in the ability to buy. Thus, even if spending should increase as predicted, it would be difficult if not impossible to determine which change was the effective one. In addition, as we have pointed out in Chapter 7, one of the purposes of saving is spending, and years of accumulating reserve funds are occasionally interrupted for individual families by a year of spending more than the family's income.

In presenting the counterargument—that large savings would not result in increased spending, or in dissaving—we must likewise distinguish between two possibilities. First, rising levels of aspiration following accomplishment mean that a family after having succeeded in accumulating some liquid assets sets its sights higher. Needs may grow and with them dissatisfaction with the size of available reserve funds may increase. Second, habits of saving play a role. The wealth of most American

[13] The theory of the dependence of spending and saving on the size of assets was originally associated with the English economist, A. C. Pigou. Chapter 8 of *Psychological Analysis of Economic Behavior* contains many further references. It may be mentioned that the theory is related to the prediction of rapid postwar inflation which has been cited at the beginning of Chapter 3. Through saving unprecedentedly large amounts during the war the American people were thought to have accomplished nothing more than the postponement of inflation. Sooner or later, the argument continued, the large accumulated bank deposits and war bonds would be spent—the prewar equilibrium would have to be restored—and therefore the wartime accomplishments of the American people served only to transfer the burden of inflation to the next generation. The fact that total liquid assets had not been reduced in any postwar year did not seem to have made this argument any less convincing. The finding that many people hold savings permanently in liquid assets likewise did not impress the theorists.

people, and most of their liquid assets, were not inherited; they were saved out of income. People who have saved substantial amounts in the past will tend to continue to do so; past behavior patterns often provide a clue for future patterns.

Despite the obvious difficulties, it was possible to arrive at an empirical answer to the question of what effect the possession of liquid-asset holdings had on subsequent saving or spending. For this purpose we did not rely on subjective expressions of satisfaction or dissatisfaction with large or small amounts of savings (as cited in Chapter 7); these findings are helpful but not sufficient. Nor did we rely on comparing the aggregate amounts of saving at different times with different amounts of wealth because of the many other differences between two periods which could not be eliminated. Our studies were directed instead to a comparison of the amounts saved by groups of people with different amounts of liquid assets. Our aim was to compare two groups, one with small liquid assets and one with large liquid assets, both similar in income. How did the subsequent saving performance of the two groups differ?

Studies with this question in mind were carried out first in 1948 and were repeated several times, especially in 1955, 1956, and 1957. In order to produce reliable data the same sample had to be interviewed twice so that one variable, the size of initial liquid-asset holdings, could be measured in the first interview and the second variable, saving or change in liquid-asset holdings, in the second interview. In analyzing the findings we eliminated those people who had no liquid assets at all as well as those with annual incomes of less than $3,000. Both groups frequently break even (neither save nor dissave) and could hardly represent instances of saturation. In comparing middle- and upper-income families having small liquid-asset holdings (less than $1,000 or $2,000 per family) with families having large liquid-asset holdings, uniform results were obtained in the studies carried out in different years. We found that most of the families with small assets either saved a small proportion of their income (added small amounts to their liquid assets) or dissaved a small proportion of their income (reduced their liquid assets by small amounts). In the second group, among families with large initial assets, on the other hand, large positive and large negative savings predominated. It was not the proportion of savers or the proportion of dissavers which showed marked differences between the two groups, but the extent of both saving and dissaving. Holders of large assets were characterized by a much greater variance in saving behavior than holders of small assets.

To mention a few quantitative data: in 1955 and 1956 among urban middle-income families (excluding self-employed) the proportion of those who saved in discretionary forms was about 35 per cent among families with liquid assets of less than $2,000 as against approximately

45 per cent among families with more than $2,000 in liquid assets; the proportion of dissavers was approximately 25 per cent in both groups. But the proportion of those who saved more than 10 per cent of their income was only 13 per cent among those with small liquid assets as compared to 32 per cent among those with large liquid assets; and the proportion of large dissavers was likewise considerably higher in the latter group.

Table 12 presents data from a reinterview section of the 1957–1958 Surveys of Consumer Finances. The size of bank deposits, shares of savings and loan associations, and government bonds was determined for the same people both in early 1957 and in early 1958. Only those spending units who in both surveys gave consistent accounts of their savings were included in the tabulation. They represent about 80 per cent of the two broad income groups considered. The cells are small, but the crucial differences shown in the proportions of large savers and large dissavers are nevertheless greater than required for statistical significance.

We find that among holders of large liquid assets (over $2,000) 31 and 37 per cent were substantial savers (added more than $500), a far greater proportion than among holders of smaller liquid assets. We find further that in the first group 30 and 41 per cent were substantial dissavers (withdrew more than $500); again many more than in the second group.[14] Thus there are families who behave as the theory of diminishing utility predicts: some families with large initial liquid-asset holdings were found to have dissaved substantial amounts. But equally frequent were the families with large liquid-asset holdings who had saved substantial amounts. This suggests an interpretation of findings contrary to the theory of saturation. It appears that habits of saving are continued except when interrupted by the spending of large proportions of reserve funds. There is no evidence that the will to save was impaired by large reserve funds.

What are the circumstances under which holders of large liquid assets will add to their assets and what are the circumstances under which they will reduce them? Studies by Morgan and Klein demonstrated interaction between liquid-asset holdings and changes in income.[15] Multivariate analysis was carried out separately for families with income increases and with income decreases. In the second group saving was negatively correlated with the size of initial assets, but not in the first group. In other words, if a family having sizable reserve funds suffers a decline in income (in a generally good year) it will tend to draw on its assets; with families whose income has increased, such behavior is much less likely.

[14] Some people, of course, may have reduced their liquid assets so as to invest the amounts rather than to spend them.

[15] J. N. Morgan in L. R. Klein (Ed.), *Contributions of Survey Methods:* L. R. Klein in *Econometrica* of 1954.

TABLE 12. RELATION OF INITIAL LIQUID ASSET HOLDINGS TO THEIR SUBSEQUENT CHANGE

Change in liquid assets 1957	1957 income: $3,000–7,499			1957 income: $7,500 and over	
	Liquid assets early in 1957			Liquid assets early in 1957	
	$1–$999	$1,000–$1,999	$2,000 and over	$1–$1,999	$2,000 and over
Added $1,000 or more	5%	7%	16%	14%	28%
Added $500–$999	6	16	15	12	9
Added less than $500	44	20	24	37	9
No change	8	30	5	4	4
Reduced by less than $500	36	30	10	28	9
Reduced by $500–$999	1	15	10	4	12
Reduced by $1,000 or more	—	9	20	1	29
Total	100%	100%	100%	100%	100%
Number of cases	(252)	(64)	(137)	(144)	(141)

SOURCE: 1957 and 1958 Surveys of Consumer Finances.

136

These findings have direct implications for the problem of inflation. It is not permissible to argue that large liquid assets generally and necessarily promote inflation. This notion is contradicted not only by the finding that many large holders of liquid reserves add to their holdings, but also by the fact that in inflationary times income declines are infrequent. No doubt, if for other reasons inflation sets in, it may be fed from large available liquid funds; but the existence of such funds in itself does not stimulate excessive demand and inflation.

Returning to the saturation principle it must be emphasized that our empirical findings contradict its general validity but do not demonstrate that gratification of needs cannot result in saturation. What the studies of liquid-asset holdings and of durable goods as well teach us is that it is possible for gratification of needs to result in raising our sights and aspiring for more assets or goods. But this need not happen, and good times are not necessarily self-perpetuating. Saturation, that is, a subjective feeling of having enough goods, may occur—under the impact of adverse attitudes. The feeling of saturation itself is an attitude closely linked to anxiety, insecurity, and a pessimistic evaluation of prospects as well as of prevailing conditions. The mechanistic assumption of a direct relation between need gratification and saturation is unwarranted. Intervening variables determine what happens following gratification of needs. Under the influence of adverse attitudes people may feel saturated. Similarly, being attracted by new goods or new features is not an automatic consequence of technological developments, but is dependent on receptive and optimistic attitudes.

CHAPTER 9

Rational Behavior

Traditional economic theory deduces the properties of the economic system from a few general assumptions about human behavior. The fundamental assumption is that of rationality. It states that an individual chooses from among the range of alternatives open to him the one whose consequences he prefers. One aspect of rationality is its *end:* a person chooses what he considers best, that is, he maximizes utilities. Another aspect concerns the specific *means* involved in rational behavior, a subject which we have not yet discussed.

How does the rational individual postulated in economic theory proceed? He first lists all conceivable courses of action and their consequences; he then ranks the consequences and chooses the best; finally, he sticks to his choice in a consistent manner.[1] Similarly, a business firm is supposed to choose from among all possible courses of action the one which maximizes its profits; it does so either by carefully calculating the optimum outcome or by ordering the probabilities with which the consequences are expected to occur.

Dissatisfaction was frequently expressed with the theory postulating that economic behavior consists of a steady flow of rational calculations. Often it took the form of asserting that economic behavior is commonly irrational and impulsive. Objections of this type made, understandably, little impression on economic theorists. Examples of impulsive buying (purchases made on the spur of the moment because of emotional needs or persuasion) as well as of inconsistent or unintelligent behavior (faulty calculations or action contrary to one's best interest) could be disparaged. They were thought to occur when the choice was unimportant, or to reflect human frailty, and to be of little relevance for the functioning of the economy in the long run.

[1] Many references could be given but it may suffice to call attention to recent discussions by K. J. Arrow, and especially to the section entitled "The Principle of Rationality" in Arrow's article on "Mathematical Models in the Social Sciences." The consistency of choice referred to above is called by economists and mathematicians transitive ordering of choices: If I prefer A to B and B to C, then I also prefer A to C. The author discussed the concept of rationality in greater detail in his "Rational Behavior and Economic Behavior."

We shall find that rational calculations and irrational behavior are not the only alternatives. We shall also raise the question as to whether intelligent, purposive behavior is correctly described in the traditional theory of rationality. If this were the case, we could seriously assert that a gambling room—say, the Casino in Monte Carlo—is the most propitious locale for finding rational behavior. A gambler at the roulette table may list all the possible choices, may calculate the odds attached to each of them, and decide accordingly.[2] Is this the prototype for action by businessmen and consumers? Does the listing of alternative courses of action and weighing their consequences characterize economic behavior?

Psychological studies help to clarify the problem. Psychologists look to scientific discovery and the thought processes of scientists as yielding the most clear-cut examples of sensible or intelligent behavior. The contributions of psychology to the analysis of rationality stem from the distinction between (1) problem solving and thinking and (2) associative learning and habit formation.[3]

Habitual Behavior and Genuine Decisions

The basic principle of one form of behavior is repetition. The strength of a habit depends on the frequency of its repetition, as well as on its recency, and on the degree of resultant success or satisfaction. In this area it is correct to say that the best way to know what a man will do is to know what he did the last time in the same situation. Habits, once established, are fairly inflexible. To be sure, as we shall discuss presently, habits can be broken. But when we behave habitually it is not because we have made a choice or decision. Habits tend to be carried out quite automatically, without being influenced by motives or attitudes.

In contrast, problem-solving behavior is characterized by the arousal of a problem or question, by deliberation or thinking which involves reorganization in a specific direction, by understanding the requirements of the situation, by weighing alternatives and taking their consequences into consideration, and, finally, by choosing among alternative courses of action. Problem solving may result in action which is new rather than repetitive. It is relatively rare, occurs under the influence of strong motivational forces—for instance, of new developments which make a person

---

[2] We do not say that gamblers behave that way, but only that they are sometimes in a position to do so. Experimental situations similar to gambling have frequently been used to study rational decision making (e.g., by Mosteller and Nogee).

[3] See M. Wertheimer, *Productive Thinking*, and the analysis of scientific discoveries in that book. Cf. also G. Katona, *Organizing and Memorizing*, and the discussion of the relation of gestalt psychology to the analysis of economic behavior in *Psychological Analysis of Economic Behavior*.

dissatisfied with traditional or habitual ways of action—and is subject to group influence. Motives, attitudes, and expectations as well as emotional factors influence problem solving and decision making, both by creating an awareness that there is a problem and by pushing people in a definite direction when problem solving is attempted.

It follows that making a deliberate choice is not the only and not the most common form of human behavior. Studies of animal and human behavior in a great variety of situations disclose that routine behavior is frequent. What has been done before is done again, long-established patterns of behavior being repeated more or less automatically. Then we are not aware of any problem, and alternative courses of action do not even come to mind. Therefore, there is no deliberation and no choosing. Stimuli elicit responses along well-established pathways, unaffected by changing motives and attitudes. This kind of behavior follows the path of minimum effort; it serves to reduce uncertainty and helps escape from vacillation and conflict by reliance on procedures which have proved themselves in the past. Yet sometimes a bell rings; we stop, look, and listen before going along in the usual way. Habitual forms of behavior may be abandoned when we perceive that a new situation prevails and calls for different reactions. Deliberation, weighing alternatives, and choosing among them, often studied by analyzing the solution of scientific problems, also occur occasionally in a great variety of situations which we encounter in everyday life.

Problem-solving behavior or genuine decision making is then characterized by certain features, such as taking consequences of alternative courses into consideration, which have been included by economists in their definition of rational behavior. Yet the two are not the same. Rather than being a trial-and-error process in which *all* possible courses are listed and weighed against one another, the essential feature of problem solving, the reorganization or restructuring of the situation, is a highly selective process. By utilizing certain (not all) clues from the environment, an item of information is seen in a different context and therefore in a new light; this leads to a new way of ordering of alternatives and to changed behavior. Problem solving is a flexible process rather than a rigid one. It represents adaptation by the organism to changing conditions; it represents intelligent learning, often rapid learning, rather than consistently sticking to choices once made.

The following conclusions derived from studies of problem solving are relevant for an analysis of economic behavior:

1. Problem-solving behavior is a relatively rare occurrence.

2. Its main alternative is habitual behavior rather than whimsical or impulsive behavior.

3. Problem-solving behavior is recognized most commonly as a devia-

tion from habitual behavior under the impact of strong motivational forces and new events.

4. Changes in behavior due to problem solving (genuine decision making) tend to be substantial and abrupt rather than small and gradual. They will occur among many people at about the same time because of group belonging and group reinforcement.

In order to demonstrate the importance of these principles for the analysis of economic behavior, we shall turn our attention first to business behavior, where rational calculations have always been thought to be more relevant than in consumer behavior. Yet following established procedures or rules of thumb and acting in a routine manner have often been described in studies of business behavior.[4] If businessmen were to consider every item of information they receive—every piece of news, letter, or telephone call—as giving rise to a problem which needs to be studied and analyzed, they would have no time to conduct their business. In larger firms delegation of authority is necessary; employees of lower rank are often given rules to follow rather than permitted to make independent decisions. Many such well-established business procedures find their origin in conventions that prevail in the entire trade or industry, others have been used for long periods in the firm, and others again develop over relatively short spans of time. Similarly, consumers often follow ways of spending and saving that prevail in their country, their family, among their friends, or are acquired through personal experience. Decisions once made determine in advance a variety of actions undertaken much later.

We may enumerate some few forms of habitual business behavior which have been described recently. Price setting by manufacturers, wholesalers, and retailers frequently falls into this category. First, there exist accounting conventions—such as division of costs into variable and fixed costs, each of which is defined in specific ways—and second, there exist rules about the usual margin to be added to fixed costs in order to determine the price.[5] What is true about "markups" often applies also to "markdowns." Retailers have developed habitual practices that determine the selection of goods offered in clearance sales as well as the extent of the price reductions. Fixed accounting principles exist also as to depreciation charges, and habits have been developed with regard to the relation of

[4] See Committee on Price Determination, *Cost Behavior* (a volume published by the National Bureau of Economic Research in 1943); G. Katona, *Psychological Analysis of Economic Behavior;* and the discussion of programmed decision making by H. A. Simon in his "The Role of Expectations in an Adaptive or Behavioristic Model."

[5] See G. Katona, "Psychological Analysis of Business Decisions and Expectations." Recently studies of pricing by giant corporations, directed by A. D. H. Kaplan (*Pricing in Big Business*), added considerably to our knowledge of routine pricing procedures and the development of pricing policies.

depreciation charges to replacement costs. Inventory control and decisions about changes in inventories represent a further area in which principles, rules, and habits govern the procedures used on a wide scale.

Not much is known about how these forms of habitual practices developed. It is conceivable that they all originated in calculation, careful analysis, and extensive deliberation. New ideas devised by one or the other theoretician or practitioner may have been first tried out tentatively, then formalized in memoranda or books, and finally accepted as standard practices.

Yet sometimes business firms deviate from their traditional methods, say, of price setting or of making capital outlays. This is a matter of major decision, deliberation, and choice, usually undertaken by the top command under the impact of new developments. War or major political changes, technological innovations, changes in the competitive position of a firm, or the perception of radical changes in the business cycle connected with changed attitudes and expectations, were found to provide occasions for such genuine decisions. Problem-solving behavior is not an everyday occurrence in business life, but when it occurs it may be of great importance for the economy.

Habits, tradition, and inertia have recently been found to be powerful forces in determining business practices as regards borrowing from banks.[6] A survey in which top executives of a representative sample of large business firms were interviewed about their borrowing practices disclosed that practically all firms fall into one of the three following categories: First, there are conservative firms which strongly believe in the principle of using exclusively internal funds. They abstain from borrowing and even abhor borrowing. The expression *"firms* which strongly believe" was used intentionally: we are describing the climate of opinion prevailing in a firm, sometimes established by the founder and followed by several generations of executives, rather than the opinion of one or the other executive. Second, there are firms which borrow from banks for the purpose of replenishing working capital (for discounting receivables and for inventory or seasonal credit). The conviction that bank credit serves these purposes, and no other purposes, is held for long periods of time without ever being challenged. Third, some business firms use short- and medium-term bank credit for expanding their facilities and financing capital expenditures. In this case, the conviction that business consists of using other people's money rules the businessmen's thinking.

The conclusion was drawn from these studies that business behavior does not consist of a continuous stream of genuine decisions or calculations of the best possible move. Long-established principles, rules of

[6] See G. Katona, *Business Looks at Banks.*

thumb, and habitual practices are occasionally abandoned, but only under the influence of powerful motivational and attitudinal forces.

A further aspect of business behavior must be mentioned because it too sheds light on consumer behavior. Personal and emotional factors appear to influence even major decisions of large firms. The actions of business firms are colored by the personality of those who run them. Personality traits of business executives, for example, conservative as against progressive inclinations, or a tendency toward risk taking as against orientation toward security, must be considered together with the nature of the business in which the firm is engaged (old industries, such as banking or railroading, as against new industries, like electronics).

Of equal importance in influencing business behavior are interpersonal relations. Customers, competitors, or banks are not seen simply as factors which enter into calculations, but as people—friends or enemies. Their personal characteristics and the subjective image business leaders have of them are of great influence in business transactions. To cite just one example: the widely prevailing stability of banking connections was found to be partly the result of tradition, loyalty, inertia, and reluctance to change. In addition, business firms (manufacturers, wholesalers, retailers, etc.) and their banks were found to constitute effective groups in which feelings of belonging and mutual reliance developed. The "personality" of the bank played a role in determining whether a firm sought advice from the banks and even whether it borrowed from them. Changing banking connections appeared to a large extent to be a matter of interpersonal relations.

Deliberation and calculation are no doubt more frequent in large firms than in households. If large firms make major decisions based on tradition, habit, or personal relations, the same must be true of buying decisions by consumers. Yet among consumers as well, we do find problem solving and weighing of alternatives. Habitual practices and lack of concern are occasionally abandoned in favor of circumspect behavior. And the principles and habits guiding the housewife in her daily routine are rarely whimsical or impulsive.

A large part of the consumer's dollar—perhaps as much as one-third—goes to buy what has been called convenience goods. Groceries, drug items, cigarettes, gasoline, and paper products are examples of the kinds of goods so classified. Convenience goods do not cost much; they are purchased frequently; they are available in many stores; they are usually bought soon after the buyer thinks of buying them; they are bought without family consultation. Habits are conspicuous in these small and often recurring purchases.[7]

[7] See the report *Convenience Goods Purchasing* issued by the Foundation for Research on Human Behavior in 1957.

If the same purchase is made frequently, there is an opportunity to repeat the same behavior often and thus to develop strong habits. The small expense involved in each purchase may create the feeling that what we buy and when we buy it does not matter much and may therefore tend to eliminate the arousal of a problem situation. A notion that different brands do not really differ from one another may also contribute to the development of certain habits, for instance, to the purchase of gasoline at the same conveniently located gasoline station. Many further consumer practices tend to reinforce habitual behavior. The practice of budgeting, for example, consists not only of allocating definite amounts of money for food, clothing, and the like, but may also lead to regularly spaced visits at stores or supermarkets and similar purchases during each visit. Scanning newspaper ads for sales and discounts and adjusting one's shopping plans accordingly are likewise frequently habitual.

Yet an analysis of the act of purchasing and its antecedents reveals some different features as well. Weighing alternatives; discussion and consultation with family members, friends, or dealers; shopping around; seeking information about quality or serviceability; and concern with price also occur, though such practices are not repeated for each single purchase. The busy housewife would find no time to engage constantly in circumspect buying. Satisfaction with past practices—with a brand or a store—reinforces her purchasing habits. To do again what has proved to be satisfactory in the past represents the simplest way to overcome the tension and insecurity expressed by the questions Did I buy the right thing? and Did I pay too much? The housewife's reliance on advertising, her brand loyalty, or her store loyalty may appear exaggerated to an expert observer, but they do not necessarily persist; habits may be broken if a new situation arises and a problem is seen.

In addition to past experience with types of goods, brands, and stores, personal factors, such as inner needs and emotionally colored images of brands and stores, play a role. Strong group factors—assurance about buying well is promoted by doing what friends and neighbors do—and "in-the-store" factors such as the arrangement of displays or wrappings also influence the choices. But impulse buying, in the sense of whimsical and ununderstandable purchases is of lesser importance for the economy than occasional genuine decision making and very frequent manifestations of habitual behavior.

Does it follow from what we have said about convenience goods that purchases which consumers make rarely or which involve large amounts of money are always preceded by careful deliberation? Recent studies indicate that lack of deliberation does occur even in buying such durable goods as automobiles and household appliances.[8] In a fair number of

[8] E. Mueller, "A Study of Purchase Decisions."

these purchases there was no discussion among family members, no long planning period, no consideration of alternatives, no information seeking, no shopping around in several stores, and no consideration of different brands. Why should this happen? Are high-income people or people with certain personality types those who do not care and purchase their large household goods without deliberation? More important factors than the income and personality of the buyer were found to account for absence of deliberation. These were urgent need for an article, the notion that a unique opportunity to buy was available, and, also, satisfaction with a similar article previously used. These were some of the major conditions under which problem-solving behavior was not resorted to. In the absence of these conditions problem solving was sometimes fragmentary or superficial, but rarely entirely lacking. This was true of the great majority of purchases of durable goods.[9]

Yet problem solving seldom consisted of a careful consideration of all the diverse aspects of purchasing a household appliance. It was a highly selective process. Information seeking, deliberation, and weighing of alternatives were restricted by some buyers to price considerations, and by others to mechanical properties and performance or to appearance. Usually only a limited number of brands or stores were considered. Habitual practices often influenced the form of circumspect buying.

Two major forms of conflict must be resolved in buying automobiles, household appliances, furniture, or in deciding about additions and repairs to the house. First, there is conflict because we usually desire or need several things rather than just one at a time. We may, for example, want a new car as well as new furniture, and at the same time may want to increase our savings and reserve funds. Second, the timing of purchases commonly causes conflict or at least vacillation: Is it a good time to buy now or should I wait? The questions What should I buy? and When should I buy it? raise problems, and problem solving or genuine decision making is a process subject to the influence of attitudes and expectations.

Is the consumer rational or is he irrational? This is not the right question to ask. The consumer is a human being, influenced by his past experience. Sociocultural norms, attitudes, and habits, as well as his emotions and his belonging to groups, all influence his decisions. He is apt to prefer short cuts, follow rules of thumb, and behave in a routine manner. But he is also capable of acting intelligently. When he feels that it really matters, he will deliberate and choose to the best of his ability.

[9] R. Ferber ("Factors Influencing Durable Goods Purchases") has found that among purchases of durable goods costing over $25, 28 per cent were made without advance planning and an additional 10 per cent with less than one month's planning. What Ferber considered impulse purchases of durable goods was estimated to represent roughly half of all unplanned purchases.

Is the Consumer Ignorant?

Intelligent behavior would hardly be possible if people were generally ignorant and uninformed about what goes on in the economy. It is fairly easy to provide demonstration for the thesis that very many people have a low level of economic information. For instance, when asked whether they followed "news about how business is going in the country," in 1956 only 38 per cent of a representative sample said that they did regularly follow such news, and even among the people saying this there were some who, in response to a follow-up question, could not name any business news they had heard during the preceding few months. When people's economic intelligence was tested—by using a method which discouraged them from guessing and yielded many answers such as "I do not happen to know"—some recent important economic developments were found to be unknown even to many well-educated people with high incomes. Table 13 shows that this was true especially about the stock market; the proportion informed about changes in automobile sales or unemployment was likewise not too large.

On the other hand, it is possible to interpret Table 13 in a somewhat different manner. One might say that people were quite well informed about crucial developments. In the spring of 1955 the majority of people in all income groups knew that business conditions had improved and that prices had not risen. Early in 1957 the majority not only knew that industrial production and incomes had increased but also were correctly informed about the rise in interest rates. At the same time, most people irrespective of income and occupation knew that the cost of living had advanced.

What is economic news? Anything that happens to business about which information is transmitted may be the answer of the expert. For most people, however, only striking or unexpected news is news. If this is true, we may understand that in 1956, for instance, the majority of people answered that they had not heard any economic news. Only unfavorable developments would have been news at that time, and most people had not heard of any such developments. Toward the end of 1957 and in 1958, however, more than one-half of all people interviewed, and many more in the upper-income groups, could report on news about changes in business conditions. Substantial changes in conditions, such as the recession of 1958, increased interest in and awareness of economic news. When something happens which really matters, people are not ignorant.

The same point may be demonstrated by looking at the data on correct information about stock market movements. In the spring of 1955 the market advanced greatly; toward the end of 1956 and early in 1957 the market hardly changed and was not front page news. It may be seen from the findings included in Table 13 that many more people were correctly informed about the market in the first period than in the second. The relatively widespread information about higher interest rates in 1957 must likewise be understood in terms of the unexpected nature of the

TABLE 13. EXTENT OF ECONOMIC INFORMATION

Item of news	Family income		
	$3,000–5,000	$5,000–7,500	$7,500 and over
	Per cent of urban people correctly informed about each development		
In June, 1955: During the last few months:			
Stock prices went up..........	34	45	63
Unemployment did not increase..	62	66	69
Business conditions improved....	57	65	72
Cost of living was stable........	53	59	75
In February, 1957: During the last few months:			
Stock prices did not change much	26	29	44
Fewer cars were sold in 1956 than in 1955....................	26	33	48
Unemployment did not increase..	35	45	60
Industrial production increased...	49	56	63
On the average incomes increased	57	74	79
Interest rates rose..............	62	62	79
Cost of living rose.............	88	91	91

NOTE: Most of the people not included in the percentages given—for example, the 66 per cent of people with incomes between $3,000 and $5,000 who did not know that stock prices had advanced in the spring of 1955—did not have incorrect information; they simply had no information at all about the matter.

SOURCE: Survey Research Center panel study.

news and of the headlines as well as the advertisements (especially on the part of savings and loan associations) to which it gave rise.

News transmitted by the mass media is not the only source of economic intelligence and probably not the most important one. People commonly find out what is going on in business through word of mouth. When people are asked for their reasons for optimistic or pessimistic expectations about business conditions, they refer to what is happening at their place of employment, or in shops or stores in the neighborhood, and to what they have heard at such places. News about business transmitted from person to person carries a stronger emotional undertone than news read in papers or heard over radio or television. The expert may be dissatisfied with the information people gain in this manner, but there can be no doubt that when there are significant changes in the economy, most people know about them and judge them correctly. Again we must conclude: Although people on the whole are not so well informed that their economic behavior is solidly based on sound knowledge, neither are they so completely uninformed that their economic actions must be predominantly emotional and irrational.

We know far too little as yet about the specific kinds of economic information which masses of people are aware of and are not aware of. In 1951 researchers were surprised about the very widespread knowledge people had about Regulation W relating to minimum down-payment requirements and maximum maturities of installment credit. Yet it was also established that information about the level of interest charges paid in connection with installment buying was practically nonexistent. On the other hand, in the years 1956–1958, many people in the middle-income brackets, interested in new or better housing, knew of the prevailing interest rates on mortgages. No doubt institutional practices, personal concern, as well as group factors, contribute to an explanation of the selective nature of economic intelligence, which requires further extensive study.

Much has been written about the ignorance of the consumer regarding quality and serviceability of specific products, and some consumer practices have been often cited as proving that the consumer is irrational. But acting without information, being easily persuaded and suggestible, or following slavishly what others do contrary to one's own interest, occur primarily when the choice does not appear to matter much. Two major practices of present-day American consumers, emphasized in this book and sometimes cited as proof of their irrationality, are well motivated and understandable. One of these, buying on installment and paying high interest charges even though cash is available or could be accumulated fairly soon has been mentioned in Chapter 7 and may be called "super-rational" rather than irrational: it appears that many consumers take their own shortcomings into account (namely, that they would not save money if they were not pressured to save). The other, reluctance to purchase when price increases are expected, has been mentioned before and will disclose through detailed analysis in Chapter 12 inherently conservative and sane consumer traits rather than behavior contrary to the consumer's own interest. In addition, we may also refer to the widely used practice of diversification, which implies not backing the most probable development or the most preferred course of action with all the means one has. This is, of course, a sensible way of action in consumer as well as in business behavior.

The frequent occurrence of such practices makes the analysis of eco-nomic behavior more complex than following the simple models either of traditional economic theory or of mechanistic stimulus-response psychol-ogy. But understanding human behavior cannot progress if a one-to-one correspondence between stimuli and responses is postulated and the student is intent on deriving the response from its stimulus without taking intervening variables into account. Motives and attitudes influence the perception of a situation and change themselves according to the felt requirements of the situation.

Temporary or Permanent Income and Surprises

The uncertainty of the future which affects all economic behavior has not yet been sufficiently considered. That the future is uncertain and that one cannot foresee what will happen have often been cited as major reasons why it is not possible to behave rationally. Conversely, rational behavior in the face of the uncertainty of the future has been the very problem modern economic theorists have attempted to solve.

At all times we have a time perspective. Our psychological field encom-passes some of our past experiences, our perceptions of the present, and our attitudes toward the future. The inherent uncertainty about what the future will bring is, then, "handled" in two ways. First, many of our motives, attitudes, and habits, which have become part of our personality, persist over long periods of time and influence our behavior irrespective of prospects and the greater or lesser uncertainty attached to them. Second, we often "solve" the uncertainty about what will happen in the near future by having expectations about the probable direction of personal as well as general developments. These expectations, which are usually not precise (one may, for instance, anticipate a salary increase but not the exact size of it) and are often not held with great assurance, influ-ence our behavior rather than determine it.

The relation of consumption to income—to present, past, as well as future income—is of central importance for economic studies and has been the subject of theories of rationality. Before discussing some newer theo-ries of the consumption function, earlier studies carried out by the author and based on the psychological principles of time perspective must be reported briefly.[10]

An income increase or an income decrease may subjectively be viewed as either temporary or permanent. Income changes should not be con-sidered in isolation—the meaning of a stimulus is determined by the greater whole of which the stimulus forms a part—but within the per-spective of the income receiver. In the studies just mentioned, then, the

[10] See "Effect of Income Changes on the Rate of Saving."

following operational definitions of two kinds of income changes were given and tested in relation to spending on durable goods and saving: If a family's current income was higher than the previous year's income and its next year's income was expected to be at least as high as the current income, the income increase was called permanent. If a family's current income was higher than the previous year's income and its next year's income was expected to be lower than the current income, the income increase was called temporary. Similarly, a distinction was made between permanent and temporary income declines.

How does spending and saving behavior vary under the influence of these differences in income changes? As reported in Chapter 7, people with temporary income declines were often found not to adapt their consumption to their reduced income; they drew on past savings in order to avoid reducing their standard of living. People with permanent income declines, on the other hand, cut down especially on their expenditures for durable goods. Relatively many families with permanent income increases were found to have bought durable goods and have dissaved sizable amounts. The smallest proportion of spending on durable goods and of dissaving was found among people whose income had not changed and was not expected to change.

We conclude that lack of symmetry prevails in consumer reactions to income changes. Many forms of consumer expenditures are sticky downward and flexible upward. This difference will be particularly pronounced in good times when a great proportion of income declines are considered to be temporary on the part of younger or middle-aged people. When an income decline is seen as temporary, people resist cutting their habitual expenditures and borrow money or, if they have liquid reserves, draw on them. On the other hand, discretionary expenditures tend to increase more than proportionally when income increases and is expected to increase further.

The quick adjustment to subjectively permanent income increases will be discussed further in Chapter 11 as a major feature of prosperous times. At this point we focus our attention on the finding that consumers tend to disregard subjectively temporary or transitory declines in income and do not allow them to make much difference in their behavior. This is, of course, how rational people should behave, and this principle (regarding transitory income increases as well) was used recently by Milton Friedman and others as a starting point for a theory of consumption, which introduces the concept of planned or permanent consumption and states that such consumption is determined by rather long-term considerations.[11]

That one of the basic aspects of this theory is in full agreement with

[11] M. Friedman, *The Theory of the Consumption Function;* F. Modigliani and R. E. Brumberg, "Utility Analysis and the Consumption Function."

an underlying principle of the studies in which this author has been engaged for many years may be seen by quoting how Solomon Fabricant, director of research of the National Bureau of Economic Research, interprets Friedman's theory in his annual report: "It is evident that Friedman abandons the conception of the consumer as a mechanical link between current income and consumption, a notion that Keynes set forth in 1936 and that played a large role in economic thinking in the years following." [12]

But what does, in Friedman's theoretical model, take the place of a mechanistic theory according to which consumption is influenced by nothing but current income? Definite, long-term expectations by consumers, the prevalence and influence of which appear to be overestimated. The theory assumes that on the whole consumers differentiate sharply between permanent and transitory components of their income. On this basis Friedman believes that the latter can be treated as accidental, chance occurrences, which are short-lived and cancel out in the long run or for large groups and therefore do not influence consumption. He argues that transitory income does not correlate with permanent income. The latter— expected income over several years, or over a large fraction of lifetime, or even the average lifetime value of income—is the one to which consumers are thought to adjust their behavior.

The emphasis on long-range planning and on definite expectations rules out flexibility and learning as well as uncertainty. It not only relegates current income to a minor position in explaining current saving and consumption but also disregards the probable impact of change in motives, attitudes, and expectations on expenditures. It is not argued here that it is impossible for consumers to think in terms of many years or their lifetime and to behave in such a superrational way. But since the current American economy is a dynamic one, in which consumers frequently find cause to change their motives, attitudes, and expectations, it does not appear to be rewarding to base the study of fluctuations in consumer demand on an acceptance of the concept of permanent income, or the "average income levels consumers expect in the future." [13]

While theories of permanent income tend to disregard the effects of unexpected developments, other recent economic theories attribute a

[12] National Bureau of Economic Research, *Investing in Economic Knowledge*, p. 3.

[13] In our discussion of long-range expectations, an important difference between Friedman's and the author's position has been overlooked. Friedman's thesis that "if consumers believe their current incomes to be below the average levels they expect in the future, the ratio of current consumption to current income will be higher than usual" (we again quote from the summary in the report of the National Bureau of Economic Research) sounds similar to the author's thesis that optimistic expectations stimulate expenditures on durable goods. But expenditures on durable goods are considered by Friedman as savings rather than as consumption (only the rental value of the services of durable goods is viewed as consumption).

great role to the element of *surprise* in explaining business trends.[14] Not enough is known as yet about the impact of surprises, and further research will no doubt yield new insights. Yet the following findings, which indicate that unexpected developments do influence consumer decision making, may be reported:

1. How can it be explained that relatively many people who had said that they did not expect to buy a car during the next twelve months actually purchased a car during that period (as shown in findings reported

TABLE 14. EFFECT OF UNEXPECTED INCOME DEVELOPMENTS ON
AUTOMOBILE PURCHASES

Income in 1948	Intended to buy new cars *		Did not intend to buy new cars *	
	Bought †	Did not buy †	Bought †	Did not buy †
Received more than expected	27%	17%	63%	30%
Received the same as expected	50	40	20	37
Received less than expected	17	32	4	22
Income or expected income not ascertained	6	11	13	11
Total	100%	100%	100%	100% ‡

* Early in 1948.

† During 1948.

‡ Those who did not intend to buy a car and did not buy one represent, of course, the largest group in the population.

NOTE: The differences between those who bought and those who did not buy may be overstated because income is not held constant.

SOURCE: J. B. Lansing and S. B. Withey, "Consumer Anticipations," p. 428.

in Chapter 6)? Lansing and Withey used Survey Research Center data to compare the income expectations expressed at the time when purchase intentions were determined with incomes received during the following year and found a substantial effect of unexpected income developments. The crucial figures are in boldface in Table 14. Families with unexpected favorable income developments were frequent among nonplanning purchasers of automobiles; and families with unexpected unfavorable developments, among planning nonpurchasers.

2. These findings were confirmed in 1954–1955 with the help of a somewhat different approach to unexpected developments. A representative sample was asked the following questions: Looking back over the

[14] See G. L. S. Shackle, *Expectation in Economics*.

past twelve months, did things work out pretty much as you expected financially or did anything unexpected happen? What was that? Any pleasant surprises? [15] Among people who had bought a car between June, 1954, and June, 1955, although in June, 1954, they had said that they did not intend to do so, in June, 1955, 23 per cent reported unexpected good events and 15 per cent unexpected bad events. On the other hand, among people who neither bought nor expected to buy a car only 9 per cent reported unexpected good events but 27 per cent unexpected bad events. (Over 60 per cent of the families reported no unexpected events.) [16]

3. Among people who in June, 1955, reported that they had had favorable surprises, we find that 34 per cent had bought a car during the previous year (as against 23 per cent among all other people) and 35 per cent a large item of household appliance (against 25 per cent among all others). Substantial differences in the purchases of the two groups remain after income is taken into account.

The findings just described concerning the impact of unexpected developments are hardly surprising. Following a fixed or preplanned course of behavior, uninfluenced by unexpected events, appears as improbable as not learning from experience and not changing one's behavior according to what one has learned. That windfall gains are not used for additional consumer expenditures—both on durables and on nondurables and services—likewise appears improbable in view of what is known about the effects of good news on behavior. [17]

Today life in the United States is replete with changes. Income variability is known to be very great. When the Survey Research Center determined the income of each family in a representative urban sample in three consecutive years (1954, 1955, and 1956) through three interviews,

[15] During the good years 1955–1957 many more people reported unfavorable than favorable surprises in reply to the first question. Since general conditions were good, many people did not classify favorable developments as unexpected. Therefore a further question (Any pleasant surprises?) was added and elicited some additional replies.

[16] C. Lininger, E. Mueller, and H. Wyss, "Some Uses of Panel Studies in Forecasting the Automobile Market," p. 421.

[17] There is not much evidence on the relation of windfalls to consumption. Some tentative data seem to show that windfall gains obtained through National Service Life Insurance dividends in 1950 and through tax reductions in 1954 did stimulate consumer expenditures. (Irwin Friend called attention in this connection to Survey of Consumer Finances data for 1950 in his "Comments on a Theory of Consumption Function," p. 457.) An analysis based on the 1950 Survey of Consumer Expenditures of the Bureau of Labor Statistics—undertaken by Ronald Bodkin as part of the extensive research project of the Wharton School and not yet published—confirms that the veterans have spent most of the unexpected dividend receipts. Klein and Liviatan showed some influence of windfalls on consumption in Great Britain (see "The Significance of Income Variability on Savings Behavior," p. 156).

Bristol found that one-half had had a change of at least 25 per cent over three years.[18] Only 14 per cent of the families reported incomes for 1956 which were within 5 per cent of their 1954 incomes; the 1956 incomes of 60 per cent of the families were higher, and of 26 per cent lower, than their 1954 incomes. An income increase from 1954 to 1955 was almost as frequently followed by an income decline from 1955 to 1956 as by an income increase. Thus, reversals of income trends do occur frequently. Even though the old theory according to which current income and its recent change alone determine consumer expenditures must be abandoned, we should not assume that the frequently occurring major income changes have no impact at all on consumers. This impact is reflected, of course, in people's attitudes and expectations, the analysis of which represents the major task of this book.

Consumers, as all human beings, learn and adjust their behavior to changing circumstances. The assumption that rigidly planned behavior— over one's lifetime or even over three years—is rational behavior should be supplanted by the notion that adaptability is the prototype of intelligent behavior. Adaptability implies flexibility and learning. Human beings are capable of developing under the influence of changing conditions. This generalization is supported by the study of changes in consumer behavior.

[18] R. B. Bristol, Jr., "Factors Associated with Income Variability."

CHAPTER 10

Group Belonging and Group Influence

It has been said that the major economic decisions are made by households, business firms, trade unions, or units of the government, rather than by individuals. This statement should not be understood to mean that economic decisions are always group decisions, arrived at by consultation or give and take among group members. More important, the individual is a member of a group, and group belonging exerts a powerful influence on his decisions and behavior even without consultation or discussion. In addition to the primary groups or face-to-face groups to which individuals belong, reference groups influence them. In many instances, group influence takes the form of similar stimuli affecting all group members and similar needs arising in them. This may be true also of "statistical groups"; therefore similarities in the behavior of income groups, age groups, and life-cycle groups were included in our studies of group influence.

Family and Friends

The most important face-to-face group to which we belong, with which we identify ourselves, and with which we share a common fate is the family. The family has become smaller over the last fifty or one hundred years. It is much less common today than it once was for several generations to live together and for the family unit to include uncles, aunts, and cousins. There are many incomplete families—single persons living without any blood relations, widows and widowers living with their children, etc.—but the typical family consists of husband and wife with or without children living with them. Who makes the economic decisions in these families?

Among the many studies of family organization, the one carried out by the Survey Research Center is most relevant for our purposes.[1] It shows that in general the family is a well-integrated economic unit. Major economic decisions are often made jointly by husband and wife; when there is a division of responsibility, this is frequently understood and approved

[1] E. H. Wolgast, "Do Husbands or Wives Make the Purchasing Decisions?"

by both partners in marriage; husband and wife frequently have the same opinions and expectations about important matters and know of each other's opinions and plans. Conflicts about major spending-saving decisions appear to be much less frequent than mutual adaptation of desires and wishes. Whatever the disagreements that may separate husbands from wives in our society, the question of what major purchases should be made with the family money is not one of the principal sources of conflict.

Specifically the study showed that in the opinion of both husbands and wives the decision to buy a car is most commonly made by the husband, and the decision to buy household appliances and furniture by the wife. Handling family expenses is done by the wife alone somewhat more frequently than jointly or by the husband alone; decisions about saving are made together in the majority of cases, yet in lower-income groups often by the wife alone and in higher-income groups (investment decisions) by the husband alone. Joint decisions are particularly frequent among younger couples. Responsibilities become divided in the course of marriage, which may be due to the development of agreement about each marriage partner's province rather than to domination of an economic area by either husband or wife.

The common notion that wives have many more buying plans than husbands may be incorrect. Substantially the same number of plans, as well as desires, were reported by representative samples of husbands and of wives. Husband and wife appeared to be well informed about each other's buying plans, and both talked about family plans. The differences found in the rate of fulfillment of buying plans reported either by husband or wife were not large; on the whole the plans reported by the wife were fulfilled somewhat better. (This was found to be true even of plans to buy a car!) Unanticipated purchases were equally frequent irrespective of whether purchases were compared with plans reported earlier by husbands or with those reported by wives.[2]

With most families consisting of only two adults, the strongly felt need of belonging is often satisfied in groups of friends, neighbors, and colleagues. Friends tend to think alike, as was shown for instance in studies of political behavior in which it was found that most friends of a Democrat belonged to or leaned toward the Democratic party and most friends of a Republican to the Republican party. We make friends with people with whom we have something in common. Those are our friends who interpret the news as we do, or as we want it to be interpreted. Irrespective

---

[2] From these and other findings it follows that for surveys concerning economic motives, attitudes, and plans, husbands and wives are equally good respondents. Husbands must be interviewed, however, if one wishes to determine the amounts of income, assets, and debts.

of whether it is primarily because of the way we select our friends, or because a strong group develops if group members share each other's experiences and goals, the result is the same: a group of friends, and also of colleagues or neighbors, usually has similar needs, attitudes, and expectations. The desires and satisfactions of others in our group become important to us, and the appraisal of our behavior by other members of our group matters. Many aspects of consumer behavior which appear to an outsider as imitation or as craving for prestige find their explanation in such principles of group dynamics.

In studying information seeking on the part of buyers of large household appliances (TV sets, refrigerators, washing machines, kitchen ranges), Eva Mueller found that more than half of the buyers turned for advice to acquaintances and in most instances also looked at the appliances used by them. A third of the buyers bought a brand or model that they had seen in someone else's home, often the home of relatives. Information seeking through shopping around in stores appeared to be of lesser importance than information seeking from relatives, friends, and neighbors.

Another illustration of the influence of friends on consumer behavior was found in studies of purchases and intentions to purchase newer household goods (clothes dryer, dishwasher, freezer, room air conditioner, garbage disposal).[3] When a representative urban sample was asked Do your friends have any of them? more than 60 per cent answered in the affirmative at a time when less than 25 per cent of the urban population actually owned at least one of the items in question. Probably some people wanted to show off, which means that prestige surrounds the ownership of such goods. More important, an affirmative answer to the question just quoted, in conjunction with an affirmative answer to the question of whether the friends liked the new appliances, was strongly correlated with intentions to purchase them. Desire to own what one's friends have may not be a matter of "invidious consumption" described by Veblen many years ago. Friends serve as sources of information and often also as salesmen. Acceptance of innovations is promoted when we have personal contact with a product and learn from people we trust how it has worked out. Seeing a new product in a friend's house and hearing her praise it may be a much more powerful influence than advertisements.[4]

William H. Whyte, Jr., gave evidence of the salesmanship function of groups of neighbors. He presented maps and photographs of a Philadel-

[3] See the two studies by E. Mueller, "A Study of Purchase Decisions" and "The Desire for Innovations in Household Goods."

[4] Similar processes may prevail regarding leisure activities and therefore the purchase of yachts, motorboats, power tools, hunting, fishing, and photographic equipment, as well as summer houses, but quantitative data showing the influence of friendship groups on such purchases are not available.

phia suburb showing the clustering of room air conditioners among neighbors in the same block and their absence in other blocks inhabited by people with similar income and occupation.[5] It does not follow that people are a bunch of sheep but, as Whyte puts it, that "the web of word of mouth" represents a most powerful influence. "Social traffic is common to every block."

What our friends own we own too or shall own soon—this seems to be true also of ownership of common stock. Asking a person whether his close personal friends own any common stock often results in the same answer as asking him whether he owns any. Ownership of common stock, and thereby of wealth in general, is highly concentrated among a relatively small proportion of American families. The 1 per cent of American families with the largest stock holdings own stock worth considerably more than the remaining 99 per cent—most of whom do not own any at all. Altogether, about 12 to 14 per cent of American families own stock, but many of them are small employee stockholders or own stock worth only a few hundred dollars. Only a small proportion of high-income families are important stockholders. Stock ownership is very rare among families in low- and even in middle-income groups.[6]

The higher the income the more frequent are stockholders, but income is not the only determinant of stock ownership. Even among families with an income of more than $15,000 only 55 per cent owned publicly traded stock in 1957. Many people with sizable reserve funds do not invest in stock because they consider stocks speculative, risky, or suitable only for people with inside information. Such notions, particularly frequent among young people, seem to remain effective unless counteracted by group influence. Having friends and colleagues who own stock and who have fared well through investments in stocks appears to be a most powerful influence which dissipates the notion that stock ownership is suitable only for business tycoons or speculators.[7]

[5] See *Fortune* magazine of November, 1954, an article reprinted in *Consumer Behavior,* Vol. II.

[6] For detailed data see the book by Butters, Thompson, and Bollinger; the monograph by Kimmel; the article by Katona, Lansing, and de Janosi, and the report on the 1957 Survey of Consumer Finances. These studies consider only publicly traded stock; in addition, about 3 per cent of American families own privately sold stock, that is, are business owners whose firms are incorporated. Trust funds and institutions are omitted from consideration. Much incorrect information has been published over the last few years about the allegedly substantial stock holdings of lower-income people. Stock ownership should be studied on a family basis and not by individuals because wives and children of a rich man should not be considered as low-income stockholders. Also, ownership of a few shares worth less than $1,000 should not be equated with ownership of thousands of shares.

[7] Even beyond the influence of income and wealth (or size of liquid-asset holdings), it was found to be true that the more education a person has, and the older he is, the

As a final example of the influence of face-to-face groups on consumption we may refer to Whyte's well-known studies of coherent suburban communities, inhabited primarily by young executives and "made in the image of organization man."[8] There is *esprit de corps* among neighbors and outgoing life rather than privacy in these communities in which children and their needs play a great role. The practice of buying on the installment plan and thereby budgeting a considerable part of their income in advance, as well as reliance on personal loans in case of emergencies, these suburbanites share with many other young couples. One important feature emphasized by Whyte seems to have developed in the new suburban communities though it may have recently spread to other areas of the country, namely, "inconspicuous consumption." Members belonging to a cohesive group behave in the same way. This means that nobody wants to attract attention through being different and conspicuous. Group belonging makes for uniformity of needs and for similar purchases satisfying those needs.

A discussion of the influence of face-to-face groups would not be complete without a reference to two further most influential groups which are relevant for economic psychology though less for consumer psychology. The importance of *work groups* for production was first emphasized by Elton Mayo, who called the desire to associate with others one of the strongest motivational forces influencing the behavior of individual workers. During the last two decades studies of morale in factories and offices and of management-employee relations have provided important insights into group dynamics, both group belonging and leadership. The study of the *business firm* has likewise profited greatly from applications of the psychology of groups. A corporation is not only a legal entity and an institutional organization, but also a group in the sociopsychological sense. The firm or the corporation is seen as acting and persisting, as having objectives of its own. Usually management, and sometimes even

---

more probable it is that he owns common stock (M. E. Kreinin, "Factors Associated with Stock Ownership"). College-educated people associate primarily with other college-educated people, and the friends of older people are older people. Group belonging may, however, not be the only relevant factor which influences the acquisition of stock ownership. A further finding of Kreinin that achievement-oriented people tend to own stock more frequently than security-oriented people (the two groups being defined as in Chapter 6 of this book) tends to support the notion that personality factors are also influential.

[8] What Whyte calls suburbia in his book *The Organization Man* applies to newly developed communities rather than to old suburbs or to the millions of people who have moved from central city locations to outlying districts of towns during the last ten years. So many people live today in suburbs that in many respects suburbanites do not differ from those not living in suburbs. But the average income is higher in the suburbs than elsewhere.

lower-level employees, identify themselves with the firm and strive to promote what is good for the firm (even if they have no ownership interest in it). Within most firms there are subgroups. The location of power and of decision making in the firm as well as communication within the firm have recently been studied from the point of social psychology, and there can be no doubt that this approach will greatly increase our knowledge of management.[9]

The Rich and the Poor

The finding that close friendship groups share experiences and goals and sometimes practice inconspicuous consumption does not contradict the notion that keeping up with the Joneses is a powerful factor in consumer purchases. Our standards of behavior, and of consumption as well, may be determined by reference groups to which we do not belong rather than by face-to-face groups. Certain consumer goods are status symbols and are purchased either to prove our status or to raise our status. In addition to the strong impact of belonging, there is also an effect of the desire to belong, and purchases motivated by prestige considerations do occur. Possibly, however, this aspect of consumer behavior has sometimes been given an exaggerated importance.

It has been a common procedure for studies concerning various groups of European as well as American society to divide the society into socio-economic classes. Although class distinctions have been thought to be somewhat less useful for an understandng of social as well as economic processes in America than in Europe, here too it has been argued that the upper classes dominate the economy and set the standards to be followed and imitated by others. (Alternatively, it has also been postulated, however, that the upper class is oriented toward the past, the middle class toward the future, and the lower class, preoccupied with problems of subsistence, toward the present.) Lloyd Warner and his school, classifying groups according to occupation, source of income, and housing, found that most Americans fall into either the lower-middle or the upper-lower class. While this classification has been valuable in many sociological studies, it is neither psychologically nor economically sufficiently clear-cut for the purpose of studying consumer behavior. This purpose is better served by differentiating among groups according to one or two clearly defined factors, such as income, education, or occupation.

The first question to be answered concerns the influence of the upper classes or of people in the upper-income brackets. Are the rich the opinion

[9] See H. R. Bowen, *The Business Enterprise as a Subject for Research;* H. A. Simon, *Models of Man;* R. Likert, "Developing Patterns of Management." The influence which groups of businessmen, belonging to different firms, exert on business decisions will be discussed in Chapter 14.

leaders, or the taste leaders, in economic matters? It has been argued that influence moves downward from those with high status to the masses. In other words, the mode of living of top-income people is imitated by others; ten or twenty-five years later similar modes of living will be found among broad population groups. The importance attached to upward mobility by very many Americans may be viewed as confirming the notion that the rich are the opinion leaders, and some observations about behavior in the nineteenth century and the early twentieth century seem to indicate that middle-class people did follow the customs and practices of upper-class people.

But experience during the last few decades appears to contradict the thesis. Fifty years ago conspicuous consumption—large mansions with many servants, lavish parties, high expenditures on dress, jewelry, as well as art objects—characterized the mode of living by the rich. There is hardly any evidence that such expenditure patterns were subsequently adopted by the broad middle- and upper-middle-income groups. Possibly they have disappeared by now even among the very rich. More important still is the other side of the argument. Many new and generally accepted forms of living were not initiated by the upper classes. The use of labor-saving household equipment, shopping in department stores and super-markets (rather than in exclusive specialty stores), vacation trips by car with stops at motels (rather than trips to resort hotels), or fishing and camping trips—these are some examples of ways of life in which broad groups of the upper-middle-income brackets (say, with $4,000 to $10,000 annual income) appear to have been the leaders.

Katz and Lazarsfeld contradicted the notion that the process of influence is a vertical process and demonstrated the existence of horizontal opinion leadership.[10] In the latter case, influence does not move downward from high-status or high-prestige levels. Marketing leaders and taste leaders were found in almost equal numbers in high-, middle-, and low-status levels. The authors concluded that each status level had its own core of opinion leaders.

A study of historical developments is outside the scope of this book. It may suffice to refer to the discussion in *The Lonely Crowd* by David Riesman, who provides us with valuable insights into the changes that have taken place in predominant character types as well as in style of life. Riesman shows that American society has become increasingly consumption-minded and that there has been a growing tendency toward uniformity—irrespective of class—and toward the acceptance of a standard package of consumption goods.

From the point of view of an analysis of short-term economic change, which is the central problem of this book, leadership in innovation is of

[10] E. Katz and P. F. Lazarsfeld, *Personal Influence.*

particular interest. About the pioneering group, the very first people who acquired, say, a TV set or an air conditioner, we know very little. About the first group of followers, those who purchased new consumer goods before they were generally accepted, we have some survey information which indicates that this group did not consist exclusively of the upper classes or the rich. Innovation-minded people who accepted new household appliances before they came to be regarded as something every well-furnished home should have, were frequently in the middle-income brackets. They were usually young and well educated. In addition, and most important, they were found to have positive aspirations and expected their financial situation to improve.[11]

The automobile is perhaps our most conspicuous possession. Only a few relatives and friends visit our home while all our neighbors, colleagues, and acquaintances see what kind of a car we are driving. Even if husband and wife should be immune to the desire to impress others by their car, their teen-age children may exert pressure on them because they may fear to lose status if their parents do not drive a late-model car. In contradiction to such widely reported social influences, the claim has been made more recently, and especially during the automobile slump of 1958, that the automobile has lost its fascination for the American people, or that the Joneses are no longer as compelling as they used to be.

We found ample evidence in our surveys that most Americans are fond of their cars and that many are interested in the annual model changes in cars. Only relatively few people look at model changes as forced obsolescence, that is, as a process through which the auto manufacturers diminish the value of cars in use. Many more people greet the new models year after year as representing improvements in operation as well as in appearance. As we said before (Chapter 3), the reception of new models was most favorable in 1955 when the longer and lower cars, as well as what the trade calls "jewelry," were thought to represent distinct differences from older models as well as improvements. But when people like something, it does not follow that they will also like more of the same. In the years following 1955, in the opinion of people, cars became more and more alike; there was no assortment to choose from.[12] Although those who bought cars tended to prefer the longest, lowest, and fanciest models, the rate of automobile buying and the interest in new models declined. The Survey Research Center found that in December, 1956, only 38 per cent of a representative sample said that the new auto models differed greatly from the previous models. In December, 1957, prior to the auto slump, the proportion fell to 20 per cent. (Data collected in December, 1958, showed a modest improvement to 29 per cent.)

[11] See E. Mueller, "The Desire for Innovations."
[12] The Cadillac with its distinct prestige may have represented an exception.

It does not follow from these findings, or from the growing sales of small foreign cars and Ramblers, that in 1957 and 1958 the American people wanted nothing but small cars. Some people no doubt did, while others were fully satisfied with what they got. Vacation travel is increasing in frequency and is overwhelmingly done in the family car. The big and powerful cars are approved for this purpose as well as for many other purposes. But there is a rapidly growing trend toward two cars in the family even among middle- and upper-middle-income families, and it is improbable that any family would want to keep up with the Joneses with both of its cars. The second car, if used for short trips to schools and supermarkets or for commuting to nearby offices, was looked upon in a different light from the first car. It is regrettable that mass manufacturing finds it difficult to satisfy minority preferences: in 1957 and 1958 the Big Three in the automobile industry failed to cater to one segment of the market.[13]

Income was found to play a relatively small role in the kind of car bought. True, the higher the income, the larger the proportion of buyers of new cars and the smaller the proportion of buyers of used cars. But in 1957, for instance, as many families with high incomes (over $7,500 a year) drove cars bought used as lower-income families (less than $5,000 a year) drove late-model cars bought new. New car buyers were found in high-, middle-, and low-income groups, and in each group the same average amount of money was paid for new cars. This is explained partly by the fact that the differences in car prices—say, between the price of a Chevrolet and a Buick—are much smaller than the differences in incomes. In addition, many high-income people bought Fords, Chevrolets, and Plymouths in 1956–1958. Whether this was due to the opinion of many people that low-priced cars and higher-priced cars were pretty much alike, or whether the finding shows that cars are no longer viewed as status symbols by some people is not known.

Naturally, high-income families spend more money on most things than low-income families. Not the absolute amounts but the proportion of income spent on different commodities must be compared in order to discover differences in behavior. In this respect our thinking has been dominated for almost one hundred years by the famous Engel's law which says that the lower the income, the greater the proportion of income spent on food and necessities; the higher the income, the greater the proportion of income spent on other things. But recent findings already reported in Chapter 2 indicate that on consumer investment items—automobiles,

---

[13] Nevertheless, two-car familes continued to grow in number, and consisted most commonly of families owning one car bought new and one car bought used. Desires for a second car will be discussed in Chapter 11.

household durables, and additions or repairs to homes—most income groups spend substantially the same share of their income.[14]

Many significant social influences are related to income levels and income differences. One of these is exemplified by the saying: The richer the economy, the more ways there are to be poor. In a rich community absence of certain goods and conveniences which are not missed at all in a poor community makes people poor. Being poor is defined better as belonging to the lowest decile or quintile of the income distribution rather than by absolute income levels. In periods of prosperity being poor has a different meaning than it has in periods of depression. Differences in prevailing income trends have a pronounced influence on the meaning of income changes. When everyone else enjoys income increases, stable income may represent a calamity. Detailed studies of these influences are greatly needed.

Differences between income groups regarding level of information or economic intelligence, shown in Table 13 in Chapter 9, reflect primarily differences in education. More income-determined are differences in the degree of optimism or pessimism. As expected, at all times more people in the upper- than in the lower-income groups reported being better off. Also regarding personal financial and business expectations and the evaluation of whether the market was favorable for buying—but not regarding price expectations which we shall discuss in Chapter 12—more people in the upper- than in the lower-income brackets give optimistic answers. These differences, though interesting and not fully explained, do not touch upon our major concern with regard to the different income groups, which is whether or not there are any differences among them as to the *changes* in their attitudes. In other words, can it be said that the rich, the poor, or neither, lead the way in expecting, and thus signalling, an upswing or a downswing in the economy?

It has been argued that the attitudes of upper- and upper-middle-income groups should be considered exclusively when change in attitudes is used for the purpose of predicting durable goods purchases because these income groups spend much more money (in absolute amounts) on durables than the lower-income groups. One might also assume that upper-income groups would be more sensitive in perceiving an incipient or impending upturn since they receive more economic information than people with lower income. But with respect to a downturn it might be the other way around since a recession hurts those with lower incomes more severely and perhaps earlier than those with higher incomes.

The findings available up to now are not fully conclusive. During the upturn of 1954 there were attitudes regarding which people in the upper-income brackets became optimistic somewhat earlier and to a greater

[14] See J. N. Morgan, "Consumer Investment Expenditures."

extent than those in the lower-income brackets. Yet the trend was not general and did not extend to expressed intentions to purchase automobiles and durable goods. In the upturn of the fall of 1958 upper-income people again led the lower-income people, inasmuch as the personal financial attitudes and buying intentions of the former improved to a greater extent than those of the latter. But there was not much difference between them as to business expectations. During the downturn of 1957 there were no substantial differences in the rate of deterioration in the various attitudes and expectations of different income groups. Probably the most useful conclusion to be drawn from presently available evidence is that it does not seem advisable to restrict studies of attitude change to upper-income groups alone. The rich are not the only buyers of durable goods, they are not the only opinion leaders, and they are not the only ones who are sensitive to changes in the economic climate.

The Young and the Old

All items of consumer durables are bought by a larger proportion of younger than of older families. In the last few years the frequency of purchases was the highest when the head of the family was between twenty-five and thirty-five years old. Married couples bought durables more often than single people, and, for most durables, having children was likewise associated with frequent purchases. All these considerations were taken into account when Lansing and Morgan distinguished six stages of the life cycle into which most American families could be divided: [15]

1. The bachelor stage; young single people.
2. Newly married couples; young, no children.
3. The full nest I; young married couples with dependent children.
4. The full nest II; older married couples with dependent children.
5. The empty nest; older married couples with no children living with them.
6. The solitary survivor; older single people.

Voluminous statistical data are available on the differences in the rate of purchases of these six groups. Usually the dividing line between young and old is set at forty-five years. Table 15 is presented so as to illustrate the extent of differences among the six stages. It must be kept in mind, however, that some of the differences shown in the table are due to income rather than the life cycle. The average income in Stage 1 and Stage 6, among younger and older single people, is significantly smaller than in the other groups.

[15] J. B. Lansing and J. N. Morgan, "Consumer Finances over the Life Cycle"; J. B. Lansing, E. S. Maynes and K. E. Kreinin, "Factors Associated with the Use of Consumer Credit"; A. Enthoven, "Instalment Credit and Prosperity."

TABLE 15. DIFFERENCES IN DURABLE GOODS PURCHASES DURING THE LIFE CYCLE (IN 1956)

Life cycle stage	Distribution of spending units	Proportion of purchasers of						
		New cars	Used cars	Furniture	Refrigerator	Kitchen range	Washing machine	TV
1. Younger,* single............	10%	6%	9%	5%	3%	3%	3%	5%
2. Younger, married............	8	8	11	13	10	17	9	11
3. Younger, with children......	35	44	49	50	51	41	56	47
4. Older,* with children.......	12	14	15	11	11	15	12	12
5. Older, no children..........	21	23	10	16	18	20	16	17
6. Older, single..............	14	5	6	5	7	4	4	8
Total †.................	100%	100%	100%	100%	100%	100%	100%	100%

* Younger means head of family under 45; older, over 45.
† The total of 100 per cent does not include all spending units; there are some who do not fit into any of the life-cycle stages and are omitted from consideration.

NOTE: Since, for instance, Stage 3 constitutes 35 per cent of the spending units considered but bought 44 per cent of new cars, it purchased more than its share.

SOURCE: 1956 Survey of Consumer Finances.

Differences among families in different stages of the life cycle are especially pronounced in installment buying. As an illustration it may suffice to cite the proportion of families in each stage who have had installment debt in 1956: 40 per cent in Stage 1, 56 per cent in Stage 2, 65 per cent in Stage 3, 53 per cent in Stage 4, 27 per cent in Stage 5, and 16 per cent in Stage 6. Similar differences prevailed in all postwar years and remained significant in multivariate analysis (after eliminating the effect of income, for instance). On the average, young married couples with dependent children appear to save at a lower rate than older people, but they too accumulate liquid reserves and it is not correct to argue that, intent on purchasing durable goods, they are not savings-minded.

Little need be said about the causes of the high purchase rates among young married couples. Household formation creates substantial needs, and with children the need for a variety of goods increases. Most frequently, right after marriage couples rent an apartment; buying a house comes somewhat later and creates further substantial needs for furniture and appliances. Uniform needs are created, not only by situational factors, but also by group influence. Small as well as adolescent children form cohesive groups, as frequently do their parents as well. Within such groups the need for similar things tends to spread, and young middle-income families all over the country acquire what Riesman has called the standard package of consumer goods. The late twenties and the thirties represent age groups in which advancement in job and career and corresponding income gains are frequent, and with them great expectations and upward mobility.

Information about the purchasing habits of different life-cycle groups must be considered in conjunction with population trends. As is well known, the baby boom reached its peak in the forties, during and shortly after World War II. The years of household formation and of substantial durable-goods purchases on the part of this unusually large crop of babies will begin by 1965. Until that time, however, our major interest for the prediction of more immediate trends in purchases of consumer durables must be in the rate of purchases by those families who have younger and those who have older children. The composition of the American population by age of children has undergone great changes in the recent past and will change further in the near future. These changes have been cited as having contributed to the recession of 1958 as well as yielding dire predictions for the next few years.

We shall look at four age groups, (1) children under 5 years, (2) children between 5 and 9, (3) children between 10 and 14, and (4) children between 15 and 19 years of age. During the five years up to July, 1944, Group 1 increased greatly, while the other three groups did not show any gain. During the next five years again Group 1 increased most, but

Group 2 also gained substantially. During the five years up to July, 1954, the largest relative increase took place in Group 2, with Group 3 following and likewise greatly exceeding the gains in Group 1. In the three years up to July, 1957, Group 3 was the largest gainer, while population projections for the years 1957 to 1964 indicate that during those years the relative increase will be most pronounced in Group 4.

It has been assumed that in the first few years after marriage, when the children are small, people spend a lot on equipping their houses and on buying automobiles. Teen-agers, on the other hand, have been thought to need more food and clothing as well as larger expenditures on education and recreation; therefore their parents would be compelled to restrict their expenditures on durables. This argument justifies pessimistic predictions for durable goods in view of the assured increase in the number of families with teen-agers in the near future. But it is also possible to argue as follows and therefore to arrive at a different prediction: Teen-agers have growing needs and wants for consumer goods, especially automobiles; fathers of teen-agers usually have higher incomes than those of younger children, and mothers of teen-agers often resume working.

What do statistics show about recent past purchases of families with older children and those with younger children? We shall compare Group A consisting of families with children aged less than 10 years with Group B consisting of families with children aged 10 to 19. Of course, many families have both younger and older children; in this case they were put in Group A. In other words, the age of the youngest child determined the classification, and Group B was made to consist of families who have only children older than 10. We find from the Survey of Consumer Finances that in 1956 new cars were purchased somewhat more frequently by Group B than Group A, and used cars by Group A more frequently than by Group B. Furniture and most household appliances had a somewhat higher purchase rate in Group A than in Group B (especially washing machines, refrigerators, and TV sets). Even though these findings appear to hold good within most income groups, the most striking fact is that the differences between Groups A and B were small.[16] The average expenditure on automobiles, household appliances (including radio and TV), and furniture by households with children less than 10 years old was $558 in 1956 according to the *Life* magazine-Politz study as against $552 for households with children 10 to 19 years of age.[17] (The difference is somewhat larger if the ratios of expenditures to income are compared because the average income is higher in Group B than in Group A.)

[16] University of Michigan master's thesis by Jessie Dalman.

[17] *Life* Magazine Study of Consumer Expenditures of 1956, conducted by Alfred Politz Research, Inc.

Having children at home as against not having children at home makes for far greater differences in purchases of durable goods than whether the children are younger or older. Even if the 1956 purchase rates of families with children under 10 and those with children over 10 were to be repeated in, say, 1960—which is far from certain—the fate of the automobile and appliance industries would not be substantially influenced by changes in the composition of the population.

We must conclude therefore that population trends and differences in the purchase rates of the life-cycle groups cannot explain short-range fluctuations in the purchases of durable goods. The study of these changes must concentrate on fluctuations in ability and willingness to buy.

Our discussion of group influence is far from complete. We have not considered any differences in the consumption of occupational and educational groups, which are related to differences in the consumption of income groups but need not be the same, nor differences between large metropolitan centers, small towns, and rural districts. Nor have we concerned ourselves with differences in the consumption of Negroes and whites, or with regional differences. The degree of uniformity in consumer behavior in the East, the Middle West, and the West represents an important topic of inquiry. This author believes that the economy of many European countries is influenced to a much greater extent by regional differences than is the economy of the United States, even though the geographical distances are much smaller in Europe than in America. Whether this hunch is correct, and if it is correct, how the uniformity among American regions came about, are questions meriting study.

A final warning is needed. We have recognized the powerful influence exerted by groups as well as the frequent occurrence of joint decisions by small coherent groups. These findings do not imply that the individual plays a minor role in economic behavior and that thinking, problem solving, and decision making by individuals may be neglected in economic analysis. Much of group influence is the result of uniform stimuli reaching people in similar situations rather than of imitation and striving for prestige. We should not forget that groups are formed and led by individuals who, although they occasionally submerge in groups, remain the basic units of behavioral studies. We have neither made the value judgment that group decisions are good nor presented the historical argument that personal responsibility has declined and plays a smaller role in today's American economy than at earlier times. What we have done is to recognize that the individual is a member of face-to-face groups and a part of society; therefore no real analysis of his motives, attitudes, and decisions is possible without taking into consideration the framework within which he functions.

Economic Fluctuations

PART FOUR

Economic Fluctuations

CHAPTER 11

The Psychology of Prosperity

Demand depends both on ability to buy and on willingness to buy—this has been the basic thesis of this book. It follows that prosperity cannot prevail without confidence and optimism. As one of the most perceptive analysts of business trends, Arthur F. Burns, put it recently, "If prosperity is to flourish, people must have confidence in their own economic future and that of their country."[1]

But confidence alone does not suffice. Even the combination of high incomes providing the ability and confidence providing the willingness to buy does not tell the whole story of prosperity. The story is not complete until we have explained what we mean by confidence. If confidence were to mean no more than a vague emotional bias having no roots beyond changes in one's own personal situation, there could clearly be no dependence on its persistence. Lasting prosperity calls for *sustained* high demand, that is, for an extended period of general striving for higher standards of living. It could not prevail if, after achieving some improvement in their situation, people were to cease to strive for more. The optimistic attitude must have a solid foundation, and the fulfillment of striving must serve to nourish rather than to dissipate the underlying motives and attitudes. In other words, prosperity requires self-reinforcing optimistic attitudes based on sound reasons. The economy must derive dynamic force from a widespread and strong conviction that more and more is obtainable. Understood in these terms, we may speak of prosperous times even if they are interrupted occasionally, for short periods, by mild recessions. The ability to overcome a recession quickly, before it causes real damage, is one of the major features of sustained confidence.

The New Climate of Opinion

At the beginning of Chapter 3 we discussed the pessimistic forecasts which were prevalent in 1945, toward the end of the Second World War. The expectation of postwar depression and unemployment was explained there in terms of the anticipated contraction of the war economy. But

[1] *Prosperity without Inflation*, p. 27.

173

those expectations had deeper roots as well. Many economists thought that the end of the war would mean a return to the conditions of the thirties and recalled that in the decade before the war the depression had endured and millions of people had remained without employment for years at a time. The experts also remembered that after the First World War there had been important new developments, such as rapid electrification and the transformation of the automobile into a necessity for the masses, which had provided tremendous impetus to the economy of the twenties. But no such new industries were foreseen in 1945. Imagination at that time was not bold enough to envisage any new impetus which might lead the economy out of stagnation.

Today we know what we did not know in 1945 and we can now point with hindsight to the rapid increase in population, the trend to the suburbs, and the multitude of expensive leisure time activities which, together with a number of new industries—electronics, plastics, frozen foods, etc.—transformed the American economy during the decade after the war. Yet the continuation of the baby boom over many years and the unrestrained growth of suburbs, entirely unexpected in 1945, are nothing but manifestations of a new climate of opinion. Where should we look for the *élan* which made the climate of the years after World War II so different from what it was in the years before it?

World War II did not represent a simple interruption after which the economy would resume where it had left off. Psychologically, it was a break with the past. In the minds of the people the depression of the early thirties and the stagnation of the late thirties were over. The economic lesson they learned was not that war can make wheels turn and provide employment. They learned that the government can do so. How this conviction developed and what credit may be attributed to New Deal legislation or even to Keynesian economic thinking, is hard to tell. What we know is that right after the war, and much more strongly in the fifties, the great majority of the American people believed that depressions were not inevitable. They reasoned that if full employment could be achieved in times of war, when much of the production was wasted, the same could be done to even better effect in times of peace. They felt that they were entitled to full employment—a conviction shared by Congress, which incorporated this view among the responsibilities of the government in the Employment Act of 1946—and looked with confidence to the government, and to some extent also to business, to give them prosperity.

At various times in the early fifties the Survey Research Center asked the following question of representative samples of American families: Do you think that something like the depression of the thirties is likely to happen again during the next five years or so? That in those years very many people would consider the recurrence of a severe depression improbable was expected. But the researchers were nevertheless surprised by the answers they received. Close to 60 per cent of all respondents, and an even higher percentage among those in the upper-income brackets, said flatly that nothing like the depression of the thirties *could* happen again. (Only 13 per cent of all people and 8 per cent of those with incomes over $7,500 said that such a depression might happen during the next five years; the rest were uncertain or said that it would probably not happen.)

Why did many people think that the depression of the thirties was a unique occurrence which could not recur? When asked the usual question Why do you think so? only a small minority referred to the prevailing good times, to high incomes, or to the extensive needs of consumers and business firms. Most people expressed themselves in quite different terms, although many found it hard to give clearly reasoned answers. "We know how to avoid a depression" was the most common reply. "We have learned many things since the thirties" was another frequent expression. What did these people have in mind? Who is "we"? Further questioning revealed that most of them had the government in mind. "The government can avert a depression and would do so if need be," they said. In short, the firm conviction was found to be widespread that the government had learned that there are means with which to fight a depression and never again would it fail to use those means.

The nature of the means to be used was often expressed in ways which an economist would not consider adequate, but which nonetheless shed interesting light on postwar thinking. Two aspects stood out clearly. First, references to war and rearmament were rare. Only relatively few people said that a severe depression would not or could not occur again because the production of military hardware would create employment. Second, the most frequent replies were in terms of public works—schools, highways, and many other forms of domestic expenditure which the government could and would undertake to create employment opportunities and make large-scale unemployment impossible.

Similar results were obtained by asking other samples a somewhat different question, Do you think that the government can do anything to keep unemployment low and make for prosperous times? This was asked during the slight recession of 1953–1954. More than 70 per cent said Yes—and stressed public works—while 10 per cent said No, and the rest were uncertain. All social classes were equally convinced that the government had vast powers over the economy.

Obviously, the question referring to "a depression such as in the thirties" was formulated in rather extreme terms. To some respondents the question may have suggested a catastrophe rather than cyclical fluctuations. Usually, therefore, the question was asked in a milder form:

Looking ahead, which would you say is more likely—that in the country as a whole we'll have continuous good times during the next five years or so, or that we will have periods of widespread unemployment or depression, or what? The answers to this question fluctuated to some extent over the years according to the economic climate prevailing at the time it was asked. But the distribution of replies obtained during the height of prosperity, 1955 and 1956, is worth reporting. In those years almost 50 per cent of the people said without qualification that the next five years would be good, and less than 10 per cent that they would be bad. (The rest said they didn't know—"Who am I to say?"—or gave conditional answers.) Among those people with an income of over $5,000 only a handful, 5 per cent to be exact, thought that widespread unemployment or a depression were probable during the following five years.

The fairly large proportion of people who answered the question about five years' business prospects in conditional terms most frequently said that whether or not we would have good or bad times depended on the international situation. Further probing made it clear that the impact of the threat of war, or of an intensification of international conflict, was usually viewed as unfavorable for the economy. In discussing the economic attitudes during the Korean War in Chapter 3, we have already reported that most people did not think of war and rearmament as turning wheels and creating domestic employment. Rather they spoke of the disrupting effects of war production which would hamper what they meant by "good times," namely, rising living standards. (The one time this was not true was toward the end of the Korean War, when there was a military stalemate for several months and relatively favorable opinions were expressed about the influence of rearmament on the domestic economy.) Conflicts and uncertainties shorter and milder than the Korean War— Berlin airlift, Formosa Straits, Suez and Lebanon, to mention a few— without exception brought forth a majority opinion that their impact on the domestic economy was unfavorable.

We are confronted here with a process of generalization. War, the threat of war, international conflict—all these obviously create misgivings, if not anxiety. The general feeling then is that nothing good can result from such evils. Furthermore, people associate war as well as rearmament with high taxes which are viewed as subtracting from their well-being. Studies conducted over several years make it abundantly clear that the American people have not attributed the prosperity of the fifties to high defense spending and correspondingly high government budgets.

Let us turn back now to the effects of the depression of the thirties on postwar attitudes. As we have said, one major form of social learning that resulted consisted of the conviction, "We have learned how to avoid depressions." Other studies disclosed that much further learning had taken place—even though, when questioned directly, people were hardly aware that they had actually acquired new insights through their collective experience with the depression and with New Deal legislation. One aspect of the new postwar climate of opinion relates to social security legislation. Unemployment insurance and old-age insurance are now generally taken for granted and considered as inevitable rights, rather than as relatively recent reforms. Second, most people are convinced that government bonds and bank deposits are safe. Even when interviewers tried to probe about misgivings, for instance toward small savings and loan associations, no trace of mistrust was found. The more rapidly these institutions grew, and the more mortgage loans they granted in their community on easy terms, the greater was the confidence. That many people had defaulted on mortgages and depositors of thousands of banks had been wiped out in the early thirties no longer appeared to be part of living memory. It was found to be practically unknown that government bonds could go down in price—even though they had done so to a considerable extent during the fifties after the pegging of bond prices had been abandoned. People did reveal an awareness of war bonds and savings bonds, and considered the fact that their interest rate was stable and that they were always redeemable at fixed prices as the normal state of affairs.

In one respect only did we find widespread opinions which seemed to indicate that some aspects of the depression of the thirties had not been entirely forgotten. We have reported before that very many people considered the stock market a place of speculation where "insiders" made prices go up or down. Thus the mistrust of investments in common stock has not disappeared entirely. But even in this respect great changes were noted. When in 1946 for the first time questions about the advisability of investing in common stock were asked in interviews, the researchers were surprised by the frequent references to the crash of 1929 and even to the "very many people" who had jumped from skyscraper windows when the market broke. As years went by such references as well as stories about how much father or uncle had lost during the stock market crash became very infrequent.

Although common stock is still considered as speculative, even by many upper-income people, mass attitudes toward business are no doubt different today from what they were after the crash of 1929. The fight of the New Deal against the "money changers" is forgotten. That big business rules the economy, or that the little man is dependent on manipulations by big business and that he is affected by speculative excesses in which financial and industrial leaders indulge—such notions as these are practically nonexistent today. On the contrary, many people say that business helps to avert a depression (though more say that it is the government which does so). When in 1950 survey respondents were given a list of institutions—government, big business, large trade unions, farmers, etc.—and were asked to rank them according to the power they have, government was considered the most powerful and big business was given a middle position in the power hierarchy.[2]

In a study carried out in 1955 general questions about the causes of price increases and inflation were followed by specific ones about the role of speculation and about business practices which might have driven prices up. Only a very small proportion of the people was found to place any blame on business. References to collusion among business firms and to monopolistic exploitation of power by big business were still more infrequent.

In this postwar climate it is felt that, except among utilities, competition does exist and is a good thing. When asked what competition is, most people speak of rivalry between producers or sellers of the same good—competition between Ford and Chevrolet, for instance—and discuss such beneficial effects as lower prices and better products. Competition among retailers is especially welcome, and the large chain stores are praised by many because they are competitive. There exist ideological objections to bigness on the part of many people, but buying from big business is favored, trust in the brands produced by big business is general, and big business is thought to be a desirable employer for one's children. Competition is rarely viewed as cut-throat competition or as something which needs to be regulated. Surveys have shown that regulation and control of business are approved in general terms (the government it was thought should be more powerful than business) and are strongly supported as emergency measures (price control, for instance, was popular in 1951), but most people know of no specific evils which would make the introduction of controls over business necessary.

Confidence in Personal Finances

The psychological climate that emerged after the war as the result of the experiences of the depression, the New Deal, and the war itself has thus far been characterized in terms of attitudes toward the economy in general. As a second vital factor in nourishing the psychology of prosperity let us look now at the impact of the war on the American people's attitudes toward their personal economic situation and prospects. During the war they had saved a substantial proportion of their incomes and had thus emerged practically debt-free and with sizable liquid-asset holdings. When it was over they therefore not only believed that a gen-

[2] See B. R. Fisher and S. B. Withey, *Big Business as the People See It.*

eral depression need never occur again, but also felt secure and confident about their own future.

During the war there were wage controls, and a sense of patriotism caused all elements of the American working public to exercise a certain restraint in demanding higher wages and salaries. As soon as it was over such demands were freely made and readily met. Year after year one round of wage increases followed another and people accepted the new fact of steady and fairly rapid rises in income. Constant increases in wages and salaries came to be viewed as natural and as the just due of all workers. A year in which hourly paid workers failed to get a wage increase or salaried employees got no raise was looked upon as a bad year. Similarly, business owners and managers were dissatisfied with a year in which profits did not rise, even if the year was as good as the previous one, which in turn had been the best ever experienced!

Inflation, of course, did take place during this decade and the increases in wages, salaries, and profits were related to the increases in prices. In most years incomes rose more sharply than prices although there were some years when the former did not keep pace with the latter. But even when there was a direct connection between the two as, for instance, when a labor contract provided for cost-of-living adjustments, many workers failed to see the connection. Interviews revealed that increased income was considered as the reward for accomplishments, while price increases were seen as something apart which detracted from the enjoyment of the fruits of one's labor.

As we have reported before, optimism about personal financial prospects fluctuated with regard to the immediate future. But when people were asked how their jobs and incomes "a few years from now" would compare with the situation at the time of any one of the surveys of the past ten years, the answers varied little. Most people said either that their incomes would go up or that they would remain the same. To mention a few figures which were practically the same in different years and among people in the upper- and the middle-income brackets: about 50 per cent said that their incomes would be higher in a few years, 40 per cent that they would be the same, and less than 10 per cent that they would be lower. Older people represented a considerable proportion of those who expected their personal financial situation to deteriorate.

Some of the expected improvement in the financial situation may reflect attitudes characteristic of the younger generation. "A few years from now we will be in a better situation"—so said, for instance, a twenty-five-year-old worker. "Everyone works to get ahead; there wouldn't be much use to living if you didn't advance." Others explained that in a few years they would have more education or skills; others again that their wives would resume working after the children had grown up. Most answers indicated not only an optimistic frame of mind but also a determination to work for the desired improvement in the economic situation and confidence that it will be achieved.

A few further statistics should be cited. They were collected in June, 1954, toward the end of the slight recession of 1953–1954, in a period of relatively stable prices and incomes. Did you ever have an income higher than your present income? was one of the questions asked. Among all nonfarm respondents 50 per cent answered No. (Farmers were not prosperous at that time; therefore we restrict the data to urban populations.) The remaining 50 per cent included older people as well as many who suffered temporary income reverses in 1953–1954.

Job mobility, and occupational mobility as well, was very extensive. Many people changed jobs to raise their incomes. Some changed jobs because of better prospects in the new job, even if they had to sacrifice income at first. In 1954 among all urban families in the labor force (excluding self-employed, housewives, students, and the retired) 28 per cent said that they had had their job less than 2½ years, 36 per cent that they had had it for 2½ to 9½ years, and 36 per cent for 10 years or longer. Job mobility is not unrelated to residential mobility, although each exists without the other. How extensive residential mobility has been we have shown in Chapter 8.

The data on job mobility do not reflect the growing importance of second jobs. During the fifties many people in the middle-income brackets took up, occasionally or regularly, an income-producing activity in their spare time. Others worked overtime and relied on it to supplement their earnings.

When asked Have you ever been unemployed? in the group most commonly hit by unemployment—blue-collar workers—23 per cent said "Yes, repeatedly" in 1954 (and an additional 8 per cent said that occasionally, for short periods, they were unemployed). Thus prior to that year the great majority of the American people has never had the experience of being out of a job. It is easy to understand that people on the whole were satisfied. The answers to four questions on satisfactions, which were asked of urban families, are presented in Figure 10.

A small proportion of people refused to give a clear answer to each of the questions, replying in essence that nobody can say or that everything has two sides. Considering the definite answers, as presented in the figure, we see that only a minority said that their occupational progress was not satisfactory, that they had had bad breaks, that their income should be higher, or that their standard of living should be better.

Another aspect of the same story is shown in the absence of financial worries. In June, 1955, urban people were asked a question in a form which was meant to elicit many replies expressing economic worries. Survey respondents were given a card and were told, This card contains a list of things some people worry about nowadays; please mark those about which you or other people around here worry. There were, of course,

Figure 10. Satisfactions of urban people in June, 1954

(Percentage distribution of answers)

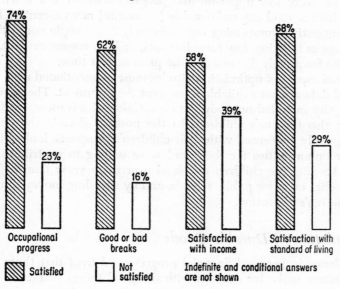

| Occupational progress | Good or bad breaks | Satisfaction with income | Satisfaction with standard of living |

⊠ Satisfied   ☐ Not satisfied   Indefinite and conditional answers are not shown

THE QUESTIONS WERE:

1. Considering what you looked forward to, would you say that you made good progress, or that you are not quite satisfied with your progress?

2. Would you say that you've had bad breaks, or have you had good breaks on the whole?

3. How do you people feel about your present income; do you think it is about what you ought to be getting or not?

4. The things we have—housing, car, furniture, recreation, and the like—make up our standard of living. Some people are satisfied with their standard of living, others feel that it is not as good as they would like. How is it with you people?

SOURCE: Periodic Surveys of the Survey Research Center.

some people who worried about several things. Nevertheless, altogether only 20 per cent marked inflation and high prices; about 15 per cent, unemployment; and 10 per cent, depression or recession in the near future. These proportions indicate how little worrying about economic problems may prevail at certain times; many more people became worried in 1956 and 1957.

Optimism about personal financial progress and about business conditions is associated with a favorable picture of the economy. Unfavorable news does not become salient or is suppressed. We may recall the discussion of social learning and the current of opinion in Chapter 5. To mention one more finding on the subject: toward the end of 1955 less than one out of every five upper-income people answered Yes when asked, Did you hear or read any unfavorable [economic] news recently? In spite of this suggestive questioning only relatively few people could think of such things as inflation, low farm incomes, or high consumer debt, which were quite frequently discussed in the press at that time.

One final aspect of optimistic attitudes must be mentioned even though statistical data are not available to support the argument. The psychology of prosperity included not only the expectation of advancement for oneself, but also for one's children. In the postwar decade the American people, greatly concerned with their children's prospects, looked forward to better opportunities for them and were willing to contribute to this goal by keeping the children in school over more years than before, by voting higher taxes for public schools, and by spending money directly on their children's education.

Accumulation of Durable Goods

Confidence in personal financial progress and trust that there will be no depression make for concern with the good things of life. In our society—we must acknowledge this even though some of us may deplore it—many good things are material rather than spiritual. Comfort is one aspect of the desired higher standard of living that encompasses many needs—a comfortable home and comfort in housekeeping and in transportation. Fun and enjoyment of life are other aspects of higher standards of living which likewise require the accumulation of a great variety of goods and are therefore expensive. Most of our cherished leisure-time activities cost a great deal of money.

Striving toward higher living standards represents, then, the prevalence of positive motives. Instead of being driven to avoid hardship and being satisfied with restoring an equilibrium, in an era of prosperity people are spurred by rising levels of aspiration. They are overwhelmingly satisfied, as testified to by their answers to direct questions (Figure 10), and nevertheless they are not saturated. Upwardly mobile people are not those who are dissatisfied with their income, as we have seen in Chapter 6, and people who are attracted by new features of durable goods are not the have-nots, as we found in Chapter 8. The process of upgrading and of accumulating more and more things may become cumulative and self-reinforcing.

When people were asked in repeated surveys what they would like to have or on what they would like to spend money, the number of things they mentioned was no greater shortly after World War II, that is, after years of deprivation when their cars and appliances were old or non-existent and their furnaces or roofs in bad condition, than in the fifties following years of accumulation. In 1946 and 1947 an automobile represented the most frequently desired item, but desire for an automobile was expressed just as frequently in later years when other desires as well became widespread. Similarly, most people after purchasing a house for their own occupancy did not settle down and rest content. Many people within a few years bought still better houses. The improvement of new homes, as well as of older ones, went on year after year. Fulfilling one project became an impetus for turning to another. Power tools, yachts, motorboats, and summer cottages are some of the many things about which few people dreamt immediately after the war, but which very many people purchased in the decade that followed. Desire for intangibles emerged at the same time. Especially the desire for expensive vacation trips increased greatly on the part of middle- and upper-middle-income families.

Prosperity is material and can therefore be measured quantitatively. Let us list a few relevant survey findings to indicate how general prosperity has been. In 1946, about 50 per cent of the then 38 million million nonfarm families lived in a house they owned; in 1958, 59 per cent of the then 49 million such families lived in their own homes. The number of homeowners had risen by approximately 10 million between 1946 and 1958. That in the top-income group—families with an annual income of more than $10,000—the proportion of homeowners was a high as 76 per cent in 1958 is much less important than this other finding: among families in which the head was 55 to 64 years old, 67 per cent were homeowners in 1958, irrespective of income. Though many homeowners had little equity, repayment of mortgages proceeded at a rapid pace: in 1958 about half the homeowners had no mortgage debt. In every single year in the fifties at least 60 per cent of homeowners reported to have spent money on the maintenance and improvements of their homes; in every year about 20 per cent of homeowners spent more than $500 on additions and repairs.[3]

For the purpose of studying purchases of durable goods we may arbitrarily define a major expenditure for durable goods as a net outlay (price less trade-in allowance) of $100 or more for automobiles, furniture, or

---

[3] It is frequently forgotten how important the home repair and improvement industry is. Total expenditures for these purposes were estimated at over $10 billion in 1957.

household appliances. In every year since 1950 approximately 50 per cent of all families made such expenditures.[4] If we omitted low-income families, the proportion would be higher still, but again the most important finding is that the proportion rises close to 66 per cent when we consider families in the age group of 25 to 34 without regard to income.

Automobiles are, of course, the most important of the durable goods expenditures. While the proportion of families buying a new car has varied substantially during the last few years (12½ per cent was the highest figure reached in 1955), the proportion buying used cars has been much more stable (close to 20 per cent was the highest figure, also in 1955). At this point, however, we are not so much concerned with fluctuations of demand from one year to another as with the extent to which that demand can be sustained over extended periods of prosperity. Let us illustrate with data collected over a span of slightly more than 2½ years (from July, 1954, to February, 1957). In this period 60 per cent of all urban families bought a car, either new or used. (Families that bought more than one car were still counted only once.) Among the remaining families some owned no car at any time during those years; only 22 per cent of those who owned a car in June, 1954, did not buy one during the following 2½ years. Replacement proceeded at a quick pace. If we consider those families who in June, 1954, owned a recent new car (1952, 1953, or 1954 models), we find that during the following 2½ years 64 per cent bought a car—most commonly a new one.

When we find that year after year one-half of all families have made a major expenditure on durable goods, it follows that many of them must have made one every year. In the three years 1954, 1955, and 1956 one out of every five urban families bought cars twice or more often. Large durable goods were purchased in one of the three years by 83 per cent of urban families, in two of the three years by 57 per cent, and in each of the three years by 21 per cent. Considering only families with children at home, where the head was under 45 years old, the figures are 94 per cent, 73 per cent, and 28 per cent, respectively. Let us repeat: these data refer to all families, including those with low incomes, who purchase much less frequently than those with high incomes. They are presented this way so as to indicate how general consumer investment is in prosperous years.[5]

[4] Strictly speaking, the figures quoted in this paragraph, taken from the Surveys of Consumer Finances, refer to spending units, not families. Close to 10 per cent of families consist of more than one spending unit, that is, contain related adults other than wife who have their own income and keep their finances separate. Since many durable goods, as for instance refrigerators, are bought only by primary and not by secondary spending units, the quoted statistics understate the proportion of families purchasing durable goods.

[5] For data on automobile purchases between 1954 and 1957, see Lininger, Mueller,

When in 1958 auto sales slumped, prophets of doom became vocal and contended that the time had passed when the automobile was the most important possession of Americans. It is most relevant to show, therefore, that the process of need satisfaction generating new needs applies to the automobile as well as to other commodities. In 1948 only about 2 per cent of American families owned two cars each. In 1958 about 15 per cent, altogether close to 8 million families, owned two or more cars each. The number of multiple car owners of course rises with income; it is also disproportionately high among families with more than one earner, among families living in suburbs and outlying areas of big cities, and in the middle-age group. Multiple car owners have become a major factor in automobile demand. In 1957 about 36 per cent of all new cars sold were bought by families who at the end of the year owned more than one car.

The rapid growth of two-car owners did not saturate demand. Owners of one car—about 60 per cent of all families, since 15 per cent had two cars, and close to 25 per cent had none—were asked the following question in repeated surveys: Have you given any thought to buying a second car? About 19 per cent answered in the affirmative late in 1956. This means that close to 6 million families had given thought to buying a second car.

Having given thought to a second car is not identical with demand for a second car. It expresses neither the willingness nor the ability to carry out one's thought. But the manner in which a fairly large proportion of American families discussed the problem of a second car made it clear that the car needs of the American people had not been satisfied, in spite of the high rate of automobile purchases in the preceding years. Naturally, it was not people who lived in central districts of very large cities who spoke of the "misery" of having just one car. Suburban living and absence of public transportation resulted in expressions of a strongly felt need for two cars in the family, especially when the husband used the family car for commuting to work. Young middle-income housewives deplored being stranded in their homes without a second car. So many of them expressed their need in such strong terms that saturation of the automobile market must be considered an unacceptable generalization.[6]

In 1958, besides automobiles, the American people needed and desired many more things than ten years earlier. But, with the exception of goals accomplished through do-it-yourself activities and power tools, the newly

---

and Wyss; for repeat buying of durables, see G. Katona, "Repetitiousness and Variability of Consumer Behavior."

[6] Many foreign cars were purchased as second cars in 1957 and 1958; American-made economy cars may likewise serve to satisfy desires for such cars.

aroused needs were not substitutes for cars. Living in a suburb, enjoying a motorboat or sailboat, fishing and hunting, having a summer place, or going on an extensive vacation trip—all of these generally require a car. Large families, to which many more young fathers and mothers aspired in the fifties than ten or twenty years earlier, likewise do not represent goals which take the place of the material things of life but make it more necessary than ever to have a nice home, equipped with a variety of appliances and laborsaving devices, and even a car or two.

Prosperity requires enduring confidence and optimism by masses of people, cumulative needs and desires, and striving for higher incomes. Installment buying has become the means by which the desired improvement in living standards has been accomplished without delay. Its wide use has already been discussed, as well as the fact that young married couples in particular learned to consider it as a necessary part of life. We may add here an often misunderstood finding: it was found year after year in the fifties that a larger proportion of people with installment debt had plans to buy durable goods than of those without debt. This is not a paradox; debt does not induce people to buy. But those people who incur debt are precisely those who need many durable goods. Especially young families with children buy on the installment plan and continue to make large expenditures year after year. Durable-goods purchases and installment buying are stimulated not only by the stage of the life cycle, but also by an upward trend of incomes and confidence in its continuation.

In Figure 11 a set of relationships is presented which was found to prevail in every one of the last ten years, irrespective of fluctuations in the extent of durable goods purchases or in optimism. The families were divided each year, without regard to absolute income level, into three groups: those whose incomes had gone up, those whose incomes had remained the same, and those whose incomes had gone down as compared with the preceding year. Major expenditures on durable goods were found to be the largest in the first group. They were somewhat smaller in the second group, among people with stable incomes, than in the third group, people with declining incomes. Income stability represents an absence of dynamic conditions and therefore an absence of stimuli. Income gains represent the strongest dynamic condition as well as increased ability to buy. The relationships presented in the chart prevailed in every income group except the highest. Families with substantial ability to buy are not greatly influenced by income changes.

A similar analysis was made of the extent of installment buying in relation to past and expected changes in income. The families were divided according to income changes (or absence of changes) that had taken place in comparison to the preceding year (up, same, or down); changes

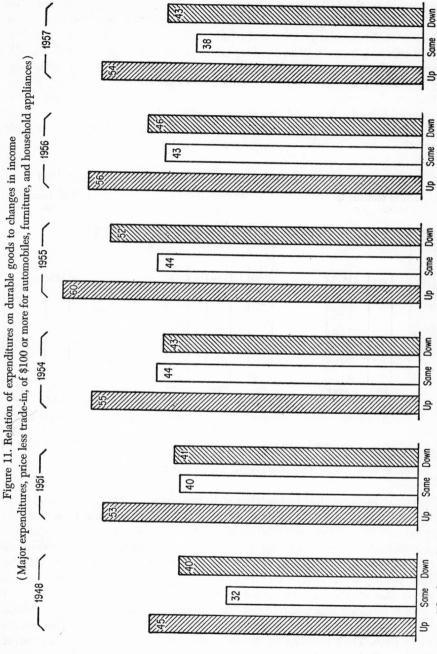

Figure 11. Relation of expenditures on durable goods to changes in income

(Major expenditures, price less trade-in, of $100 or more for automobiles, furniture, and household appliances)

NOTE: The figure shows the percentage of spending units making major expenditures, first, among spending units whose income has increased against the preceding year (up); second, among spending units with unchanged income (same); and finally, among spending units with decreased income (down). SOURCE: Surveys of Consumer Finances, *Federal Reserve Bulletin*, July, 1958, p. 769.

expected in the following year (up, same, or down); and a combination of the two (both up, both the same, both down). The results, illustrated in Figure 12 for one year typical of all the years in which this relationship was studied, indicate that the largest proportion of families with installment debt occurred among (1) those whose incomes had gone up, (2) those whose incomes were expected to go up, and (3) those whose incomes had gone up *and* were expected to go up. Similar relationships were obtained when middle-income families alone were considered and also when, in place of families with any installment debt, only those with relatively large installment debt were taken into account.

Figure 12. Relation of installment debt to past and income changes, 1956

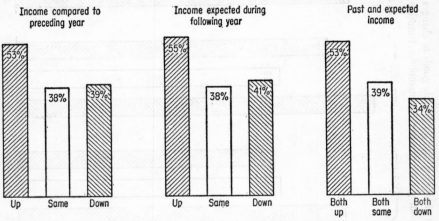

NOTE: The length of each column indicates the proportion of spending units in the respective group (families with income change—up, same, down—compared to the preceding year, expected changes in the following year, and a combination of the two) who had installment debt early in 1956.

SOURCE: G. Katona, "Attitudes toward Saving and Borrowing," Table 21.

The data presented in the charts do not presume to indicate that past or expected income increases are the causes of purchases of durable goods or of buying on installment. Both types of income changes are particularly frequent among young married couples. The problem of discriminating among the different variables and discerning what the true causes are is rather complicated. Our purpose is simply to demonstrate that apparently different aspects of prosperity go together: upward income mobility is associated with improvement in living standards, which in turn is often achieved through durable-goods purchases on the installment plan. Then purchasing durables on installment represents a prompt response to income increases and to expected increases as well.

Dangerous Dynamism?

Is the picture presented here one of overconsumption with inevitable dire consequences? During the past ten years installment buying has been repeatedly blamed for inducing people to consume excessively and thereby to mortgage their own futures and lead the economy to collapse. Alternatively, continuous large consumption has been seen as a manifestation of inflation and a cause of inflation. It must be admitted that the rate of durable-goods purchases could conceivably become excessive. Dynamic elements in the economy can become dangerous. But the psychology of prosperity which we have tried to describe in this chapter differs from the psychology of inflation and need not contain those tendencies which make a slump inevitable.

Overbuying is a concept which cannot be defined meaningfully. When industry builds new factories, industrial capacity increases. If, then, demand declines, there is overcapacity, but not if demand increases. By the same token we have seen that consumers, in the very process of fulfilling their needs and desires may stimulate still further needs and desires and may not reach the point of an "oversupply." Consumers, of course, because of trade-in practices and lack of space in their homes, usually discard their old consumer goods when they purchase new ones rather than maintain them as "reserve capacity." Our research has confirmed that neither a high level of consumer debt nor increased rate of durable-goods purchases in itself brings forth an adverse reaction. If such a reaction comes it is because of other developments as, for instance, a pessimistic turn in attitudes and expectations. As we have said before, saturation is an attitude. Under the influence of certain attitudes, needs and desires decline in frequency and intensity. Under the influence of failure and frustration, they may even appear exhausted. In a psychological climate of prosperity, however, neither heavy buying nor heavy debt should be expected to lead to economic collapse.

It is also possible for large consumption to persist throughout long periods of prosperity without stimulating inflation because of one common feature of strivings and desires which we have mentioned before but must now emphasize: Levels of aspiration are usually only *slightly* above levels of accomplishment (see point 4, page 130, Chapter 8). The tendency for desires and felt needs to exceed considerably what one has is a characteristic of inflationary psychology as we shall describe it in the next chapter. In the absence of inflationary attitudes, however, desires and strivings are usually reality-tested. When one new need becomes salient after another one has been gratified, when one small advance in income and living standard creates the desire for another step ahead, the process is commonly characterized by calculation and self-regulation.

This is what happened after 1955, the year of the automobile boom, in which the installment debt of the American people rose by the unprecedented amount of $5 billion. Many experts demanded then that the government clamp down and introduce controls over installment buying so as to make it impossible for people to continue "excessive" buying. Nothing was done and yet the proportion of income earmarked for repaying installment debt rose no further. (Total installment debt rose somewhat in 1956 as well as in 1957, but not out of proportion to income increases.) Of course, there were some people who overextended themselves. Most people, however, calculated carefully the size of time payments they could afford. The desire to save was not impaired by installment buying. The blame for the price increases in 1956 and 1957 can hardly be attributed to installment buying.

Additional findings cast further doubt on the notion that depressing effects resulted from the large increase in installment debt in 1955. In the fall of 1955 and again in the summer of 1956 people with installment debt were asked whether they found it a hardship to repay their debt. A fair proportion, close to 30 per cent, of debtors replied in the affirmative.[7] Yet further analysis revealed that this opinion was not related to the proportion of income needed for the payments. It was related to level of income. Low-income people usually said debt caused hardship, irrespective of its size. Among families with an income of over $5,000— which, of course, is not a high income—only 13 per cent complained of any hardship.

As shown before, installment buying is associated with the expectation of income increases. Often what we expect to make in the future rather than what we make today is used as the basis for calculating what size monthly payments we can afford to make. If there had been no income increases in the two years following 1955, the installment debt might have proved to be "too high." If incomes had gone down, no doubt the debt would have caused trouble. But the debt in itself was not the factor making for a recession. Installment debt is likely to become an important problem only after incomes fall; it is a reinforcing influence rather than an initiating cause of instability.[8]

Self-regulation regarding installment debt is one of the restraining features which may prevail during prosperity. Of more general significance is the finding reported in analyzing the developments of 1957 that optimistic attitudes constantly require new stimulation. We may recognize

[7] The wording of the question was as follows: Some people find it quite a hardship to make the required payments on their debt, others are not much bothered by their payments; how is it with you? The question was asked after purpose and size of installment debt were determined.

[8] See G. Katona, "Attitudes toward Saving and Borrowing," p. 471.

here an aspect of the process of *habituation*. People may become accustomed to news about increases in GNP, in production, and in retail sales. They may come to expect such news, and news about lesser gains than before (deceleration of upswing) or about stability at record levels may be disappointing. Since the higher a given level, the larger an absolute increase is needed to produce equal percentage gains, one might almost speak of automatic features which counteract a runaway boom. In addition, there seems to be a disposition to pay great attention even to slightly unfavorable news when things are very good and have been good for a long time.

A final consideration must be mentioned in contradiction of the notion that the dynamic features which characterize the psychology of prosperity necessarily lead to excesses. Is people's underlying trust that incomes will go up as time goes by unjustified and unrealistic? We do not consider here price increases due to which stable income means reduced purchasing power, even though we should recognize that some price advances are a normal and common feature of prosperous years. Thinking in terms of what economists call real income, we must consider the increase in productivity of our industrial plant. There are great difficulties involved in calculating this increase, but most experts agree that productivity has improved during the last decade by 2 or 2½ per cent a year (on the average). Most people who feel that an improvement in their standard of living is a necessity and that unchanged levels of living mean deterioration, do not think of rising productivity and of their desire to participate in it. But in view of growing productivity, may one say that the people are wrong in expecting their living standards to improve? Finally, it is doubtless not a one-way street from increased productivity to higher incomes. Rising expenses and higher aspirations often result in an inclination to work harder with the result that productivity improves.

Certain basic differences between the American and the European societies have frequently been expressed by saying that in the United States, in contrast to Europe, there exists a culturally induced discontent with low status. No doubt, for many decades the American people have been unwilling to accept permanent class differences and have been strongly impelled to emerge from low economic status. What has been described here as the psychological basis of prosperity is perhaps an extension of these strivings. What we have is not good enough, even if it is not poverty but rather middle-class comfort or perhaps, compared to what we had before, even affluence. Only to move up and to acquire more and better things and higher status satisfy us. The postwar decade has demonstrated that such sentiments represent the heart of the psychological climate in which prosperity flourishes.

CHAPTER 12

The Psychology of Inflation

The study of inflation represented one of the starting points of economic psychology. It was in this area that the decisive influence of expectations and the inadequacy of economics without psychology could first be demonstrated. History, from ancient times to the present, has provided many instances when the supply of money has grown faster than the flow of goods and prices has risen. Economic theory accordingly taught that if incomes grow faster than the quantity of goods produced, purchasing power exceeds supplies and prices are likely to rise. Some psychologists, on the other hand, held that if people are convinced that prices will rise substantially, their readiness to spend increases and prices are likely to rise. Neither the older teachings of history and economics, which disregard expectations, nor those of social psychology, which make expectations all-powerful, tell the whole story; only by considering them together can the process of inflation be fully understood. Additional purchasing power need not inevitably compete for goods; a gap between incomes and supplies represents a potential for inflation which requires certain predispositions to be activated and may be nullified by other predispositions. Nor is it necessarily correct that what enough people expect, will happen, whether it was going to happen or not. Unjustified rumors may generate inflationary expectations, but the expectations will hardly ever endure and bring about sustained price increases over long periods of time unless the rumors are warranted. Inflation—a general, sustained, and rapid increase in the price level—is neither a purely financial nor a purely psychological phenomenon. It is the joint result of a gap between incomes and the supply of goods *and* of inflationary expectations.

Inflation has thus far been described in its traditional meaning. Today, however, this traditional inflation is commonly designated as "galloping" or "runaway," to distinguish it from a slow, long-run trend of gradual price increases—sometimes as little as 1 or 2 per cent a year—which has come to be known as "creeping" inflation. The psychology of traditional inflation has previously been discussed at great length.[1] The psychology

[1] See the following publications by the author: *War without Inflation; Price Control and Business;* Chapter 10 of *Psychological Analysis of Economic Behavior* and, in popular form, *The People versus Inflation* by G. Katona and A. Lauterbach.

of creeping inflation has been studied more recently and will be described here. There are significant differences in the psychological climate of the two types of inflation. Only after studying the psychology of creeping inflation will we be in a position to judge whether there is any danger that it may develop into runaway inflation.

Reactions to Changes in Prices

For an understanding of any kind of inflation it is important, indeed essential, to study the reactions of the people to what we may call the inflationary stimuli. Such financial developments, for example, as debasement of coin, excessive use of the printing press to manufacture money, government deficits, credit expansion, as well as past price increases, represent inflationary stimuli. Yet none of them in themselves, irrespective of whether they occur at a great and rapid or a small and slow rate, automatically result in higher prices. Galloping and creeping inflation alike are "man-made" in the sense that they both depend on how consumers and businessmen react to financial developments and to past or expected price changes. This basic fact has rarely been denied. What has been denied has been the necessity to study those reactions. The assumption has been that they could be predicted without investigation. It has been thought that the concept of rational man or economic man implied what these reactions must be and that common sense sufficed to confirm the theoretical deductions.

Let us recall traditional teachings and see how far they lead us. It follows from the so-called law of supply and demand that, other things being equal, if prices go down the quantity demanded will increase and if prices go up the quantity demanded will decline. This is usually demonstrated for the entire economy and the general price level as follows: If the money available to buyers does not change and is fully spent in one period, and if prices then go up, a smaller quantity only can be bought in the period of higher prices. This reasoning is, of course, correct under the assumptions made. But will the reaction of buyers to price increases be the same, and will it be predictable, if incomes were not fully spent prior to the price increases?

What is the traditional teaching with respect to expected, rather than past, price changes? How will people react if they expect prices to go up or to go down? The usual assumption is that if people confidently expect prices to go up, the quantity demanded will increase. This will be so because it is prudent to buy before the price increase takes place and some people, at least, will be in a position to do so. Contrariwise, if people confidently expect prices to go down, the quantity demanded will decline.

In this case, people will wait with some postponable purchases until the prices have declined.

Past price increases and expected price increases jointly characterize inflationary processes. As we shall show later, either may occur without the other. But, most commonly, the two occur together, and inflation consists of price increases which are expected to continue. But, as we have just seen, according to traditional teachings past price increases make for smaller and expected price increases for larger demand. We are not told how the economic man would react if prices have gone up and also are expected to go up.

Experience with runaway inflations in many countries and in many times has clearly shown, of course, what happens when prices advance sharply and there are ample reasons to expect them to continue to do so. Then inflationary fever makes for scare buying and hoarding, which drive prices up still higher. But how do people react to small price increases and small expected price increases? This crucial question of creeping inflation cannot be answered by historical studies or deductive logic. The answer may not be the same under different conditions and can only be determined empirically.

We shall present, first, some of the generalizations justified by extensive studies carried out by the Survey Research Center and postpone the presentation of quantitative data supporting the generalizations. But let it be clearly understood that the findings and generalizations pertain to the behavior of the American consumer in recent years; we are not presenting generalizations about human nature.

1. *Threshold.* In economic behavior, as in other kinds of behavior, there is a threshold, that is, a point at which an effect begins to be produced. In terms of inflation, then, it is not justified to assume that any and all changes in prices influence consumer behavior. In the first place, consumers are often not aware of price changes which are a matter of record. Even public announcements of increases in automobile prices or in the cost-of-living index may go unnoticed by the majority of consumers. The reverse is also true. At some times many, or even most, consumers may be convinced that certain or all prices have increased even though according to the record they have not.

It follows that studies of inflation must begin with a determination of whether there is an awareness or *perception* of price changes. But even generally perceived price changes may be viewed as insignificant. The prevailing *attitude* toward them may be one of no concern. Then we should not expect any reaction to the changes. Similarly, it may happen that many people expect prices to go up or down but feel no concern about it and so do not react.

We may not assume that the threshold is constant. It will vary with experience. Following inflationary experiences, people may become more sensitive and their threshold may be lower. The threshold will also vary with respect to individual articles. Both the absolute difference in dollars and cents and the percentage change may matter. Advertising may affect the threshold inasmuch as people may become sensitive to widely advertised price reductions. We should know much more about this important aspect of consumer behavior than we do, but studies of the threshold have thus far been rather inadequate.

2. *Resentment of price increases.* A housewife who does a lot of window shopping feels cheated when she finds that a dress or a piece of furniture in which she is interested is priced higher than it was a month or two earlier. Her disappointment or even anger represents the root of an unfavorable emotional reaction to price increases. General price increases make people feel worse off; the money they have does not go as far as it once did. The adverse emotional reaction, often expressed in the words "Prices are too high," will be particularly pronounced if the price increases are seen as unjustified. Rising prices are more generally accepted in times of war than in times of peace. Unjustified price increases are resented, and this adverse emotion reduces the willingness to buy.

Price increases are generally seen from the consumer point of view. When the question is asked whether or not rising prices are good for the economy, most people, including businessmen and their wives, say that they are a bad thing. That production and profits usually increase in times of rising prices is not in the forefront of their thinking.

What is true of past price increases applies to expected price increases as well. They, too, are considered to be bad for the economy. People argue: Prices are going up; we shall have to pay more for meat and necessities; we shall have less to spend on other things. This reaction again holds even for people who benefit from the price increases, that is, those whose incomes advance more than the prices.

We must remember that we are considering here small price increases. When it is expected that prices will go up by a few dollars or a few per cent, the thought of buying before prices go up is less powerful than the adverse emotional reaction. This is particularly true because price expectations are not held with certitude. The opinion "Prices will probably be higher next year than today" expresses anxiety about something which threatens to happen rather than the possession of reliable information on the basis of which one can act with confidence.

The adverse reactions to small price increases are part of a broader framework. During the last two decades masses of people in America have held the conviction that inflation was bad. This conviction was not shaken by the fact that the years of inflation were good years. In the

opinion of most people, those years were good for reasons other than inflation and despite inflation.

3. *Bargains.* The window-shopping housewife is elated when she finds
a dress or a piece of furniture priced lower than what she almost paid
for the same article a month or two earlier. The feeling of getting more
for one's money or of being offered a bargain evokes pleasurable reactions. Lower prices are seen as good for the economy. One major reason
for this view, as expressed in interviews, is that when prices are reduced
people can buy more. Expected price declines bring forth the same reaction. People think they will be better off because prices will go down,
and their willingness to buy increases.

An exception to the favorable reaction to price reductions cited in the
literature is not of major interest to us, namely, that lower prices may be
viewed as implying reduced quality. It is often true that the cheaper one
of two similar articles offered at different prices is seen as being worth
less. But in the case of price reductions for the identical article, considerations of loss in quality do not arise.

There is, however, another situation in which reduced prices do not
evoke a favorable response: if a price reduction is seen to be the first
phase of an ongoing movement, to be followed by further price reductions, it does not stimulate demand. This is known best from studies of
business behavior. Price cuts of copper, tin, and the like have often resulted in everybody waiting for further price cuts rather than in purchases. It is also known from studies of the deflationary spiral in times of
depression, when price reductions are viewed as a response to bad times
which will result in a further worsening of economic conditions. But in
good times price reductions will not generally evoke the expectation of
further price cuts. Bargains are characterized as temporary price reductions. Consumer elation takes the form of perceiving a unique opportunity to buy. The notion that things cost less than before and may cost
more again stimulates buying. The favorable affect is augmented if the
buyer feels that he alone, or only a few people, are given the unique
opportunity to buy. Special discounts, increased prices for articles traded
in, and the like, in place of reductions in list prices, make use of such
notions.

Suppose price reductions take place during what people consider an
inflationary period, that is, following some years of price increases and at
a time when many people think that in several years prices will again be
higher. Then, with no anticipation of a downward spiral of prices, consumers greet price reductions as a welcome interruption of inflation.

4. *Reliance on stable prices.* If the housewife thinks that the price of
a certain article today is what it has been for a long time, she feels that
the price is right. People become accustomed to prices which have per-

sisted for quite a while and gain confidence when they expect prices to remain stable. Absence of anxiety about overpaying creates a climate favorable to purchasing. Generally, the experience that prices have been stable coupled with the expectation that they will remain stable stimulates buying.

"Right" prices or "normal" prices, as well as prices which are "too high," have psychological meaning even though from an economic point of view they are undefinable concepts. If, after prices have gone up and have been felt to be too high, the price advance does not continue, people may become accustomed to the new price level. This process of habituation is slow and gradual. Following inflationary experiences it takes time until reliance on prices is restored and people again come to consider them to be right and just.

Recent Fluctuations in Price Expectations

Let us look now at the quantitative data from which these generalizations about people's views of price changes and their reactions to them were drawn. Some of the relevant data have, of course, already been cited in Chapter 3.

The American people are well aware of the fact that they have had inflation. Practically without exception they all said in interviews conducted in the fifties that prices were much higher than ten or twenty years earlier. In describing inflation people focused their attention on the rise of food prices and at certain times particularly on the price of meat. When asked about the reasons for the price increases they most frequently mentioned two factors, rising labor costs and the high demand for goods. This was the case both soon after World War II and in 1955–1957. Except during the early phases of the Korean War relatively few people thought that either government, or trade unions, or business had caused prices to go up. In a survey conducted in 1955 most respondents specifically denied that profiteering had been a cause of price increases; they thought that business was interested in stable prices or even in lowering prices, rather than in raising them.

As to when during the past decade the price increases had taken place, in retrospect most people did not know the correct answer and could not differentiate between periods of inflation and periods of price stability. Yet when at different times during the past ten years they were asked about changes in the prices of food, clothing, household goods, etc., during the preceding year, the answers were substantially correct.[2] For

[2] The question was worded as follows: We'd like to know what's happened to prices of food [or household items] here in [city] during the past year. Have they stayed about the same, gone up, or gone down?

instance, in 1951 most people said that prices had gone up. In December, 1952, they reported that prices had been stable. In 1956 and 1957 the answer, "Prices have gone up," was again much more frequent.

People's price expectations fluctuated still more than their notions about past price changes. Variations in the frequency of expecting price increases are shown in Figure 13. The figure shows the proportion of people who expected price increases at various times. In addition, there were always a few people who expected prices to fall, some more who said they didn't know, and many more who expected prices to remain

Figure 13. Trend of short-run and long-run price expectations, 1951–1958

(Percentage of families expecting prices to go up during the next year and during the next five years)

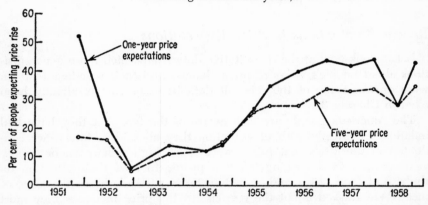

THE QUESTIONS WERE: What do you expect prices of household items and clothing will do during the next year or so—stay where they are, go up, or go down? Looking further ahead—do you expect that, say five years from now, prices of the things you buy will be higher than they are at present, lower, or just about the same?

SOURCE: Survey Research Center, Periodic Surveys.

unchanged during the succeeding twelve months. The question about longer-range price expectations ("say, five years"), likewise shown in the figure, brought forth many more "it depends" answers and answers that prices would be lower than the question about short-range expectations. The changing frequencies of expecting price increases give a good indication of the sharp fluctuations in inflationary sentiment. From mid-1952 to mid-1955 most people were not concerned with inflation. The same was true in 1948–1949, as previously reported but not shown in the figure.

The difference between one-year and five-year price expectations is worth studying (Figure 13). At all inflationary periods there were many people who expected prices to rise in the near future but to be unchanged or even lower in five years. "What goes up must come down" was the usual explanation for this divergence of opinion. In November, 1951, for example, 52 per cent of the respondents expected that prices would be higher within the next twelve months; only 17 per cent that they would be higher five years later. In December, 1956, the respective percentages were 44 and 34; and in October, 1958, 43 and 35. The greatest divergence in the number of people holding both opinions occurred in 1951. The proportion of people expecting longer-range price increases reached its highest levels in 1956, 1957, and 1958. Yet even in those years only about one-third of all respondents believed that we were living in a period of continuing and enduring price advances. The idea that price increases are a chronic feature of our economy has gained adherents but has not become general. The theory which postulates that union power, high government debt, and spending inclinations of Congress are enduring features of our society and make for an inflationary age has thus far not entered into the thinking of the majority of the American people—not even of those in the upper-income brackets.

There were times when most people expected prices to do in the near future what they had done in the recent past. For instance, in 1951 and toward the end of 1956 most of those who said that prices had gone up also expected them to go up still further. But the expectation of rising prices also prevailed following price stability—for instance, in 1955— and there were times when most people who said that prices had gone up expected no further increases (early in 1952, for instance, as well as in June, 1954). It appears that expectations of inflation sometimes originate in perceived price trends but at other times have a different origin. Price expectations cannot be inferred from perceptions of past price movements (nor can they be inferred from actual price movements).

That most consumers, excepting farmers, consider higher prices for food—whether past or expected—to be undesirable is easy to understand. Similarly, it is not surprising that past advances in other prices—say, clothing or household goods—arouse consumer dissatisfaction. But how about the reactions to expected increases in these prices? People who said that they expected prices of household goods and clothing to go up during the succeeding twelve months were asked in repeated surveys, Would you say that these rising prices would be to the good, to the bad, or what? A similar question was asked of people who expected prices to remain unchanged or to decline. Substantially the same answers were obtained to these questions at different times. The average answers from four surveys conducted in 1956 and 1957 are shown in Figure 14.

Intentionally, the question was not formulated precisely. People were not given a frame of reference; neither their own financial situation— would rising prices be good or bad for themselves—nor the situation of the entire economy was specified. Nevertheless, the question appeared to be meaningful to practically everybody. Answers to the follow-up question—Why do you think so?—indicated that the question concerned something which for most people was not at all controversial. Experts disagree about who is hurt by creeping inflation and some even argue that such inflation is good for the economy. But relatively few consumers agreed with this opinion. The great majority felt that inflation was bad. "When prices go up it is harder to make ends meet"—this was how the consumer point of view was overwhelmingly expressed. Not only wage earners but the self-employed as well argued in this manner. Many of

Figure 14. Reactions to expected changes in prices of household goods and clothing

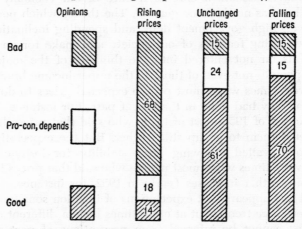

THE QUESTION WAS: Would you say that rising (unchanged, falling) prices would be to the good, or to the bad, or what?

NOTE: Average data from four surveys conducted in 1956 and 1957.

SOURCE: E. Mueller, "Consumer Reactions to Inflation."

those who expected prices to decline used a comparable line of reasoning: a reduction in prices would be to the good because then consumers could purchase more and thereby improve business conditions. Only a small minority thought of any adverse effects declining prices might have on production and business. Finally, we may note that most people in the relatively small group who said that unchanged prices would be to the bad argued that prices were too high and therefore it would be an unfavorable development if they were to remain unchanged.

Let us emphasize: when asked about rising or falling prices the respondents had small price increases in mind. They were specifically asked about the extent of expected price changes and replied that they would go up or down a little.

In explaining why price increases were undesirable a fair number of people maintained that when prices rise wages tend to lag behind. Data collected about income increases in years of rising prices do not seem to bear out this opinion. In 1957 a new question was therefore included in a survey. We asked, Some people can be fairly sure that their income goes up when the cost of living rises; is this the case with the income in your family? Surprisingly, only 12 per cent said Yes; 14 per cent, including many self-employed, did not give a clear-cut answer; and 74 per cent said No. Many people answered in the negative even though they had had substantial income increases during the preceding year. In their opinion, the improvement in their incomes had been due to reasons other than inflation. Attributing higher wages, salaries, or profits to the good work one performs and even to lucky circumstances ("good breaks") appears more frequent than considering them to be a compensation for higher prices or a consequence of inflation.

An analysis of replies to the questions Are you people making as much money now as you were a year ago, or more, or less? and Are you people better off or worse off financially than a year ago? confirmed that people do not generally feel that higher incomes compensate for higher prices. In 1951, an inflationary period, for instance, only one-half of those who reported that they were making more than a year before said that they were better off and one-third with unchanged income complained about being worse off. In 1955, on the other hand, following a year of relatively stable prices there was a close correspondence between the number of people reporting income increases and the number feeling better off. In 1957, after another period of rising prices, the gap between the two answers was again larger.

Survey research reveals that opinions about price changes are occasionally strongly related to opinions about business conditions. In 1949 and 1954, for instance, the expectation of good business conditions was associated with falling or stable prices and in 1951 and 1957 the expectation of less favorable business conditions, with rising prices. At certain other times (1952 and 1955, for example), this relationship was much less pronounced, indicating that sensitivity to price changes may sometimes remain below the threshold.

In studying the relation of attitudes toward prices to purchases, let us look first at the influence of past price changes on the purchases of new automobiles. Automobile prices are not easy to determine because the "price" of a new car depends on trade-in allowances and discounts. Nevertheless, many people have definite opinions about car prices. When people were asked, for instance in the spring of 1956, whether "it costs more or less to buy a new car now than a year ago—considering new car prices, trade-in allowances, and discounts," 36 per cent said "more" and

15 per cent "less." (The others said "same" or "can't say.") In the fall of 1957, 45 per cent said "more" and 7 per cent "less." The latter distribution of opinions was followed by a period of much lower car sales than the first distribution.

Turning to the influence of anticipated automobile prices, Figure 15 shows the fluctuations in expectations and in the evaluation of market conditions for automobiles. The winter of 1954–1955 saw a boom in automobile sales. At that time, many more people said that times would be good to buy cars than that they would be bad, and many more said that

Figure 15. Attitudes toward automobile prices, 1954–1958

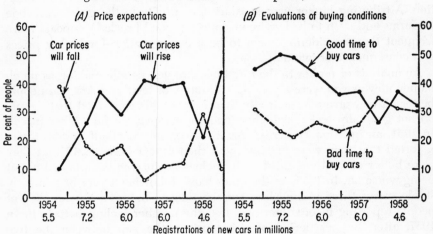

THE QUESTIONS WERE: Now about auto prices, what do you expect they will do in the next twelve months or so? Thinking now of the automobile market—do you think the next twelve months or so will be a good time or a bad time to buy a car?

SOURCE: Survey Research Center, Periodic Surveys.

car prices would fall than that they would rise. The first half of 1958, on the other hand, was the period of the lowest automobile sales in the fifties. In December, 1957, the opinion "bad time to buy cars" exceeded the opinion "good time," and the expectation of price increases greatly exceeded the expectation of price declines. The chart also contains data about these attitudes in 1958, which will be discussed in the next chapter.

Changes in expected car prices do not, however, always contribute to an explanation of fluctuations in automobile sales. Nineteen fifty-seven, for instance, was a fairly good automobile year, even though at the beginning of that year many more people expected prices to go up than to go down. At the same time, the majority of consumers thought that it would be a good time to buy cars. The explanations given for this appraisal of market conditions revealed that most people were at that time concerned with considerations other than prices (income increases, prosperous times, etc.). Price expectations, even though they could be elicited through direct questions, were not salient.[3]

A last piece of evidence about the relation of attitudes toward prices to purchases of durable goods may be found in the rate of purchases of groups of people who prior to purchasing had different attitudes. This comparison can be made when successive interviews are available with the same people. Most relevant are the data of the purchases by the following two groups of people: those who expected prices to rise and said that this was "to the bad" and those who expected prices to fall and said that this was "to the good." Having made the measurement of price expectations in June, 1954, Eva Mueller found that during the following twelve months the rate of durable-goods purchases (automobiles and household appliances) was 0.87 for the first and 1.09 for the second group. (The figures represent ratios of number of purchases of durables to those estimated according to the incomes of members of the two groups; this is the same method of calculation which was used in Chapter 6, page 84.) The purchase rate of the first group was below average, that of the second above average. People who expected no change in prices had a purchase rate of 0.95. Although similar data are not available for periods in which the expectation of price increases was very frequent, the data suggest that the expectation of *small* price increases tends to restrict demand for consumer durable goods.[4]

Scare buying and hoarding are reactions which are released by the confident expectation of *substantial* price increases and shortages. Shortly after the outbreak of the Korean War, under the influence of news about military defeat, people did react in this way, but not in earlier or later years when most people thought that small increases were probable.

The data about attitudes toward price changes have been presented as they relate to the entire population. How about the attitudes of different economic groups and especially possible differences between low- or middle- and high-income families? Those with high incomes might be thought to be better informed about, and therefore more concerned than others with, past and threatening inflation. This assumption is not borne out by the facts. Although high-income people are better informed about economic developments than low-income people and their knowledge does influence their attitudes toward prospective business trends, it does

[3] L. R. Klein and J. B. Lansing, "Decisions to Purchase Consumer Durable Goods," also showed that the influence of price expectations on spending behavior may vary from time to time. Price expectations must be considered in relation to recent price movements, income expectations, and the general economic setting.

[4] E. Mueller, "Consumer Reactions to Inflation."

not seem to bear upon their attitudes toward prices. Most of the time those with high incomes expressed substantially the same opinions about past as well as expected price trends as those with middle and low incomes.[5] The opinions of the various groups were similar also regarding the favorable or unfavorable impact of rising or falling prices. Therefore, in presenting data on price expectations and their influence on expenditures for durable goods, we were justified in not differentiating between economic classes. Such a differentiation must be made, however, in considering the influence of attitudes toward inflation on saving and investment.

Investment Preferences

During the runaway inflations in Germany, France, China, and many other countries, people converted their bank deposits into common stock, real estate, gold, and foreign exchange. Intent on safeguarding their funds against inflation, by their very action they accelerated the rate of depreciation of money. In the United States, neither in 1950 nor at any time during World War II did investors and savers turn away from investments with a fixed value. Several years of creeping inflation and of widely prevalent opinions that prices would increase still further failed to shake people's trust in the dollar. Only on the part of some high-income people did preferences shift in the direction of investments with a variable money value, while the great majority of savers maintained their confidence in bank deposits and government bonds.

We shall analyze expressions of investment preference rather than investments actually made. The available data on changes of personal investment are inadequate. How much money consumers—as distinguished from business owners and trust funds—put into common stock or real estate each year is not reliably known. But it is possible to state that the bulk of consumer savings was put into banks and savings and loan associations even in such years as 1951 or 1957 when most people expected prices to go up. It is also known that the proportion of families owning common stock increased at most by a few percentage points during the postwar decade and that in all income groups, except among families earning more than $15,000 a year, only a minority owned stock.

The following question was asked in several nationwide surveys conducted between 1948 and 1958: Suppose a man has some money over and above what he needs for his expenses; what do you think would be

[5] But toward the end of 1958 and early in 1959 people in the upper-income brackets were more concerned with inflation than people in the middle and lower brackets. In 1959 the majority of upper-income people thought that the prices of things they buy would advance somewhat over the next five years.

the wisest thing for him to do with it—put it in a savings account, buy
government savings bonds with it, invest it in real estate, or buy common
stock? The question was followed by detailed queries about the advantages and disadvantages of each of the four forms of investment.

Among the people queried—the question was asked only of people
with an income of at least $3,000—60 to 73 per cent answered that the
wisest thing would be to put savings into fixed-value investments (banks,
government bonds, or both). The highest proportion, 73 per cent, was
obtained in 1948 and again in 1954—years of a relatively low rate of
inflationary expectations—and lower proportions in 1951 (65 per cent) and

TABLE 16. POSTWAR FLUCTUATIONS OF INVESTMENT PREFERENCES

Kind of investment	Preferences among people with							
	Income over $3,000				Income over $7,500			
	June, 1951	June, 1954	June, 1957	June, 1958	June, 1951	June, 1954	June, 1957	June, 1958
Fixed value	65%	73%	60%	63%	46%	55%	44%	50%
Variable value	18	16	29	26	33	25	42	34
Other combination..........	17	11	11	11	21	20	14	16
Total	100%	100%	100%	100%	100%	100%	100%	100%

THE QUESTIONS WERE: Suppose a man has some money over and above what he
needs for his expenses. What do you think would be the wisest thing for him to do
with it—put it in a savings account, buy government savings bonds with it, invest it
in real estate, or buy common stock? Why do you make that choice?
SOURCE: Survey Research Center, Periodic Surveys.

in June, 1957 (60 per cent) when inflation was more commonly expected
(Table 16). Looking at families with incomes of $7,500 or more, we find
that 60 per cent opted for fixed-value investments in 1948 and 55 per cent
in 1954; the frequencies were under 50 per cent in 1951 and 1957. Thus
inflationary expectations had some influence on investment preferences,
but the influence was neither substantial nor enduring.

The proportion of those who thought that the wisest thing would be
to put the money in stock or real estate fluctuated between 13 and 29
per cent for people with over $3,000 income and between 19 and 42 per
cent for people with more than $7,500 income. The people classified in
Table 16 as giving preferences for other investments are mainly those who
specified that savings should be put in both banks and stock, or in all four
of the types of investment referred to in the question.

The finding that investment preferences do fluctuate somewhat according to inflationary expectations was strengthened by the additional finding that among people who said that prices would be higher in five years, there were more in favor of variable-value investments than among those who thought that prices would not be higher. Further studies revealed, however, that only a small part of the expressed preferences for common stock was due to inflationary expectations.

When people who expressed preferences for common stock were asked for their reasons, only relatively few mentioned inflation. Somewhat more spoke of the prospects of capital appreciation. This may in some cases have been related to inflation, while in others it was explained by such statements as "It is wise to invest in common stock; those who did have fared well recently." The largest proportion of those who expressed a preference for stocks gave the high returns on them as their reason.

When asked about the advantages of putting savings into banks or bonds, people referred to convenience and liquidity ("The money is always available") and first of all to safety. Such expressions as "Government savings bonds are safe" or "Money in banks is safe" were used spontaneously by the majority of the people at all times during the postwar decade. The closing of the banks in the early thirties was apparently forgotten. Yet the expression "safe" meant something else as well: when buying stocks or real estate one may lose money; the value of those investments can go down; this cannot happen to money in banks or bonds. Experts know that it was an innovation introduced during World War II to create war bonds with a constant redemption value, rather than permit their prices to fluctuate according to the supply and demand on the bond market. Today for most Americans this new feature is a "natural" property of bonds: savings bonds are a good investment because their price can never fall—in fact, it goes up steadily because of accrued interest. The thought that money might be lost on savings bonds or bank deposits did not enter very many people's minds during all these years. When asked who had done better, those who had bought savings bonds or those who had bought common stock ten years earlier, the answers fluctuated according to what people thought stocks had done in the recent past, and inflation was not generally taken into consideration.[6]

Attitudes toward savings bonds were studied further by asking representative samples the following questions: Do you see any reasons why people should buy bonds these days? and Do you see any reasons why

[6] We may also recall the finding reported in Chapter 7 that some people were not dissatisfied even though they knew that their bonds were worth less than ten years earlier; they thought that having saved something was better than having saved nothing.

people should *not* buy bonds these days? The first question was unhesitatingly answered in the affirmative by most people in 1944, as well as in 1951 and 1956. When asked for reasons for buying, the reply "To help the war effort" changed to "To help the government," and the latter gradually became less frequent than answers such as "To make a good investment." The second question, on the other hand, surprised most people. What do you have in mind? or How can there be reasons for not buying bonds? were frequent replies. The question was no doubt suggestive and, nevertheless, at no time could more than 15 per cent of a representative sample be induced to give any reasons against buying savings bonds. "The government doesn't need any money" or "The government is wasteful" are examples of the reasons most frequently mentioned; references to low interest rates followed next in frequency. Answers implying that money in savings bonds was not protected against inflation were never frequent, not even among upper-income people.

In June, 1951, when concern with inflation was quite pronounced, a rather suggestive question was asked in a nationwide survey. The question was, Do you see any connection between rising prices and whether or not people buy savings bonds? About 65 per cent replied that they saw none. Another 10 per cent pointed out that bond buying tended to counteract inflation. Most of the remaining 25 per cent said that inflation had an adverse effect on bond buying; their main argument was that people could not afford to buy bonds if living costs were high or were rising.

Similarly in answering a question about whether one should take price changes into account in deciding how much life insurance one should carry, only 4 per cent of a representative sample and 12 per cent of high-income people referred to inflation and its possible effects on the value of life insurance (in 1952). "Higher prices make it harder to keep up premium payments" was the most frequent reply on the part of people who said they did see a connection between inflation and life insurance!

It is not denied here that there are people—especially a growing number of high-income people in recent years—whose investments and investment preferences are governed by fear of inflation. Diversification of investments—putting some money in stock or real estate in addition to the funds in banks and bonds—has also been stimulated by inflation. Many American families have achieved some diversification: their main asset, supplemented by some money in savings bonds, savings and loan associations, or savings banks, is the house they own, rising in value in case of inflation partly because of the mortgage debt which then becomes less burdensome. Nevertheless a paradox remains: price increases have been among the most salient economic experiences of the American people for the past fifteen years, and yet these experiences and corresponding expectations have not been carried over to the saving and investment preferences of the great majority of them.

An analysis of how people talk about bank deposits, bonds, stocks, and inflation reveals that there are two explanations for the behavior of the masses with regard to saving and investing. One explanation applies to a minority only. These people would like to have an alternative to saving exclusively in bonds and banks but feel that other forms of saving are much more risky. Buying common stock, they say, is no way out because one may buy the wrong stock and lose money in spite of inflation. They are convinced that safety rather than defense against inflation should be the major consideration in selecting investments.

The second and most important explanation of saving and investing behavior as expressed by the great majority is the following: Inflation is not a sure thing; even if it should occur, it will be small. When directly asked about what prices will do, many people say that they will go up in the near as well as the distant future. This notion carries an unfavorable emotional undertone and influences buying inclinations but is usually not held with such conviction as to determine saving and investment policies. Depreciation of the dollar sufficient to cause substantial losses in bank deposits does not enter the minds of most people. They believe that price increases, if they come, will be too small to really affect savings. People are not worried about the value of their money in banks and bonds. In short, inflationary psychology as known in many other countries has not developed in the United States.

Fighting Inflation

Runaway inflation is one of the greatest possible evils. The misery it creates for most people and the disorganization it brings about for the entire society are well known from experiences in many countries in past centuries as well as during the last few decades. No doubt, runaway inflation must be fought with all means at the disposal of governments and people. Inflation must also be fought by all available means in times of war because it impedes the war effort. A successful fight against inflation must make use of psychological methods because fiscal policy, monetary policy, price control, and rationing will serve as effective weapons against inflation only if they elicit the desired reactions on the part of the people.[7]

But today in America runaway inflation is not our problem. Undoubtedly we must be watchful to ensure that creeping inflation does not develop into galloping inflation. This danger exists because people's re-

[7] This point has been discussed by the author in the books referred to in footnote 1.

actions to inflationary stimuli are not fixed and may undergo a change. Some social learning has already taken place—as evidenced by the dwindling gap between short-range and long-range price expectations as shown in Figure 13—and is conceivable regarding investment preferences. Therefore leaders in government and business must not passively accept the inevitability of an inflationary age. Nor should they provide universal and absolute guarantees to safeguard the population in case of inflation. If most people counted on automatic increases in wages and salaries, if the cost of living were seen to determine pensions and social security payments or even the value of bank deposits and bonds, people's attitudes might well undergo a change; no longer might they look upon price increases as undesirable. Similarly, a very different situation, favorable to the development of more rapid inflation, would prevail if business firms were to feel sure about their ability to transmit wage increases to their customers through higher prices.

Yet the danger that creeping inflation will be transformed into galloping inflation is not too great. The attitudes toward inflation which we have described are deeply ingrained and have proved fairly resistant to repeated inflationary experiences. There is a deep gulf between the two kinds of inflation. Runaway inflation is characterized by a break with the past; habits and convictions, regarding frugality and saving money, for instance, are abandoned when people think that a new situation has arisen. In a shock situation catastrophic reactions, such as scare buying and hoarding, prevail, and these reactions make people's worst fears come true. In sharp contrast to such forms of behavior, creeping inflation is characterized by a reduced inclination to buy because of the resentment of price increases. The expectation of further small price increases, an expectation not held with great assurance, makes people feel worse off rather than electrifying them into spending. In short, old habits, such as the desire to save, are not destroyed; the exigencies of the moment do not overshadow past and future.

Creeping inflation is an evil, but not a catastrophe. The past years of creeping inflation have not been years of human suffering, as Sumner Slichter has repeatedly pointed out.[8] During creeping inflation production is not disorganized and employment is not reduced. (Rising productivity may even help keep inflation in bounds.) Most wages and salaries keep pace with price increases so that the society does not consist of a few profiteers and masses of inflation victims. It is the people living on insurance and pensions who suffer most, because many owners of bank deposits and government bonds profit more from inflation in other areas than they lose on those savings. Therefore, although creeping inflation must be fought, this must be done with circumspection, so that the rem-

[8] See, for instance, his article in the *Harvard Business Review* of 1957.

edies should not result in consequences more serious than the illness against which they are prescribed.

Creeping inflation has its beneficial aspects as well. It helps to sustain certain attitudes which are essential for the creation of prosperous conditions. The belief that standards of living are rising and are bound to rise as years go by is closely related to the expectation of income gains. Expectations of higher incomes are usually fulfilled in times of creeping inflation and, as we have seen, this fulfillment is not necessarily attributed to inflation. If anti-inflationary measures should destroy such expectations, more harm than good might result. On the other hand, it should not be forgotten that rising incomes and economic growth can occur, and did occur, without any price increases. This was the case, for instance, in 1954–1955.

During the last few years much has been written of inflation as caused by constantly increasing costs ("cost-push inflation"). But rising costs of production due to rising wages are and always have been only one of the factors contributing to slowly rising prices. The other one is increased demand, and this factor has self-remedying rather than self-reinforcing features. When demand is substantial the sellers are in the saddle and often raise their prices; consumers may then respond by postponing some of their purchases and thus create a buyers' market. Even if price increases are not canceled when people buy less—though some retail prices may be reduced by way of increased discounts and more widespread clearance sales—periods of stable prices may result and interrupt the creeping inflation. Thus consumer reactions help to alleviate the damages of inflation. At the same time, the perception of interrupted price advances strengthens the people's notion that a continuous inflation is not inevitable.

Anti-inflationary measures—credit restriction, higher interest rates, tax increases—may be introduced in either of two periods: when demand is growing, or later when resentment against price increases is widespread and consumer buying inclinations are falling. Since government action is rarely fast, anti-inflationary measures are more often introduced in the second than in the first period. In 1955 when demand and the use of installment credit were growing rapidly, inflationary tendencies were not widely perceived and the government did not fight inflation. In 1957 demand and the use of installment credit were steady at a high rate, but a large proportion of consumers were aware of inflation and reacted to it unfavorably. Then government spokesmen proclaimed that inflation was Public Enemy Number 1. It is doubtful whether this was a correct assessment of the situation at that time. In 1957 the threat of recession and unemployment was much greater than the threat of inflation. Yet the government took vigorous action in the form of raising interest rates and curbing credit, which actions coincided with consumer resistance to high prices and proved to be excessive.

The government has big guns at its disposal. Transition from an easy money policy to one of credit restraint (even without the introduction of direct controls over credit) and transition from deficits to an excess of receipts over expenditures (even without tax increases) are powerful weapons which immediately become known all over the country. Being transmitted through the media of mass communication, their "announcement effect" may be even greater than their actual impact on finances. The timing of such measures constitutes a most difficult problem. Not enough is known at present to be able to specify the exact circumstances under which they should be introduced. There can be little doubt, however, that the psychology of the consumers should be taken into account. And this fact itself offers room for hope in the timing of future anti-inflationary programs. For it has been demonstrated that people's thoughts and feelings about inflation and their reactions to inflationary stimuli can be determined and need no longer remain a matter of guesswork.

Controlling creeping inflation is, then, a very difficult matter, probably more difficult than averting recessions and unemployment. This is, however, far from tragic because it is hardly correct, as we so often hear, that "the most important single issue confronting us is inflation." It way well be that a business recession causes more human suffering than creeping inflation.

CHAPTER 13

The Psychology of Recession

There can be no doubt that periodic *threats* of recession are inevitable. We have seen in studying the psychology of prosperity that misgivings about economic prospects arise frequently when the economy is stable on a high level rather than advancing further and may even arise when the rate of advance is thought to have slowed down. We have also seen in studying the psychology of inflation that small price increases, which are a common occurrence in prosperous times, are usually considered unfavorable developments and reduce the willingness to purchase. The question is whether such threats of recession, or recession potentials, must necessarily develop into over-all adverse business conditions with widespread unemployment and suffering on the part of millions of people.

It is also probable that occasional adverse developments in one or the other field of business activity will always occur. If, however, for example, automobile sales fall when everything else is expanding (as was the case in 1956), or construction declines when most other activities are rising, a recession will not ensue. But in 1957–1958 contraction took place simultaneously in exports, business inventories, business capital expenditures, residential construction, and consumer demand for durable goods. How can it happen that incipient tendencies toward curtailment in one area reinforce those in other areas—this is a crucial question of economic psychology.

Substantial contraction in economic activity may stem from different sources. Cumulative, self-reinforcing expectations are one of these. As a result of slight misgivings consumer purchases of durable goods may slacken, or capital expenditure plans of business may be slightly reduced; when the news about such decisions reaches the consumers or businessmen, it is seen as justifying the misgivings and results in additional and more widespread curtailment of expenditures. Similarly, decisions to make small reductions in inventories may bring about slight declines in production, which then are seen as reasons for further, larger cuts in inventories. Second, the transition from an upswing to stability or to a downswing may be seen as ushering in a fundamental change in the economic climate. If feelings of confidence and optimism are frustrated

212

and pessimism and anxiety become widespread, the onset of a new era, entirely different from previous prosperous years, threatens.

Neither of these sequences appears to be inevitable. We shall analyze developments in 1958 [1] and show that cumulative adverse expectations did arise at that time, causing a sharp downturn in some crucial indicators of business activity, as well as widespread unemployment. Yet we shall also show that a reversal of the underlying sentiment, which might have led to a long depression following the postwar decade of prosperity, did not take place. That adverse expectations could have been avoided cannot be proved, but expectations need not be cumulative and early countermeasures would probably have arrested the cumulative process of business curtailment. There is no guarantee that basic attitudes favorable to prosperity can be perpetually maintained. Yet the hopeful conclusion emerges from our studies that periods of deep depression are no longer inevitable.

Cumulative Processes and Unemployment

In analyzing cumulative, self-reinforcing processes we cannot restrict our discussion to consumers and shall even begin by a few references to business developments. Some evidence is available about cumulative business expectations during the winter of 1957–1958. As mentioned before, the Securities and Exchange Commission and the Commerce Department conduct quarterly surveys on the capital expenditure plans of American business. Based on a fairly complete sample, especially of large business firms, these surveys have a good record in predicting annual changes in business expenditures on plants and machinery and a fair record in predicting their quarterly changes. To be sure, it has been observed occasionally that in times of upswing the actual capital outlays somewhat exceeded the anticipated expenditures. Possibly in good times the committed large investment projects are somewhat expanded and accelerated or are supplemented by smaller projects decided upon at the last moment. In the first half of 1958 there were very large differences between anticipations and actual outlays in the reverse direction. The size of last-minute reductions can be seen in Table 17.

Specifically, the two agencies ask business firms for three kinds of data four times a year. In the middle of each quarter they ask about (1) capital expenditure plans for the next quarter, (2) capital expenditure plans for the current quarter, and (3) actual outlays during the past quarter. Thus on the basis of replies received in February, 1958, for instance, capital expenditures during the second quarter of 1958 were estimated at $32.6

[1] Only the psychological aspects of the recession of 1958 will be discussed; no attempt will be made to present a complete account of the economy during that year.

billion (annual rate), while those during the first quarter of 1958 were estimated at $34.4 billion (second anticipation), and the outlays during the fourth quarter of 1957 were reported to have been $36.2 billion.

We see from the table that business capital expenditures remained high even during the fourth quarter of 1957 when the recession was already widely visible, though they were somewhat lower than anticipated.[2] Because of misgivings about future sales and profits, in November, 1957, business firms set their anticipations for the first quarter of 1958 at a slightly lower rate ($35.5 billion). Actually they spent only $32.4 billion during the first quarter. It seems that something happened toward the end of 1957 and in the first quarter of 1958 which induced them to make

TABLE 17. DIFFERENCES BETWEEN EXPECTED AND ACTUAL CAPITAL
EXPENDITURES OF BUSINESS FIRMS

(Seasonally adjusted annual rates in billion dollars)

Quarter	First anticipation	Second anticipation	Actual outlays
III Quarter, 1957	37.9	37.2	37.8*
IV Quarter, 1957	37.2	37.5	36.2
I Quarter, 1958	35.5	34.4	32.4
II Quarter, 1958	32.6	31.4	30.3
III Quarter, 1958	30.3	30.3	29.6
IV Quarter, 1958	31.0	29.9	30.0

* All-time high.
NOTE: Data connected by thin lines were collected at the same time.
SOURCE: Surveys conducted by U.S. Securities and Exchange Commission and Department of Commerce.

substantial immediate cuts. The same process was repeated in the second quarter, when again the first anticipations were higher than the second anticipations, and the latter higher than the actual outlays.

Bad news was self-reinforcing in business inventory policies as well. Business inventories continued to expand during the third quarter of 1957 and were reduced only slightly during the fourth quarter. Thus the anticipation of lower sales induced business leaders to make small adjustments in their inventories. During the first half of 1958, the roof fell in: inventories were cut by the annual rate of $9.5 billion in the first and again by the annual rate of $8 billion in the second quarter. In the first

[2] It should be noted that business surveys of a different kind indicated a downturn earlier. According to data collected by the National Industrial Conference Board newly approved capital appropriations by business firms showed some decline already in the second quarter of 1957.

half of 1958, then, the rate of production was reduced not only to the extent that actual sales fell, but to a far greater extent so as to enable producers and distributors to carry much smaller inventories than before. Fear of adverse developments before they were actually observed led business leaders to take small steps of curtailment; when the fears proved to be justified and sales and profits fell, they repeated the same measures to a much greater extent.

Broad groups of consumers were likewise subject to cumulative adverse expectations. Consumer zestlessness was observed as early as the fall of 1956 and a weakening of consumer optimism could be detected in June, 1957 (see Chapter 3); by December, 1957, consumers on the whole were fairly pessimistic. Consumer purchases of automobiles and other durables were, however, curtailed only slightly in the last quarter of 1957 under the influence of worries about jobs, incomes, inflation, and rising interest rates. Somewhat later, when news spread about substantial increases in unemployment, consumers found their expectations justified and responded with much greater intensity. We have described before the reasons why in the course of 1957 the proportion of people thinking that times were not good to buy automobiles increased steadily. According to a Periodic Survey conducted in November-December, 1957, 9 per cent of all families expressed intentions to buy new cars within twelve months as against 10½ per cent in December, 1956. Then followed a much sharper decline: according to the Survey of Consumer Finances, in January-February, 1958, 7½ per cent of the families expressed the intention to buy a new car (7½ per cent of 52 million families represents about 4 million new cars, that is, no more than the calculated annual scrappage rate). It appears that when the news about declining automobile sales reached the people, willingness to buy cars dropped sharply. Only 2.4 million new cars were sold during the first half of 1958 as against 3.1 million during the first half of 1957.[3] Installment debt repaid on automobiles exceeded newly extended automobile credit by a full billion dollars during the first six months of 1958. People's automobiles grew older and their debts smaller—many families became debt-free—but automobile purchases were sharply curtailed.

The extent of contraction in economic activity may be illustrated by a few additional figures. As the result of the decline in automobile purchases, business capital expenditures, and business inventories, the American steel industry operated at only slightly over 50 per cent of capacity during the first half of 1958 as against close to 100 per cent at the beginning of 1957. This rate of decline far exceeded the decline in

[3] During the entire year of 1958, 4.6 million new cars were sold as against 6.0 million in 1957. The 4.6 million total included 375,000 foreign cars, many more than in the preceding year.

residential construction for which there were powerful specific reasons in the form of tight money and rising interest rates: the number of housing starts had dropped only 20 per cent from 1956 to early 1958. The extent of curtailment in steel production can only be explained in terms of businessmen and consumers "overdoing" what they had begun to do. Pessimistic expectations of business managers fed upon reduced demand by consumers; pessimistic expectations of consumers were reinforced by news of the effects of business inventory policies, and so on. Cumulative processes had been set in motion.

The most important and most visible consequence of the sharpness of the 1958 recession was the rise in unemployment. Official statistics, according to which unemployment reached a maximum of 5.2 million during the spring and summer of 1958, do not give us a full picture of its impact. When we are told that in each of several successive months approximately 5 million people were unemployed, we may suspect that many more than 5 million people were laid off, because in each month some must have been reemployed while others lost their jobs. In June, 1958, the Survey Research Center attempted to determine the impact of unemployment. Approximately 6 per cent of heads of families were found to be unemployed at that time; an additional 8 per cent reported that they had been unemployed some time during the previous twelve months. Among the 52 million families in the country, about 15 million contain only people who are either self-employed or outside the labor force (e.g., housewives, retired, students).[4] Of the remaining 37 million families at least 8 million were hit by unemployment some time in 1958 and several more millions lost some income by working shorter hours.[5]

The following groups were hit hardest by unemployment: nonwhites; young people (head of family under thirty years of age); those with some high school education; families with an income between $3,000 and $5,000 in 1957. (Those who did not go beyond grade school and families with incomes below $3,000 were not among those hardest hit; many of these are not factory workers.) Of course, some people were unemployed only for a few weeks and most of the unemployed received insurance benefits and other relief. Nevertheless, most of those who experienced unemployment in 1958 reported not only that they had cut down on their

[4] A family, we repeat, consists of people related by blood, marriage, or adoption who live together; it may consist of a single person.

[5] Further findings by the Survey Research Center may be mentioned to indicate how widespread the impact of the recession was. In 31 per cent of the families headed by blue-collar workers there was a member who had been unemployed during the twelve months prior to June, 1958, and in an additional 14 per cent there was a member whose working hours had been cut. In greater Detroit the corresponding figures were 54 and 22 per cent; in other words, in Detroit three out of every four blue-collar families were hit by the recession.

purchases—which usually means not spending money on things one would *like* to spend money on, since expenditures on necessities are difficult to curtail—but also that they had done one or more of the following: reduced their savings, borrowed money, received help from relatives, piled up bills. The sharp downturn in 1958 caused widespread human suffering.

End of an Era?

It is usual for prophets of doom to come forward when things are bad. Instead of describing the various pessimistic interpretations of prospects that were current in the spring of 1958, we shall cite just one business forecast, namely, the most pessimistic one that came to our attention. It was correctly stated by a well-known business analyst that for fifteen years prior to 1958 the American economy had been governed by sustained high confidence. This era was over, the analyst maintained; for several years, possibly a decade, American industry would operate in a different climate in which uncertainty and uneasiness would replace confidence. The sins committed during prosperity—creating excess capacity in industry, constructing too many office buildings and houses, piling up too many consumer goods in households—would require a lengthy process of readjustment, which would take place at a time when most people felt insecure and pessimistic.

The prediction of the end of an era was not to be taken lightly in the spring of 1958. It was worth while and possible to subject it to careful study. Part of a nationwide survey conducted in June, 1958, was devoted to finding out whether or not the underlying sentiment responsible for the preceding prosperous years had been destroyed or impaired under the influence of the recession.

The question whether a depression like the one in the thirties was likely to occur was asked in June, 1958, as it had been asked during the preceding prosperous years. The answers were substantially the same. Once more the great majority of the people said that such a depression would not or even could not happen again. Once more only a very small proportion of the people and even only a small proportion of the unemployed thought that such a depression was likely during the next five years. The major arguments they used in explaining their opinion likewise remained unchanged. During the recession, as in previous years, the majority maintained that something had been learned since the thirties which made it possible to avoid severe depressions.

Turning to personal financial expectations we find that in June, 1958, just as in previous good years, families fell largely into two groups: those who a few years later expected to be better off and those who expected their situation to remain unchanged. Only one in ten expected to be worse off, the same proportion as in 1953–1954 and only insignificantly more than in 1955–1956.

Unemployment in 1958 was something entirely different from unemployment in the thirties. Personal financial and general business expectations of the unemployed were only somewhat less favorable than the expectations of employed people in similar socioeconomic classes. Many unemployed thought that their chances of getting their old jobs back in the near future were good; only one out of four gave an unqualified pessimistic answer about getting their old jobs back or getting other jobs which would pay about the same. The proportion of pessimistic answers given by employed people in reply to a conditional question ("Suppose you lose your job during the next few months . . .") was similar.

As a further very important aspect of the psychology of prosperity we recognized people's growing needs and desires for durable goods. Did the rapid rate of spending during a decade of prosperity exhaust their needs and desires for more and better goods so that the recession ushered in an era of saturation, or even of wantlessness? This question again was answered by the people themselves with an unequivocal No.

Desires for material possessions were studied first with regard to housing. The studies about potential residential mobility, reported in Chapter 8, were repeated in 1958. The proportion of people who said they would *like* to buy a house or would like to move was found to be as high as before. Again not only dissatisfaction with housing arrangements but also the desire to improve fairly satisfactory housing arrangements were given as the reasons. Desires for better or bigger houses, for location in better neighborhoods, and for home ownership were expressed in 1958 as frequently as in the previous years.

When people's wishes and desires were studied further by asking them to name special or unusual expenditures they would *like* to make, the answers received in June, 1958, could not be distinguished from those of one or two years earlier. Again about 70 per cent of families described at least one, often several, desires. There was no substantial change in the kinds of things mentioned. Automobiles, additions and repairs to houses, household appliances, cottages and trips, as well as luxury and hobby expenditures were all reported as before and with similar frequency. Only the follow-up question brought forth different answers in 1958 than in 1956. After people had enumerated what they would like to have, they were asked, What are the chances that you will buy . . . in the next twelve months? The proportion answering that the chances were good or fair was lower in 1958 than before, and the proportion saying that the chances were slight or that there was no chance at all was higher. It appears, then, that willingness to buy was impaired, but for reasons other than absence of needs and wants.

Overproduction, overconsumption, and overcapacity are terms popular in explaining the onset of recessions. Excess capacity in business plants can neither be demonstrated nor disproved. Naturally, in comparison with the shrunken demand in 1958, there was much unused capacity in factories. But it does not follow that industry had overspent in previous years because, obviously, a business concern should not gear its capacity to the year of lowest demand. The theory of overspending and of overcapacity was also applied to consumer goods. It was said that consumers, after having bought recklessly for years, had acquired everything they needed and had become overburdened with debt. This interpretation of the developments of 1958 cannot be accepted.

Even though in a certain sense wants are unlimited and a surfeit of things is inconceivable, we ourselves have pointed out that under certain circumstances feelings of saturation may indeed develop. Disappointment, failure, and frustration may lower levels of aspiration and may result in a lack of desire. But in 1958 this did not happen.[6] Even though a great many people had suffered disappointment at that time, and many unemployed suffered hardships, the people themselves did not draw the conclusion which some experts drew. In people's discussions of the recession no traces were found of remorse about too great past spending. On the contrary, most of them maintained that sooner or later things would turn up again and they would then continue to improve their standard of living. They knew, even during the worst months of the 1958 recession, what needs they would satisfy and what goods they would buy when "good times to buy" would return.

Automatic Stabilizers and Stable Income

We have shown that the recession of 1958 cannot be attributed to overconsumption in the preceding years, resulting in saturation of consumer needs. Nor can it be attributed to insufficient purchasing power of consumers. Decline in ability to buy does not explain how the recession came about in 1957, nor does it explain the sharp decline in demand for durable goods in 1958. Total personal incomes reached their highest level in the third quarter of 1957. Their lowest level, in the first quarter of 1958,

[6] This is contrary to the observation of one of the most perspicacious analysts of the contemporary scene. David Riesman wrote in the winter of 1957–1958: "The basic stockpile on which our society's dynamism rests—the stockpile of new and significant wants—is badly depleted" ("Abundance for What?" p. 228). To be sure, and we shall come back to this point in the next chapter, Riesman spoke not only of the tendency "to lose zest for bounteous spending on consumer goods," but also of too many socially insignificant rather than significant wants. J. R. Meyer also wrote in the November, 1958, issue of the *Review of Economic Statistics* that "consumers and producers simply have no *obvious* large blocks of unsatiated needs to be met."

showed a decline of hardly more than 1 per cent. (In real terms and per capita the decline was somewhat larger, but still insignificant.) In the second and third quarters of 1958 national income rose again. How could this happen when unemployment was substantial, overtime was abolished in many cases, and the work week was frequently shortened?

In contrast to the thirties, the American economy today has certain features which are called automatic or built-in stabilizers. In Chapter 11 we discussed how people's views of the economy differed in the fifties from those in the thirties. These changes are related to certain institutional changes that have taken place. One of these has already been mentioned before—social security, of which the people are well aware. The unemployment insurance system operates so that in good times, when there are few unemployed, the government takes in much more money than it pays out, while in bad times it is the other way around. As a result of unemployment insurance benefits—often supplemented by industry as well as by welfare payments—the loss of income by the unemployed is reduced and they are enabled to keep up their expenditures on necessities. These benefits explain why national income did not fall very sharply but of course cannot explain why it remained stable.

Our tax system likewise has features which tend to stabilize the economy. When our incomes decline our tax payments are also reduced. This feature of individual income taxes is of course helpful in many instances but again cannot explain the stability of national income during the recession. Corporate income taxes are a somewhat different story. They amount to 52 per cent for large corporations, which means that the government picks up the check for one-half of the decline in corporate profits. The corporations' ability to pay dividends in periods of unfavorable business is thus cut by only one-half of the amount of the decline in profits before taxes. To be sure, if they are pessimistic, corporation executives may decide to cut dividends much more than what would correspond to the reduction in profits after taxes. Alternatively, since usually only a part of profits is distributed to stockholders, corporation executives may decide to keep their dividends at prerecession levels. The latter was done —on the whole, not by each individual corporation—in 1958. Therefore the sharp decline in corporate profits experienced in that year was not transmitted to the consumers in form of reduced dividends.

The reason why many corporations maintained their dividends in the face of much lower profits is not to be found in optimistic long-run attitudes alone. Business behavior, the same as consumer behavior, is dependent on certain forms of thinking which, though nonexistent a few decades earlier, have now become habitual or even traditional. One of these is that reduction of dividends should be avoided if at all possible. It was known before the recession that such a notion was part of the American business climate. In a nationwide interview survey with business executives conducted in 1956 the Survey Research Center sought opinions about the advantages and disadvantages of borrowing from banks or through bond issues as against issuing common stock. It was found that corporation executives did not feel that stock issues were more advantageous because, if profits should fall, it was possible to reduce dividends but not interest charges. We quote the conclusions reached in that study: "Many corporation executives feel today [that] dividends are fixed with respect to their lowest acceptable level—which is the current rate. 'Nowadays, it is not possible to reduce dividends,' we heard frequently. This statement means that the company's prestige, its standing in the industry, as well as the reputation of its executives, would suffer greatly if dividends were reduced." [7]

Long-range union contracts which often postulate wage increases two or more years in advance or automatic annual salary increases are further features of today's economy. Because of them there were many income increases in 1958, compensating for some income reductions. In addition, there were areas of the economy—especially agriculture and the food industry—which were immune to the recession and continued to grow. In June, 1958, 27 per cent of American families reported that they were making more money than a year before (as against 38 per cent in 1956) and 28 per cent that they were making less (as against 17 per cent in 1956). Thus there were fewer people in 1958 than in 1956 who were encouraged by income gains to increase their spending, and more who were discouraged, but in the aggregate incomes remained stable.

Stability of national income does not guarantee unchanged consumption expenditures. The decline in the ability to buy on the part of some may not be compensated for by a higher rate of spending by others; the latter may devote their income gains to saving more. The question is, Suppose, as in 1958, national income is stable and consumer expenditures on durable goods fall; will the money not spent on durables be spent on nondurables and services, or will it be saved? In 1958 it was spent, primarily on food and a variety of small items. As we saw in Chapter 7, amounts put in banks and securities—what we have called discretionary liquid saving, excluding amounts borrowed and debts repaid—did not rise during the first half of 1958 when durable-goods purchases slumped. In fact, of course, some people saved more than before while others dissaved in order to maintain their living standards in spite of reduced incomes.

That consumer expenditures on nondurables and services did not show any effect of the recession is a remarkable fact, even though the picture becomes somewhat less favorable when price increases (food prices in par-

[7] G. Katona, *Business Looks at Banks,* p. 144.

ticular went up in 1958), population increases, and the economy's long-range trend are taken into account. Why did people, collectively, maintain their expenditures rather than increase their savings? In Chapter 7 we reported findings about savings motives and derived the conclusion that amounts of discretionary liquid saving should not be expected to fluctuate cyclically. Now we may add a further explanation for what happened in 1958: The maintenance of those long-range attitudes which characterized prosperity and the belief that the recession would be temporary encouraged the consumers to spend rather than to add to their savings.[8]

Antirecession Measures

Through the automatic reduction of tax payments out of reduced incomes and through increased social security payments, the government contributed to alleviating the downward trend in the economy without taking any action. The government also introduced deliberate antirecession policies. First, monetary policy was reversed and residential construction stimulated. Much later, government expenditures, other than for unemployment benefits, were expanded. Some relatively small increases in defense expenditures must be attributed to the sputniks and the worsening of the international situation, and fairly large increases in agricultural subsidies must also be attributed to factors other than the recession. Yet as a result of such additional expenditures, higher social security payments, as well as new countercyclical housing and highway programs and public works, undertaken at a time of sharply falling government revenues, by the summer of 1958 the government was operating with a substantial deficit. While as late as the third quarter of 1957 the government was withdrawing more funds from the economy than it was contributing, in the second quarter of 1958 it made substantial cash contributions to the economy. For the fiscal year beginning July 1, 1958, the deficit was officially estimated at $12 billion.

The deficit did not result from a reduction of tax rates. Many economists as well as politicians demanded early in 1958 that antirecession action should consist primarily of a tax cut. The Eisenhower administration and influential congressional leaders in both parties were opposed, and the discussion of tax reductions was abandoned when the size of prospective deficits, which would ensue without tax cuts, became known.

Let us look first at the impact which changes in monetary policy had on the economy. In 1957 Federal Reserve authorities not only allowed *interest rates* to rise considerably but also purposefully contributed to

[8] After referring to high consumer expenditures, A. F. Burns concluded that "if there were any heroes during the recession, this distinction belongs to ordinary consumers" (in "Some Lessons of the Recent Recession").

tightening money in order to fight inflation. It was hoped that the tight money policy would achieve two goals then deemed desirable: higher rates of saving by consumers and lower rates of borrowing by consumers and business firms. In fact, the amounts saved were not affected. The relation between interest rates and saving was studied in a nationwide survey conducted in June, 1957. Two sets of questions, intentionally formulated in a suggestive manner, were asked. First, Recently many people have been increasing their savings; have you had any special reasons for wanting to save in the last few months? What were they? Even though people were pushed toward a certain answer by being told something which had not happened—namely, that savings had increased—very few people mentioned high interest rates. Most people accepted the suggestion and explained increased savings by references to saving for a rainy day or old age. Following this question, it was determined that most people were aware of the higher interest rates (75 per cent of people with an income of $7,500 or more). These people were asked, Does the increase in interest rates make a difference to you personally? The answer "Yes, we save more" was given by only 5 per cent of those with an income of $7,500 or more. Most people gave one or the other of the following two answers: "Yes, we earn more on our savings" or "No, it does not make any difference."

Many people were found to have taken some kind of action because of changes in interest rates: they had shifted their savings to institutions paying the higher interest. But interest rates were not a powerful enough consideration to make them cut their expenditures so as to be able to save more. Rising interest rates did contribute, however—as we reported before (Chapter 3)—to a feeling of uneasiness. The reaction of many was that something must be wrong with the economy which made interest rates increase sharply. Higher interest rates had no direct impact on the rate of installment buying—most people do not know what the interest charges are when they buy a car on installment—but did adversely affect the purchasing of houses. In buying a house with a long-term mortgage, an increase of the interest by even one-half of 1 per cent affects the monthly payments appreciably, and prospective buyers are aware of the difference.

It is not possible to prove definitely that higher interest rates did not influence the rate of business borrowing. Yet in the business survey referred to above, information was collected about corporation managers' attitudes toward borrowing and the conclusion was drawn that business borrowing is fairly insensitive to changes in interest rates. Decisions to invest and to borrow money were found to originate in considerations other than the cost of money. An increase in the cost of money by even 2 per cent a year—of which only one-half matters because of corporation income taxes—was found to make no difference in most projects. But many business firms did use short-term bank credit for long-range investments during the prosperous fifties, and news about tight money created some doubt about access to and renewability of bank credit, and therefore had an adverse psychological effect on some firms' willingness to expand further.

The government's tight money policy was continued as late as the third quarter of 1957 when some Washington officials still proclaimed that inflation was "Public Enemy Number 1." The policy was reversed in November, 1957. Interest rates were reduced substantially within a few months and more money was made available, primarily to the market of mortgages for new construction. There was a fairly prompt and substantial response on the part of builders of apartment houses and one-family houses, and of home buyers as well. While the rate of housing starts fell from 1.1 million in early 1957 to 0.9 million in early 1958, by July, 1958, it had risen to 1.2 million. While in June and December, 1957, the great majority of the people said that it was a bad time to buy houses, in June, 1958, upper-income people were equally divided between those saying it was a good time and those saying it was a bad time. In June, 1957, two-thirds of informed people said that it had become harder to finance house buying; in June, 1958, only one-third said so. Desires to buy houses were frequent both in 1957 and 1958; the difference in purchases between the two years was due to financial considerations. It appears that measures of monetary policy do have a prompt and strong influence on one important aspect of economic activity, namely, residential construction. Their effectiveness in fighting inflation is far from assured, even though at certain times at least they seem to be capable of promoting attitudes detrimental to spending on durable goods and may promote a recession.

When early in 1958 the severeness of the recession became generally known, very many people clamored for government action stronger than creating easy money conditions, particularly *tax reductions*. The major arguments brought forward in favor of reducing taxes were the following:

> Reduction of income tax rates would have an immediate effect on the finances of very many people, while public works would take much longer to get under way.
>
> Since the government is a less efficient spender than consumers and business firms, the initiative to bail out the economy should be left to the latter.
>
> Tax reductions would constitute a most conspicuous action, making it widely known that the government was fighting the recession.

The major counterarguments were the following:

> People might save rather than spend the amounts by which their weekly or monthly take-home pay would be increased.

Those who suffered most from the recession, the unemployed, would not profit from tax reductions.

Tax reductions constitute fairly permanent changes—to raise taxes later when inflation might threaten would be difficult.

In addition, of course, there were those who argued for measures costing less, and there was no agreement in Congress or among experts which taxes to cut by how much.

This author, probably at the same time as some others, proposed a tax refund plan.[9] He argued as follows:

The 1957 income taxes rather than the 1958 taxes should be cut. Then those unemployed in 1958 would also benefit.

To make a strong impression on consumers and to stimulate down-payments on durable goods, taxpayers should receive a sizable refund in a lump sum, instead of finding their take-home pay increased by a few dollars a week or a month.

The refund should be calculated in a simple manner from the tax returns filed by April 15, 1958, so that people would know even before the arrival of their checks how much they would receive.

A cut of 1957 taxes would be a one-shot proposition. The question of how to raise taxes later would not arise.

Congress postponed the decision on taxes until the summer of 1958. By that time the deficit was large, the economy had begun to recover, and no action was taken.

Opponents of tax reductions sometimes argued that the people themselves were opposed to that measure. This argument, of particular importance for psychological economics, deserves consideration.

Measures intended to stimulate production and employment, and thereby to combat recession, may serve to generate additional income or greater confidence. In order to be effective, antirecession measures must serve both purposes. Appeals and moral suasion alone do not work. If people are told that the recession is over or that it will end soon, they will fail to trust the statement unless they see why it should come true. Likewise, additional income provided by government expenditures or tax reductions may, if not understood, create mistrust and anxiety and therefore reduce, rather than stimulate, the willingness to spend.

It follows that the people's way of thinking and feeling about antirecession measures is important, even though it cannot and should not be taken as the sole determinant of government action. Sometimes measures may

[9] In a press release issued in March, 1958; see also the testimony by G. Katona reproduced in *Administered Prices*, Hearings before Subcommittee on Antitrust and Monopoly, 1958, p. 3126.

be necessary which are not understood by broad groups of people; in such a case careful psychological preparation should precede the measures.

The following question was included in the June, 1958, Periodic Survey: Do you have any opinion about what might be done to reduce unemployment and bring about prosperous times? About one-half of the people, and many more in high-income brackets, expressed a variety of ideas of what might be done. The majority of the various proposals made may be grouped into three categories: public works, check of inflation (both by the government and by business and labor), and business action gratifying consumer needs and stimulating consumer demand.

But many people find it hard to express themselves about such difficult matters. Therefore a number of specific proposals were also presented and people were asked about each of them, Do you think this will help a great deal in bringing about good times, help only a little, or not at all? The exact wording of the proposals and people's replies are contained in Table 18.

The popularity contest was won by "public works, like building roads and schools." In all income groups the opinion that public works would help was given most frequently and the opinion that they would not help, least frequently. Replies to the question about increased defense spending were divided. Those who said that such spending would help were counterbalanced by others who thought that it would necessitate higher taxes or who could not make up their minds about its value to the economy. Lower interest rates were thought more often to help a little than to help a lot.

The series of proposals included two which many economists would not consider antirecession measures. "For the government to economize and balance the budget" was considered helpful by one-half of the total sample as well as one-half of the upper-income group. Many fewer people thought that "to raise wages and salaries" would be helpful. The majority of upper-income respondents were strongly opposed to this proposal, and this was even true of a substantial proportion of the low-income group. That higher wages and salaries would promote inflation was the most frequent counterargument mentioned.

It was said very frequently that tax reductions would help, but a sizable minority thought they would not. Some of these people agreed that reducing taxes would have a beneficial effect on demand but thought that it was impracticable because of the necessary, huge defense expenditures. Other people, associating depression with the necessity for economizing, did not understand how tax reductions could contribute to increased demand. No doubt, if the government had cut taxes in 1958, consumers would have had to be given some comprehension of what the government was trying to do. To accomplish this task would not have been very difficult.

It appears probable that much could have been achieved if taxes had

TABLE 18. OPINIONS ABOUT VARIOUS ANTIRECESSION MEASURES, JUNE, 1958

Opinion	Public works	Increased defense spending	Tax reductions	Lower interest rates	Balanced budget	Raise in wages and salaries
A. All families						
Would help a lot............	39%	27%	37%	20%	28%	20%
Would help a little.........	38	24	24	33	18	14
Pro-con; may help..........	5	5	4	4	4	4
Would not help.............	9	22	21	18	17	51
Don't know, not ascertained....	9	22	14	25	33	11
Total.................	100%	100%	100%	100%	100%	100%
B. Families with incomes of $5,000 and over						
Would help a lot............	36%	30%	33%	22%	31%	11%
Would help a little.........	45	27	26	36	18	13
Pro-con; may help..........	4	7	5	5	4	5
Would not help.............	10	22	27	22	22	63
Don't know, not ascertained....	5	14	9	15	25	8
Total.................	100%	100%	100%	100%	100%	100%

THE QUESTIONS WERE: Here are six things people have mentioned that might stimulate business and reduce unemployment. Some of these you may have no opinion about. The first is to start public works, like building roads and schools. The second is to reduce interest rates. The third is for the government to economize and balance the budget. The fourth is to increase defense spending. The fifth is to reduce taxes. The sixth is to raise wages and salaries. For each: Do you think this would help a great deal in bringing about good times, help only a little, or not at all?

SOURCE: Survey Research Center, Periodic Survey.

been reduced early in 1958. The immediate impact of a tax remission would have been greater and its ultimate cost might have been kept smaller than that of public works programs, which tend to continue even when they are no longer needed.[10] Probably a prompt tax cut would have counteracted the development and spread of cumulative expectations which, as we have seen, made the recession severe and increased the extent of unemployment. The damage caused by the government's failure to act early and to a sufficient extent was mitigated by the fact that the underlying attitudes of the American people were not impaired by the recession. That this would be so was, of course, not known early in 1958 and there is no guarantee that it would be so again should another setback occur.

Recovery from Recession

Several important economic indicators registered a sharp advance during the early summer of 1958. The recession turned out to be V-shaped rather than saucer-shaped. The timing of the upturn was influenced mainly by the increase in the net cash outlays of the Federal government and the reversal in business inventory policy. After an excessive cut in inventories, the high level of consumption of nondurables made it necessary for business to reverse its policy. The rate of industrial production, which fell from 147 early in 1957 to 126 in April, 1958, recovered to 142 in December, 1958. Yet only part of the previous decline was made good in 1958 and unemployment remained substantial, because expenditures on business plants and machinery and those on consumer durable goods did not advance much,

Consumer attitudes and expectations were determined in May-June and again in October, 1958. The composite index of consumer attitudes and buying inclinations, which had dropped from 112.4 in December, 1956, to 91.0 in February, 1958 (see Figure 8, Chapter 3), stood at 94.5 in May-June, 1958, and rose to 99.9 in October, 1958.[11] Components of the index did not show uniform changes as may be seen from Figure 16.

Consumers' evaluation of their personal financial situation deteriorated during the first half of 1958. In view of growing unemployment and shortened work weeks this finding was expected. Correspondingly, the proportion of people who thought that business conditions would be unfavorable during the succeeding twelve months rose. Yet in June, 1958,

[10] Arthur F. Burns, former chief economic adviser to President Eisenhower, also expressed this opinion in a speech of Nov. 19, 1958 (see "Some Lessons of the Recent Recession"). He pointed out that inflationary fears and pressures seem less likely to follow a tax reduction than public expenditures.

[11] The improvement of consumer attitudes was much sharper in 1959. In May, 1959, the index reached 109.8.

many more people believed that "a year from now times will be better" than believed that conditions would deteriorate further. In this respect expectations improved substantially during the first half of 1958.

Perceptions of and attitudes toward prices represented an important aspect of improved sentiment in June, 1958. Many consumers refused to believe that inflation and recession could occur at the same time. Although during the first half of 1958 the cost-of-living index had advanced and

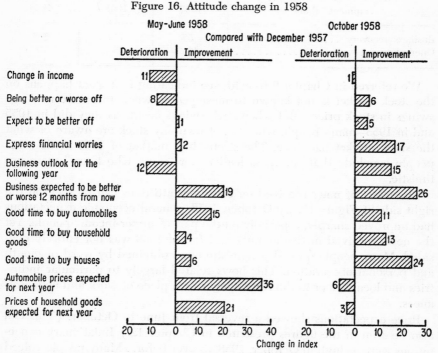

Figure 16. Attitude change in 1958

SOURCE: Periodic Surveys of the Survey Research Center. For explanation, see Figure 1, Chapter 3.

food prices in particular had gone up, fewer people than in 1957 said that prices had gone up, and price expectations became much less inflationary. Especially regarding the prices of automobiles and household appliances many people argued that a buyers' market would force them down. As a result of changed price expectations, the appraisal of whether or not it was a good time to buy also improved. Yet the frequency of definite intentions to buy durable goods remained fairly low although the proportion of people who said, "Possibly we might buy" increased.

Later in the summer and in the early fall of 1958, the media of mass communication reiterated the official government statement that the recession had ended. At the same time the stock market advanced substantially, wiping out the entire decline that had occurred in 1957. Consumers heard the news. When, following the question calling for an expression of their business expectations, they were asked, Why do you think so? the frequency of spontaneous comments changed as follows:

Frequency of spontaneous comments about	December, 1957	May-June, 1958	October, 1958
Business recovery	5%	17%	30%
Unemployment	43	35	19

We referred in Chapter 9 to evidence indicating that what happens on the stock market is not known to most people when there are no large swings in stock prices. But when such swings occur—as they did in 1955 and in 1958—many people who do not own any stock are aware of what the stock market has done. The strong bull market of 1958 made some people conclude that "business leaders" or "those who know" were optimistic.

The effect of news received on consumer attitudes can be seen on the right side of Figure 16. By October, 1958, general economic expectations had improved sharply, especially on the part of upper-income people. Yet the news received in the summer and fall of 1958 was not entirely one-sided. Many people quoted pessimistic news obtained by word of mouth and personal observation. This news related largely to particular industries and localities or to the respondent's own place of work and acquaintances.

Price expectations showed a reversal from June to October. (This can also be seen in the figures presented in Chapter 12.) Inflationary expectations were as high in October, 1958, as ever before. Many people voiced disappointment that the recession had gone by without price reductions. The prices of new cars in particular were frequently mentioned as being too high. There can be no doubt that the absence of price reductions during the recession of 1958 hampered the recovery of inclinations to buy.

Attitudes toward the respondents' personal financial situations improved somewhat by October, 1958, but the improvement was considerably smaller than the deterioration in 1957. Worries about employment and job security did not disappear. In October, 1958, 21 per cent of all families said that they worried about steady employment as against 29 per cent in June, 1958, but only 9 per cent in late 1956. When asked whether they were affected by the recession, not fewer than one out of every three families said that the recession had hurt their financial situation. The majority of these reported that they had suffered shorter or longer periods of unemployment or worked shorter hours. Yet especially among upper-income families the proportion of those who reported income increases and said that they felt better off substantially exceeded the proportion reporting income declines or feelings of being in a poorer financial situation.

During the second half of 1958 consumer attitudes toward personal finances and business conditions showed much more pronounced improvement than expressed buying intentions. Especially plans to purchase new cars and interest expressed in new cars, though more frequent or more pronounced than during the recession, failed to reach their prerecession levels. The situation toward the end of 1958 was therefore less favorable than the situation toward the end of 1954 when sharply expressed consumer willingness to purchase automobiles led the economy out of a recession.

In the winter of 1958–1959 consumers stepped up their expenditures on nondurables and services, corresponding to rising incomes. Expenditures on automobiles and other durable goods, as well as business capital expenditures, likewise increased, but remained well below their prerecession levels. Therefore there was substantial unemployment, and the growth trend of the American economy suffered an interruption. It took some time until consumers overcame their disappointment with unemployment and with the rising prices.

On the whole, the American people were not dissatisfied with government policies during the recession. When asked in October, 1958, whether in their opinion the Federal government has done a good job or a poor job in dealing with the problem of recession and unemployment, 53 per cent said "a good job" and 25 per cent "a poor job." (The rest had no opinion.) The first group referred to unemployment compensation and public works, as well as to the quick improvement in business conditions. The second group argued that the recession had lasted too long or that the government had done too little. These opinions did not differ substantially among low-, middle-, and high-income families. Whether or not a person thought he was hurt by the recession made for some differences, but the largest differences in the appraisals of government policies during the recession were found elsewhere: Among those who said they usually thought of themselves as Democrats, the opinion that the government had done a poor job was much larger than among those who said they thought of themselves as Republicans. This division of opinions occurred at the time of a national election campaign. It probably permits the conclusion that the recession of 1958 played a role in the outcome of the

November, 1958, elections. But regarding people's economic thinking the findings of the October survey suggest that government actions in the 1958 recession did not disappoint very many people.

"We did very well in fighting the recession of 1958," concluded some experts pointing to the short time span between the beginning of the downswing in 1957 and the beginning of the upswing in 1958. Others, however, were more impressed by the extent of the decline in production and of human suffering through unemployment. There can be no doubt that what happened in 1958 was not a major catastrophe. Pessimism was not on the rampage and a new era of lack of confidence not in the offing. A severe shake-up did occur, destroying complacency and making it clear that the instability of our economy is still one of our greatest problems. The recession provided a good test for the automatic stabilizers which have become permanent features of our economy. They proved their worth in maintaining income and purchasing power. But the volatile forms of demand dropped sharply and the recession of 1958 was not used to test the effectiveness of vigorous antirecession action by the government. For many people the illness was severe and left scars which were not forgotten quickly.

CHAPTER 14

Consumer Sanity

Today in the United States it is not a few powerful business leaders nor a few government officials whose decisions and actions determine what happens to the economy. Millions of consumer households contribute, through their behavior, to raising or lowering production and prices and to bringing about prosperity or recession, progress or stagnation. In addition to an increase in the number of people whose decisions matter to the economy, there has also been an increase in the availability of information. Not so long ago news spread slowly and most people were ignorant of economic developments beyond their limited sphere. Today, with rapid mass communications, every localized difficulty and incipient tendency becomes widely known within a short time.

What are the effects of these changes? What difference does it make that several million household units influence economic activity rather than a few thousand business units? Are exaggerated and excessive reactions common among consumers, and might the economy therefore be subject to uncontrolled spurts of inflation or deflation as induced by mob psychology? Is too much information received by too many people detrimental to economic stability?

Group Behavior among Business Leaders

The mass media—newspapers, periodicals, radio, and television—reach consumers and business leaders alike. That prompt and fairly uniform information is now provided from coast to coast should presumably have a like influence on both. But it might be argued that the latter also have access to additional and perhaps better information and may be more discriminating in evaluating the news they receive. Consumers, on the other hand, so it might seem, having incomplete knowledge of economic principles might well become easy victims of news, rumors, propaganda, as well as manipulation, and might serve as carriers and transmitters of rumors. On the basis of these assumptions one might expect that business leaders would not be easily swayed by others from their decisions made on the basis of solid knowledge, while the less wise mass

233

of consumers could readily be shifted from one position to another and thus have an unsettling effect on the economy. In fact, our studies revealed practically the opposite to be true.

One significant difference between business leaders and the millions of middle- and upper-middle-income consumers is that among the former there exist face-to-face groups, while the unorganized masses do not unite in cohesive consumer groups. A business manager frequently meets other business managers, exchanges information and hunches about the economy with them, and tends to form opinions through personal contact. Business groups are fairly cohesive units in which some pressure often prevails toward uniform attitudes. Each consumer, of course, knows many other consumers but typically does not discuss economic or financial matters with them. Housewives may talk about sales or bargains with each other and may complain about high prices to each other, but discussions among consumers about the probable course of the economy are infrequent—except under the rare circumstances when radical changes occur or threaten. Even though attitudes tend to change in the same direction among millions of consumers, since they all are subject to similar information transmitted to them, the process of mutual reinforcement tends to be less pronounced with consumers than with business leaders.

Economists have long been aware of the interdependence of business sentiment. In analyzing business cycles, they have often used such expressions as "errors of optimism" and "errors of pessimism." Even though, the future being uncertain, one business leader may err in an optimistic and another in a pessimistic direction, economists have noted that usually the errors of forecast are all in the same direction, all businessmen being overcautious at certain times and overexuberant at other times. Clusters of errors help explain cyclical fluctuations. If all businessmen acted in the same way, small causes may make for explosive effects, as many economists have pointed out.[1]

Turning from general statements to an analysis of recent American business behavior, we may recognize compelling reasons for fairly uniform courses of action. Following the leader may be a matter of necessity rather than of inclination or of contagion in expectations. When a major producer introduces technological innovations—such as more efficient machinery or automation—other producers must follow in order to remain competitive. The same is often the case when one large producer changes his product by adding to it new features or gadgets (one may think, for

---

[1] Among the most influential economists expressing such views are A. C. Pigou and Joseph Schumpeter. Recently the Swiss economist, W. A. Jöhr, developed a psychological business cycle theory along the lines described above (in the book *Die Konjunkturschwankungen*).

instance, of wraparound windshields). Even the unconfirmed rumor that a competitor is planning to make certain changes or introduce new products may induce other producers to take similar steps. At the beginning of World War II the United States decided to devote several billion dollars to the development of atomic bombs in the belief, which later proved to be unfounded, that Germany had embarked on a similar venture. On a much smaller scale, to be sure, industry proceeds similarly. Since there prevails widespread inertia in business life, and most producers are disinclined to replace a successful product or manufacturing procedure by something new and untested, what provides the spark which initiates such processes and explains why they are often adopted very quickly by all producers? The spark may be found in the well-confirmed observation that business managers constantly watch their competitors and are ready to adopt new procedures when they believe, correctly or incorrectly, that others are about to do so. Inertia and hesitancy are overcome by the notion that others may embark on something new and thereby gain a competitive advantage. This "atom bomb theory" of business innovations may be applicable not only to innovations by manufacturers but also to such developments, for instance, as the first large suburban stores opened by city department stores. The fact that competitors often belong to the same organizations or groups does not guarantee correct information about one another's plans; but it helps spread facts as well as rumors.

In addition to watching their competitors and speculating about their probable actions, businessmen have their ears to the ground to detect, as early as possible, the prospective moves of their customers and of the ultimate consumer. All-pervasive is the fear of not being able to satisfy old customers because of insufficient capacity or inadequate inventories, and thus of losing them to competitors. Therefore to adopt the same policies—inventory policies as well as those relating to capital investment—which others have adopted or are expected to adopt appears justified. Failing to follow the leader may lead to losing some of one's share in the market, or may even be suicidal. "What we expect others to do, we must do"—this is how a top industrialist in a highly competitive industry explained his business policy in an interview. If everyone acts on this principle and if expectations about competitors' and customers' actions are uniform, then we have an explanation of why business innovations often spread with lightning speed. We can then also understand why proposals to stabilize business investments and to formulate counter-cyclical investment policies—advocated, for instance, by the Committee for Economic Development and widely discussed during the past ten years—have not been successful. Large corporations now operate on five-year capital budget plans and give much attention to attempts to avoid sharp fluctuations in capital expenditures. Nevertheless, most business firms still expand their capital expenditures at the same time and contract them at the same time. This was the case both during the upswing of 1955–1956 and the downswing of 1958. The coincidence in changes in capital expenditures is due only partly to the fact that rising or falling profits and sales, which stimulate expansion or contraction, are an industry-wide phenomenon. In addition, business firms operate in a strong group situation in which uniform action is facilitated, while action contrary to group consensus is undertaken rarely.

It has been postulated by an exponent of a psychological business cycle theory that in times of upswing optimism, and in times of downswing pessimism, are carried over from entrepreneurs to the consumers.[2] True, individual investors may often follow a pattern similar to corporation policies. This may be true of investments in the stock market or of the operations of speculative builders. In the realm of fashion, likewise, sequences of behavior may be found for which the principles of following or anticipating others apply. But consumers do not constitute cohesive face-to-face groups, and there are good reasons, therefore, to doubt that the principles of business behavior are generally valid for consumer behavior. But before going into what we actually found to be true of consumer behavior, let us consider first the general problem of how attitudes could conceivably snowball among consumers to produce drastic effects on the economy.

Self-fulfilling Expectations

Self-fulfilling expectations were discussed before in describing the process of runaway inflation. The expectation of rising prices may induce people to buy in excess of their needs and thereby makes itself come true. What has been called the vicious circle of depression exemplifies the same process in reverse: the expectation of lower incomes and fear of unemployment cause people to reduce their expenditures; incomes then decline because they were expected to decline. Or we may recall the bank runs in the early thirties. Rumors that a bank was not sound led people to withdraw their deposits; even a strong bank could not withstand such a cumulative process in which more and more people participated and made the rumors come true by their action.

A recent explanation of the rapid abandonment of some urban districts by white inhabitants represents a most interesting application of this theory. "The prophecy of racial invasion is self-fulfilling. Belief by the whites that a Negro invasion is imminent leads them to move out of

[2] *Ibid.*, p. 425.

the neighborhood, the very action that makes the invasion possible." [3] In the words of Merton, "Confident error generates its own spurious confirmation." [4]

One may wonder whether great inflations or runs on banks are correctly described as originating in erroneous or unjustified rumors about future price increases or difficulties of banks, and one may doubt whether they were *unfounded* expectations which made themselves come true. Unfounded rumors may influence some people's behavior for a short time. But in order for the expectations of very many people to be maintained over long periods, the expectations must have a foundation and people must understand the reasons for their expectations. If this is the case, then runaway inflations and bank failures, and probably the invasion of white neighborhoods as well, are not caused by the expectations alone but by good reasons—loss of war and the printing of money, for instance, or many illiquid bank loans, or the fact that some whites in the neighborhood have sold their houses to Negroes—in conjunction with expectations. The causation is not purely psychological, but factual as well as psychological.

Yet being based on factual observations does not make expectations self-fulfilling or self-justifying. It appears probable that expectations seldom feed upon themselves and when they do we are faced with a form of catastrophic behavior rather than typical human behavior. People resist speculative fever as well as despondency unless their sanity is crushed by a series of repeated shocks. News and rumors will not sustain action by very many people over prolonged periods and will not become cumulative, except when unusual and rare circumstances favor the arousal of mass hysteria.

Let us enumerate first those instances in which cumulative, self-justifying processes were found to have characterized consumer behavior in the postwar period. They were few in number. And in each instance the bandwagon effect was arrested before the effects became very serious.

At the outbreak of the Korean War, we may recall, there was scare buying and hoarding. These manifestations of contagion and excessive behavior disappeared as soon as the fear of large-scale war and of resulting shortages subsided. In 1955, according to the findings of our surveys, favorable attitudes toward the automobile market and the news that more and more people were buying cars helped to transform desires into demand for new cars. There is evidence that people who were usually used-car buyers bought new cars that year and that people traded in their cars earlier than usual. But the process lasted for only a few months, and not

[3] M. Jahoda and P. S. West, *Journal of Social Issues,* 7, p. 136, 1951. See also E. P. Wolf, *Journal of Social Issues, 13,* pp. 7 ff., 1957.

[4] R. K. Merton, *Social Theory and Social Structure,* Free Press, Glencoe, Illinois, 1949, p. 121.

more than one million car buyers were influenced by the contagion or by cumulative attitudes. In 1958 the notion that this was not a good time to buy a car was reinforced by the news that car buying had slumped, in other words, that people all over the country were feeling the same way. Similarly, uneasiness and worry about the employment situation were confirmed and reinforced by the news about rising unemployment. Yet the recession had other causes as well and the buyers' strike was far from general and did not last long.

In contrast to the occasional occurrence of excessive behavior, we found several instances when consumer reactions resulted in small recessions being arrested early and inflationary movement being reversed after a short flurry. After it is fulfilled an expectation may disappear or even generate a reverse expectation. People may expect price increases and after prices have risen they may feel that the factors producing them have exhausted themselves; then different price expectations may arise. Thus inflation following the end of World War II generated expectations of price declines in 1948–1949, and the reduction in prices at that time was accompanied by an improvement in consumer inclinations to buy. The resistance to price increases in 1951 and the optimism that arose in 1954 during a period of relatively low levels of production are, of course, among the most important instances of reversal of sentiment noted during the past ten years. In 1949, 1951, and 1954, consumers were the decisive force in the economy; in 1956–1957, they contributed to not letting the boom get out of hand; and in 1958, they contributed to recovery through maintaining their spending on nondurables.

The Conservative Consumer

We recall two principles of consumer behavior described previously which contradict the notion that consumers are inclined to indulge in excessive behavior. We found, first, that consumers desire and expect only *slightly* more than they have. Even though aspirations rise with accomplishments, consumers do not easily lose sight of reality. We found, second, that consumers constantly need *new* stimulation. Instead of getting more and more optimistic when business improves, relatively soon they find the recurring news about growing production, sales, and profits no news at all. If nothing really new happens they tend to wonder and to become cautious.

A current of information, which overrides personal experiences, as described in Chapter 5, is probably a rare occurrence and requires confirmation and reinforcement over an extended period. At most other times, news and information are evaluated in terms of personal experiences. This is particularly true of news about incipient recessions. When newspapers, radio, and television report on growing unemployment and falling production and make dire predictions, people whose personal situations have not been adversely affected are influenced for a short while only, rather than permanently. Knowledge of unfavorable economic events may even result in seeing one's own situation in a more favorable light and may later become the basis for renewed confidence and optimism. This does not, of course, mean that a much advertised recession cannot become severe. It does mean, however, that suppressing or sugar-coating bad news for fear that it may create mass hysteria—as was advocated early in 1958— is not necessary and may even be dangerous.

Masses of consumers interpret economic news according to deeply ingrained and stereotyped notions which are fundamentally conservative. As we have said, "What goes up must come down" was a common reaction to price increases. "Trees don't grow to heaven" is a popular expression reflecting the opinion that there are limits to ongoing trends. The forces that generate economic trends are not thought to be inexhaustible. The longer a trend continues, the more are people inclined to be on the lookout for reversals.

The persistence and conservatism of mass attitudes are reflected in the widespread and stable conviction that inflation is bad. Many people experienced the best years of their lives during those recent periods in which the cost of living kept going up. Yet these experiences did not dent their attitudes toward inflation. Government deficits are likewise thought to be bad even though most years of deficits were prosperous years. We may also note that many people maintained that rearmament was an unfavorable economic development, often in contradiction to their own personal experiences.

Traumatic experiences—as, for instance, military defeat—may make for a sudden reversal in opinions and behavior. News about economic developments usually brings forth some changes in behavior, but not radical ones. Most commonly, social learning is a slow process. We have seen that inflationary experiences did not destroy the underlying belief that government savings bonds and bank deposits were safe and represented a wise investment. In 1958 many people expressed the opinion that inflation and recession could not go together, contrary to what was happening at that time.

People want to understand the reasons for the developments that take place. They are not satisfied with learning about events; they want to know why a thing happened or why it will happen—be it better or worse business conditions, or higher or lower prices. News which is transmitted without an explanation, or with an explanation that is not understood, usually does not influence people's behavior. Information must fit into people's way of thinking in order to be effective. "Recovery is around the corner" and other examples of moral suasion do not work unless people understand why they should be true.

Most people in the middle-income brackets have an over-all picture of the working of the economy which is concise and meaningful. They do not have sophisticated knowledge of economic relationships. But they usually understand what is going on, which means that they have a feeling about what leads to what. The large majority of people have a prompt answer to such questions as Why do you say so? or Why do you think so? following the expression of opinions about the trend of economic activity or prices. To be sure, their reasons are not given in terms of complex theories. Frequently they give such simple answers as "Everybody's buying," "There is more demand than supply," "The buyers are in control," or "There's lots of money around." Whether or not economic analysts are satisfied with the explanations given is unimportant. The people who say so are satisfied; they feel they know why what they expect to happen will happen. They see a connection between their experience and their expectation.

Obviously, the people's level of information is limited. Frequently misconceptions prevail rather than insight and understanding. This is particularly true of fiscal policy. The function of automatic stabilizers, and even of unemployment insurance benefits in maintaining income, is not understood by very many people. They see taxes as the consequence of government expenditures and frequently as costs of production which are transmitted to consumers in the form of higher prices. It then becomes hard for them to understand that raising the income taxes tends to reduce total demand and therefore represents a weapon against inflation, while lowering them has a stimulating effect on demand. Scholars and publicists have not yet succeeded in clarifying the economic function of government deficits among the masses.

"A little learning is a dangerous thing." No doubt, more knowledge and better knowledge is preferable to incomplete and unsophisticated information. But the little knowledge people have of the workings of the economy does not seem to lead them astray frequently. In one instance, at least, it proved to be most helpful in counteracting the operation of self-fulfilling expectations. If the masses had learned more about inflation, they might have adopted behavior conducive to spurring it on (as, for instance, through converting their bank deposits into goods and securities). Of course, people who try to beat inflation likewise do not act on the basis of a complete understanding of inflationary processes. It certainly does not follow that little knowledge is preferable to really full understanding. The general public's knowledge of inflation—consisting fundamentally of the two notions that inflation is bad and that they do not have it in their power to do anything about it—is incomplete, but not necessarily incorrect.

One further bit of evidence of the basic conservatism of the American consumer is to be found in his budgeting habits. Although only a minority of households operate on the basis of budgets worked out in detail, most consumers have some rudimentary budgetary devices. Past practices and habits—reinforced through satisfactory usage—and the fairly large share of income used to pay fixed obligations help in keeping track of finances. Installment buying, through which contractual obligations are increased and discretion for making less necessary expenditures is reduced, has become a budgetary device contributing to self-regulation. In addition, some household expenditures, especially for food, are budgeted by millions of families, and the planning of other expenditures, as well as careful shopping, are the rule rather than the exception. It seems that for many young housewives shopping has become an avocation in which they have acquired great expertness. It must also be recalled that in spite of all the lure merchandisers exert on the consumer, his will to save has not been impaired.

Consumers are not rational in the sense of operating as calculating profit-seeking mechanisms. In contradicting such old-fashioned notions, we must at the same time warn against accepting the other extreme point of view and believing that consumer behavior is governed by whims and fancies. We have seen that it is far from being the rule that the consumer is impulsive. Impulsive buying does take place, but primarily when it does not really matter because it is a question of choosing among fairly equivalent products, or making small purchases, or occasionally deviating from one's usual careful shopping to enjoy some luxury. That, as has been said, the consumer is lost in the wilderness of commodities is again a half-truth. The consumer does not care exclusively about the functional properties or the "real value" of the goods he buys, but he does not disregard them. He does not know enough about durability and serviceability, and whether or not it is worth paying a little more. Yet interest in such matters has been increasing and the number of followers of testing reports, such as those issued by Consumers Union, has risen greatly during the last few years.

About advertising, consumers usually agree that it presents exaggerated claims. Ads serve to make brand names familiar and have an influence on the choice of brands. (Whether or not they are also influential in increasing consumption is a more controversial matter, although a substantial cut in advertising to which people are accustomed may reduce interest in certain consumer goods; but let us not forget that automobile advertising was not smaller in 1958 than in 1955!) Most consumers trust old, established producers and merchants. Does this mean that they are gullible? Are consumers really manipulated by businessmen? Are they indeed pawns in the hands of unscrupulous hucksters? The belief of many people that most widely advertised products are good can hardly be considered unjustified. It is hardly true that most widely praised gadgets and product improvements are useless or that most clearance sales, discounts, and price cuts are phony. Nevertheless, in a wealthy economy in which consumers have great latitude of action, suggestion plays a role. There is also manipulation. But who manipulates whom? There can be no doubt that the consumer also manipulates the advertiser, the retailer, and the manufacturer, who all carefully watch for any slight change in consumer tastes and buying inclinations. The often-told story of the animal psychologist who spent years training his rats to respond to various stimuli only to realize that ultimately his rats regulated his life contains a grain of truth. Among consumer and advertiser, as in all interpersonal relationships, there is interaction.

In a certain sense it is, of course, incorrect to speak of the American consumer. There is no standard consumer. No two people are exactly alike, and there is hardly any motive or idea which is not held by some people. Yet this is not only a country of diversity, but also one of great uniformity. Generalizations about consumers are faulty, but they may make sense and are necessary. This is true of the conclusion that today's American consumer, though not rational and not fully logical, is conservative and sane. The much maligned, often misunderstood, and unorganized consumer is a stabilizing force in our economy.

Stabilizing the Economy

Of course, the consumer does not act with the intent of stabilizing the economy. He is not aware of his power and does not behave like a boss. The crucial point is that the consumer is not inclined to excessive forms of behavior. Because of those deep-seated and enduring tendencies which we have just described, he usually helps to mitigate inflation and recession and does not contribute to exaggerating boom conditions. Except when provoked strongly and repeatedly he does not suddenly reverse his patterns of spending and does not indulge either in overcaution or in overexuberance.

Nor, of course, does the business community serve typically and usually as a destabilizing force. Our previous description of uniformity in inventory and investment policies of business must not convey the impression that self-fulfilling expectations and errors of optimism or pessimism are the rule in business behavior. But in comparing the influence of big business with that of unorganized consumers, there appear certain crucial differences. Group behavior in our competitive system occasionally leads very many business firms to take similar major decisions at the same time, which may have an unsettling effect on the economy. This is less frequently the case with consumer action. Dynamic forces may more easily sway a small cohesive group than the unorganized masses. The more decision makers there are, the less probable are excessive reactions. The fact that today our economic fate is dependent on millions of people, the consumers, has not added to the instability of our economy. Probably, it has made our economy more stable.

Depression did threaten repeatedly during the postwar period, notably in 1949, 1954, and 1958. But it was the consumer who refused to be frightened in 1949 and kept up his purchases of durable goods. In 1954 again it was the consumer who put an end to downturn and stagnation by sharply stepping up his demand for automobiles. In 1958, finally, the consumer, though postponing his purchases of durables, maintained his rate of spending on nondurables. The belief of consumers that declining prices and large discounts provided favorable conditions for buying was a stabilizing factor in 1949 and 1954, just as the resentment of price increases and the belief that they justified abstention from buying helped to stabilize the economy in 1951, when inflation was the threat. Only in 1955 was there some justification for the view that consumers are not a stabilizing force. While in that year consumer purchases of durables may have increased unduly, in the following two years the consumer refrained from following the lead of business firms in raising his purchases further.

Over the last few decades capitalism has undergone substantial changes in Western Europe. It has tended to develop into a planned economy, or what is called in Europe a mixed economy (public *and* private ownership). The dangers inherent in too much business power were the major reason for the trend toward statism. The extent of business fluctuations as well as profiteering by monopolies, trusts, and cartels, appeared intolerable and was counterbalanced by increasing the power of the state over business. In the United States we have also acquired a growing number of regulatory agencies and a large set of legislative rules but no government control over business policies and no central planning of business investment. How can these divergent developments be explained? One answer, though probably not the whole answer, is found in the "countervailing power" of consumers.[5]

Some writers have thought that what they called "people's capitalism" has already been attained or might be attained if very many American

---

[5] This most suggestive phrase was introduced by J. K. Galbraith in his *American Capitalism* in 1952. Galbraith spoke of the power of organized labor and of the great retail concerns in counteracting the power of manufacturers and specifically denied any such power to the masses of unorganized consumers.

families were to own corporation stock.[6] If the people not only had a share in business but also controlled it, it has been suggested that the dangers emanating from the power of big business would be eliminated. This is an unrealistic argument. Even if the number of stockholders should increase greatly over the next few decades, stock ownership would remain highly concentrated among a minority of stockholders. More important still, numerous small stockholders would not control the corporations. Corporate management is a complicated technical matter which is bound to remain in the hands of professional management, which today is and will remain self-perpetuating.

Nor would the organization of consumers represent a sure way toward more economic democracy. Organizations of stockholders, and organizations of consumers in general, could easily develop into associations ruled by the organizers and exploited by them for their purposes. If masses of consumers were to embark on concerted action, for instance, by planning and timing their purchases together, we would make great strides toward a planned economy and might lose the countercyclical influence of unorganized consumer behavior.

George Romney, president of American Motors Corporation, said in a recent speech, referring to studies by the author of this book, that the "concept of a capitalistic society has been replaced by the concept of a consumeristic society."[7] There is, of course, much truth in the assertion that the consumer not only mitigates excessive economic fluctuations but also exerts a strong influence on business decisions. But is he the "boss of our economy," as Mr. Romney says, whose preferences alone determine what industry can sell and therefore must produce? Obviously, acceptance of a new product by very many consumers—be it the dishwasher or the small car—depends on consumer tastes in addition to the product itself and the methods of marketing. Yet most innovations are initiated by the engineer, the producer, and the marketer, rather than demanded by the consumer. Things which are not known to exist are seldom desired. It is hardly surprising that as late as toward the end of the last war consumers had not thought of television. Studies of people's felt needs and desires did not indicate that a few years later life without television would become inconceivable. The same is true even with respect to needs which, it would seem, should be felt by masses of people. Undoubtedly many people suffered from the heat of the summer in the past—yet they never even dreamt of air conditioning. Even after air conditioning was introduced in public buildings, there was no clamor for room air conditioning. The masses of consumers do not have much imagination—not even in demand-

[6] This was argued, for instance, in several releases issued by the Advertising Council.

[7] Speech before the annual meeting of the American Automobile Association, Chicago, Sept. 17, 1958.

ing new types of television programs—and cannot take over the function of product planning.

Consumer needs as developed in response to technological innovations and to marketing practices by business determine, of course, which kinds of goods are chosen to represent the desired improvement in the standard of living. As long as the needs are not exhausted because of failure and frustration, the economy will grow in the direction approved by the consumers. True, this direction and consumers' felt needs might not be the socially desirable ones. (Consumers might, for instance, choose larger and fancier cars rather than more books.) But this is a consideration, though of great importance in any assessment of American civilization, which transcends the scope of this book. Suffice it to say that the argument deploring the direction in which consumer influence has led this country may have some justification, though it is far too early to make a definite judgment. For social learning is possible and may bring forth more desirable choices among consumer needs. Social learning which would result in consumers making better use of their power of stabilizing the economy is likewise conceivable.

Instead of arguing that there is too much manipulation of consumers, a good case might be made for the thesis that they are not manipulated enough in the sense of not being helped to acquire sufficient information and knowledge. No doubt progress has been made in the fight against the instability of our economy, but undoubtedly again much further progress is needed if we are to accelerate improvement in the standard of living of the masses and avoid occasional substantial losses in production as well as human suffering through widespread unemployment. We have pointed to certain tendencies in consumer behavior which counteract instability in the economy. To attempt to influence consumers so that they should better understand their function and make better use of their power is a task for leaders of public opinion. Little experience exists as yet in this respect. But we need not be afraid of more and better knowledge. Much more information and many more statistical data about the economy are available today than twenty or even ten years ago. Yet additional information is still needed and must be publicized in a form understood, not only by experts and business leaders, but by millions of consumers as well.

President Eisenhower said in his television address to the American people on May 21, 1958: "In a free economy, people do not always buy just because they have money. Theirs is the sovereign right of choice. One of the hopeful developments of recent years is that new knowledge is rapidly being accumulated about the aspirations and wants and motivations of our people." [8]

[8] Quoted from *The New York Times*, May 22, 1958.

Consumer expectations and motivations are no longer shrouded in uncertainty. Though we shall have to improve our information about consumers further, already today changes in their attitudes can be measured in a fairly reliable manner. Even incipient tendencies may be recognized and may serve as clues for appropriate countermeasures by government and business. But we should not rely on such action alone. The consumers themselves, by understanding what is happening and what they are doing, provide the best hope for a continuous growth of the economy, not interrupted by severe recessions. A better understanding of economic processes by consumers would promote more farsighted behavior and represents therefore an important goal for the near future.

APPENDIX

Survey Research

Most of the data presented in this book have been collected through survey research. Interviews with representative samples of the population constitute the principal methodological tool of psychological economics. It is therefore necessary to describe the basic principles that govern data collection through surveys.

Sociologists, psychologists, economists, and mathematical statisticians are among the scholars who have developed survey methodology over the past twenty years. Surveys serve the purpose of accumulating knowledge in many areas not connected with economic processes. Although much of what will be said in this chapter is applicable to all kinds of surveys, our discussion will concentrate on the clarification of the purposes and methods of economic surveys.[1]

The Function of Surveys

Economic research is either based on records or derived from personal contact with decision makers. *Records* are prepared for practical or legal purposes. For these reasons corporations, for instance, prepare balance sheets and profit and loss accounts, and firms as well as individuals file tax returns. Business firms, trade organizations, and governmental agencies also prepare collections and analyses of records in order to conduct their business rather than for the sake of obtaining scientific insights. Thus each life insurance company summarizes the data on its own business, and associations of life insurance firms provide assistance to individual companies by preparing statistics on the total amount of premiums paid in the country. Since imports are an important source of government revenue and information on imports is useful for trade, an agency of the Federal government collects and analyzes data on foreign trade. Sometimes trade associations and government agencies organize their records according to theoretical principles and publish them in a form suitable to convey an understanding of developments. The most important example of a systematic

[1] For a more detailed discussion of the methods of the surveys utilized in this book see the articles "The Sample Survey" by A. Campbell and G. Katona and "Methods of the Surveys of Consumer Finances," as well as Chapter 15 of G. Katona, *Psychological Analysis of Economic Behavior*. On sampling, see L. Kish, "Selection of the Sample," and on interviewing R. L. Kahn and C. F. Cannell, *Dynamics of Interviewing*.

organization of economic data is the work carried out in the Department of Commerce in estimating the size of Gross National Product, national income, and many other aggregate measures of economic activity. This work provides source material for scientific research, which is then carried forward by economists in government, private business, and universities, who analyze the relationships among the variables recorded so as to test hypotheses and theories about causes and effects.

Not everything that is relevant is recorded, however, and much information is not recorded in the way it is needed. In order to determine how prices have changed, for instance, it is not enough to have access to files and archives. Enumerators of the Bureau of Labor Statistics visit a sample of retail stores and determine there the prices of a sample of commodities in order to compute the cost-of-living index. *Personal contact* with decision makers—government officials, businessmen, as well as consumers—represents the method of obtaining a variety of data not available from records. The decennial census provides some basic information through personal contact with all households in the country. But complete enumeration is an impractical and inefficient method in many instances. Today the Bureau of Census determines the number of employed and unemployed people through sample interview surveys, and other government agencies, private business firms, and independent research groups proceed in the same way both for practical purposes and for the sake of enriching economic knowledge.

Surveys collect data which are not otherwise available in order to answer the questions How many? Who? and Why? We may illustrate the function of surveys, first, with a reference to an industry which is rightly proud of the extensive archives it keeps. From its records the life insurance industry can determine the total amount of life insurance in force in the country and the total amounts of life insurance premiums paid. But it cannot find out how many Americans carry life insurance. There are people with several policies—some have more than ten—contracted with different companies. Collating the records to avoid duplications is impracticable because in view of the very substantial residential mobility of the American population the same person may be recorded at several different addresses. (The same is true of bank deposits or United States government savings bonds.) Therefore a few years ago the Institute of Life Insurance asked the Survey Research Center to find out the proportion of insured people in the entire population as well as in significant subgroups—such as income and age groups—through interviewing a representative sample of the American people.

The answer to the question How many? represents the starting point for more significant inquiries. What is the relation between income and life insurance carried? This question again cannot be answered from records, because even people with large insurance policies do not communicate changes in their income to their company. Needless to say, it is most important, especially in times of inflation, to find out how amounts spent on life insurance kept pace with increases in income. Surveys yielded data about the proportion of income used for premium payments by different income, age, and occupational groups, as well as by urban or rural families. The question about who holds different attitudes was also answered according to religious preferences or political affiliations. By thus answering the question Who?—which economic or demographic groups carry larger or smaller amounts of life insurance, for instance— we contribute to answering the question Why? But this approach to finding reasons for economic behavior does not suffice because even in demographically and financially homogeneous groups there are great variations in ownership of life insurance (as well as of other assets). Sociopsychological variables must also be considered and can be studied through survey research. The same survey in which financial data (income, amount of life insurance owned and purchased, etc.) and demographic data (age, education, etc.) are determined may serve to measure people's opinions, attitudes, and expectations. In Chapter 8 it was shown how opinions about the function of life insurance served to explain differences in life insurance ownership and thus contributed to answering the question Why?

In place of life insurance we could have taken any number of other examples to illustrate the function of survey research. Let us look at just one further example from a fairly new industry. The commercial aviation carriers and the government supervisory agencies have, of course, data on plane tickets purchased, and records enable them to prepare tabulations about passenger miles flown, but not to answer any of the following questions: How many Americans fly frequently (say, more than ten or twenty times a year), how many rarely, and how many have never flown in a plane? How greatly has the number of people traveling by plane increased during the past few years? What is the relation of business to nonbusiness travel by plane? How are air travelers distributed on the income and on the age scale? Data yielding information on these and many further questions were collected through sample interview surveys conducted by the Survey Research Center and have contributed to answering the question Why do some people fly often, some rarely, and others never? Further information relevant to this question, of particular importance for the future of the airplane industry in the jet age, was obtained by studying such psychological variables as anxiety about flying and desire for or enjoyment of speed in relation to the frequency of air travel.[2]

Having thus described the function of surveys, we may generalize as follows: The primary purpose of surveys is to obtain information on trends over time and on functional relationships among variables. This statement has, first, a negative implication: determination of a frequency or a position as it prevails at a given time is not the major purpose for which surveys should be employed. To find out how many people are optimistic at a given time or how many expect prices to go up may be of journalistic value since it makes for interesting reading, but such findings do not constitute major goals of survey research and are subject to large errors. By formulating the questions about optimism or price expectations in different ways, it is possible to change the absolute frequency obtained. But by using the same wording of a question in successive surveys, each time with a different representative sample, time series can be constructed, which yield not only important insights into economic behavior but

[2] J. B. Lansing, *The Travel Market.*

are also subject to much smaller errors. Reporting errors tend to be constant if well-trained interviewers ask the same question a few months apart, and therefore do not influence the comparisons. Relations between variables—say, between income and liquid-asset holdings, to mention two financial variables, or between age and installment debt, or between optimism and purchases of durables, to mention demographic and psychological variables—are likewise subject to smaller reporting errors than absolute measurements and are of crucial significance for science. Absolute measurements represent at best the starting point for studies. This is true both of measurements which are quite reliable, as for instance of the number of automobile owners and purchasers in a given year, and of those which are subject to fairly large errors, as for instance the mean amount of liquid assets held per family at a given time.

On the Methodology of Economic Surveys

Reporting errors represent the most difficult problems of survey research. Other errors exist, but are less damaging. Nonresponse errors, due to the fact that not everyone falling in a representative sample can be interviewed, are often small (less than 10 per cent of the sample), and sampling errors are measurable. Of course, nonresponse errors are small only if well-trained interviewers make repeated personal calls, and sampling errors are measurable only if probability sampling is used to draw a representative sample.[3] Sampling errors arise whenever a sample is used rather than a complete enumeration. Sample surveys therefore provide approximate data rather than exact measurements. Since the size of the sampling errors can be calculated in advance for different sample sizes, the researcher is in a position to decide before undertaking a study whether or not he should resort to sampling and how large a sample he should use.

The larger the sample, the smaller the sampling error, but the increase in reliability resulting even from doubling the sample size—by making, say, 4,000 rather than 2,000 interviews—is sometimes of little relevance for the problem studied. On the other hand, the smaller the sample the easier it is to make sure that well-trained interviewers use identical methods and thus reduce the reporting errors. (In addition, of course, the smaller the sample the smaller the cost of a survey.) Complete enumeration becomes an uncontrollable task as soon as anything beyond simple factual information is needed and is subject to large errors even in that case. Therefore, recently the Census Bureau used sample surveys to check up on and to correct certain data obtained in the decennial census. (This was done through a survey operation called the "quality check.")

If in successive surveys such variables are measured which are widely represented in the universe, a sample size may be sufficient which appears to laymen surprisingly small. The expression "widely represented in the universe" applies,

[3] This is done in all surveys conducted by the Survey Research Center, while some widely reported surveys make use of less expensive short cuts. A sample is a probability sample if every unit in the population to be studied has a known chance of being selected for the sample.

for instance, to purchases of durable goods or to installment buying in which substantial proportions of all population groups participate but not, for example, to purchases of common stock which are restricted to less than 5 per cent of the population in a year and mainly to high-income people.[4]

In order to determine changes in the degree of optimism of the American population the Survey Research Center sometimes restricted its samples to 1,300 families in the nation and could nevertheless obtain a satisfactory answer to the crucial question Was there an improvement or deterioration in sentiment as compared to three or six months earlier? Even though the answer was not considered to be in the affirmative unless the differences obtained between two successive small surveys were considerably above the levels required for statistical significance, it was possible to arrive at significant economic insights.

The principal drawback of such small samples lies in the difficulty of studying subgroups of the sample. If in addition to attitudes and purchases of durables by all families one wishes to study those of high- and low-income families, or even of urban and rural high-income families, one needs large samples; otherwise one "runs out of cases," as the expression goes. Two successive small samples may yield significant data for nationwide comparisons, but not for studies restricted to parts of the samples.

Obviously, scientific reports must contain information on the size of sampling errors and thereby on the statistical significance of the findings. In this book this information has been omitted because technical publications re-referred to in footnotes contain it and because our primary concern is with differences far beyond the significance level. Detailed tables on sampling errors for Survey Research Center surveys have been published in several articles and monographs.[5]

In a number of instances, however, we have presented information on relationships based on fairly small subgroups of the population. We may refer, for instance, to the data in Chapter 8 on the relation of liquid-asset holdings to subsequent discretionary saving. In such instances the sampling errors attached to the finding of a survey are of crucial importance, except when several independent observations are available to test the relationship. The studies of liquid-asset holdings and saving, as we said, were made in 1948, again in 1955, 1956, and 1957, each time with independent measurements and in several income groups. Even if the findings obtained each year were not statistically significant (i.e., it could not be ruled out that the relationship shown was due to chance), the probability that the same finding would be obtained several times in succession is very small.

In order to obtain comparable data from each member of a sample, it is necessary to prepare a questionnaire. Interviewers are not permitted to change

[4] Studies of infrequent transactions carried out primarily by high-income families are difficult, although it is sometimes possible to draw special samples.

[5] For sampling errors in the Surveys of Consumer Finances, see the articles on Methods (*Federal Reserve Bulletin,* July, 1950) and in the *Federal Reserve Bulletin* of September, 1958. For sampling errors in the Periodic Surveys, see the monographs by G. Katona and E. Mueller, *Consumer Attitudes and Demand* and *Consumer Expectations.*

sequence or wording of the questions (nor, of course, do they have any latitude in selecting respondents). It does not follow, however, that only simple and direct questions may be used or that interviewing is a simple task. For studies in economic psychology it is necessary to use well-selected and well-trained interviewers who know how to establish rapport with all kinds of respondents, know how to induce them to talk freely, and can use "open-ended" questions as well. The free answers given by the respondents to these questions are taken down as nearly verbatim as possible and are quantified later through a process of content analysis or coding. The most important open-ended questions used in the studies described in this book are the simple nondirective probes Why do you say so?, or What do you have in mind?, or Tell me more about it.

How questions should be formulated and how interviewers may be trained and supervised are fairly complicated matters discussed in technical publications. Only a few further remarks are necessary to convey an understanding of the methodology of the surveys utilized in this book. The assertion frequently made, that it is not permissible to use questions which appear biased or suggestive, is incorrect. Such questions are permissible and often most useful, provided they are not biased in relation to their objective and especially if used to measure trends over time rather than to obtain absolute measurements. (Thus, for instance, we made use of the suggestive question Have you read or heard of any unfavorable news?) On the other hand, "iffy" questions should not be asked. If a consideration has never occurred to a person and if it is foreign to his way of thinking, one does not gain anything, and may be misled, by ascertaining his reactions to that consideration. To illustrate: answers to a question inquiring about probable behavior if savings banks were to pay 10 per cent interest on deposits would be meaningless. Or: in an inflationary situation, when nobody expects price reductions, it is worse than useless to inquire about probable reactions to substantial price reductions. If the answers to such questions are based on unsupported guesses and hunches, even changes in the answers obtained in successive surveys may be misleading. Furthermore, survey questions should not imply that future circumstances and reactions are certain. One should not exclude the possibility of uncertainty and of conditional answers and should not insist on definite commitments. Only under certain, fairly rare conditions may one insist that a respondent, even though he is unwilling, must make up his mind and must choose between the alternatives which the researcher presents to him; otherwise one may falsify findings. Some people are too accommodating and say what they think the researcher wants them to say.

A most useful feature of survey methodology consists of the "funnel arrangement" of questions. One starts out with a general question to which a fairly large proportion of the sample is expected to be able to answer, rather than with specific questions, and then narrows down the scope of questioning. For example, respondents are asked to tell why in their opinion people in general save, before they are asked whether they themselves save for retirement. Or, the Survey Research Center does not ask simply about intentions to buy durable goods during the next few months, even though many more expressed buying intentions are fulfilled during the first few months after the interview than later. The questioning begins with ascertaining desires, then turns to intentions to buy during the next year—the year is an accounting concept in the minds of most people—and ends with a question about the probable timing of the contemplated purchases. From the answers to the last question the analyst may prepare a tabulation of buying intentions for the next six or three months.

By utilizing the best available survey methodology—carefully selected, trained, and supervised interviewers using questionnaires in which sequence, form, and wording of the questions is appropriate and the questions are supplemented by probes which help to convey the respondents' thoughts—it is possible to minimize but not to eliminate reporting errors. Misunderstandings by respondents or by interviewers, errors due to lack of interest or information, overstatements due to pride, understatements due to modesty, or incorrect answers due to concealment may occur in the best-conducted surveys (though, probably, more frequently in collecting such financial data as the amount of savings than in determining attitudes and expectations). As we said before, our expectation is that the mistakes due to reporting errors will remain constant when successive representative samples are asked the same questions and therefore will not influence our findings about changes over time.

Science is quantitative and the major purpose of surveys consists in obtaining quantitative data. Yet qualitative information may likewise be most useful; it has a place even beyond the one frequently mentioned in the literature, namely, in the initial phase of a study when qualitative data help in formulating hypotheses. Qualitative studies may follow the quantitative studies so as to clarify and illustrate broad categories the frequency of which has been established. How people talk about problems and what shades of opinion are included in a category may be found out by letting people explain their points of view and recording the answers received. In publishing results, reproducing the words respondents used in interviews, rather than restricting the publication to the quantified categories developed by the researcher, often helps in conveying an understanding of research findings. The explanations people give also help in avoiding misclassifications when opinions and attitudes are quantified.

Reinterviewing the same respondents or interviewing the same sample several times (panel studies) represent most useful methods for specific purposes, among which the study of change and of changers is paramount. But successive interviews with different samples, each of which is representative of the same universe, are necessary for other purposes. This is true because reinterviews and panels are necessarily deficient in newly formed families and movers and because some panel losses as well as some panel bias cannot be avoided.[6] On the other hand, the important tasks of validating survey data and of exploring the relation of verbal expressions to action can often be best carried out through repeated interviews with the same respondents.

Mail interviews are, of course, much less expensive than personal interviews. They have disadvantages, however, because (1) the proportion of nonresponse

[6] See G. Katona, "Federal Reserve Committee Reports," and M. G. Sobol, "Panel Losses and Panel Bias." The latter study contains data about the extent of panel losses and panel bias in the Survey Research Center's 1954–1957 panel, from which numerous data presented in this book have been taken.

to mail questionnaires is usually high and it is not known how those who respond and those who do not differ from each other; (2) mail questionnaires must make use of relatively simple, fairly short, and not too indiscreet questionnaires (mostly direct questions or multiple choice questions); and (3) there is no assurance that the respondents understand the written questions or that the analysts understand their replies.

This is not the place to describe the great variety of methods through which sample surveys may be made efficient tools for studying different situations and transactions and even experimenting with them. Suffice it to say that there is a vast difference between nose-counting polls and surveys permitting the analysis of relations among different variables. Experiments, the principal method of natural science, involve manipulation of variables, which is hardly possible with respect to major aspects of consumer behavior. Yet a principal purpose of manipulation can be approximated in survey research through isolating groups of people subject to different developments and observing their behavior under different conditions.

Difficulties in Measurement

It has been stated in Chapter 6 that it is difficult to devise a satisfactory test for determining the influence of attitudes on the actions of *individuals*. These are the major reasons which make for difficulties:

1. Interpersonal comparisons are unreliable. When A and B both give the same answer to the same question, we are not justified in assuming that they feel and think alike. Suppose A and B are classified as optimistic and C as pessimistic. Because of personality or other differences resulting in a different usage of the same or similar words, it is possible that the true attitudes of A and C may actually be more alike than those of A and B. Depth interviews—not carried out in our studies—might conceivably help in improving interpersonal comparisons, but even depth interviews would hardly solve the problem. Since we shall necessarily compare small subgroups of a sample in testing the effect of different attitudes on individual behavior, the result of the test will be adversely affected by erroneous classifications. In aggregative tests, however, when the distributions of answers given by large representative samples at two points of time are compared, erroneous classifications of some individual attitudes may cancel out and will be much less damaging.

2. Attitudes do not influence every type of action all the time. At certain times it is ability to buy which is relevant. Even when attitudes change independently from changes in income, certain forms of action are habitual and are not influenced by attitudes. Among purchases of durable goods, there are many which are necessary or habitual and are not subject to genuine decision making. To mention just two simple examples again: if my car, used for commuting to work, breaks down I may buy a new car even if I am pessimistic; or if I habitually trade in my car every two or three years, I may continue to do so despite my pessimism. Numerous purchases of such types contribute, of course, to the fact that several million new cars are sold even in years of

recession. In comparing the purchases of two small groups of individuals, the occurrence of necessary or habitual purchases may mask the differences in the purchase rates of optimistic and pessimistic people. In comparing differences in the purchases of all people over two successive periods, it becomes much easier to discover marginal effects superimposed, by virtue of different attitudes, on the fairly steady rate of necessary and habitual purchases.

3. We turn from technical difficulties, which arise mainly from the small size of the samples used, to problems of timing the successive measurements of attitudes and of expenditures. If today the proportion of optimists is found to be significantly higher than three months ago when it was higher than six months earlier, it is probable, as we said before, that three months from now the proportion will be higher still. We expect this to happen, in the absence of substantial new developments, because of the current of opinion described in Chapter 5 and because of feedback effects: news about the increased rate of purchases, itself, may influence the attitudes. Therefore some individuals who today qualify as pessimists may have become optimists by the time we determine their purchases. Such changes would adversely affect tests of the predictive value of attitudes for individual behavior.

4. Some optimists whose subsequent purchases we assume will be high may have been optimistic for some time before they were interviewed and may have bought durable goods shortly before the measurement of their attitudes. Such purchases will have been made by fewer of those people who were pessimistic when interviewed. Optimism remains a predisposition to action for the first group; but, having made their purchases in the period before the survey, they may not act according to their predisposition in the next period. Since there are many more people who buy a car every two or three years than there are who buy one every year, there exists what is technically called a negative serial correlation in the data on annual expenditures on automobiles, which impairs the chances of reliable findings from a comparison of the subsequent behavior of optimists and pessimists.

5. There are many specific factors, peculiar to an individual's situation, which may make a difference when the purchases of optimists are compared with those of pessimists. Personality traits, illness or good health, family situation, age, rural versus urban residence, home ownership, inventories and their condition—these are some of the factors which do not vary much in the aggregate when two short, successive periods are compared but do vary substantially from one person to another. Even aggregate income varies much less from quarter to quarter or year to year than income varies from individual to individual. It is not practicable to exclude the effect of all such variables. Yet even if all these variables were measured with very large samples and a multivariate analysis were carried out, we would not have solved our problem completely. Consider the variable "age." Age influences purchases as well as attitudes. Younger heads of families tend to buy more durables than older heads of families; they also tend to be more optimistic than older people. The same is true of income: the higher the income, the greater the purchases, and also the more optimistic the attitudes. By attributing all the differences in

purchases between young and old to age and between high- and middle-income groups to income, we make it hard for attitude effects to show. Similarly, it would of course not be permissible to attribute the differences in purchases to attitudes and then to study the additional effects of age and income. These considerations imply, then, that a multivariate analysis, designed to show effects of attitudes beyond the effects of all other variables, represents a very severe test.

In summary: Measurement of the effect of attitudes on purchases of individuals requires the exclusion of the effects of a great number of other variables which likewise influence purchases. Many specific factors peculiar to the individual's situation cancel out in the aggregate and do not influence the aggregative test. But in studying the difference in the purchase rate of relatively small groups of individuals, there may easily be so much "interference" or "noise" caused by nuisance variables that the results may not be conclusive.

Therefore the survey methods and statistical techniques presently in use cannot be expected to yield large differences in the purchases of optimists and of pessimists. Some differences in the assumed direction should show up. But even if these differences were small, we should have no reason to doubt the validity of aggregative tests which have been made, over a too short period to be sure, and reported in Chapter 3. Tests of individual behavior may supplement the aggregate tests but cannot supplant them.

On the Survey Research Center

Most of the data presented in this book have been collected by the Survey Research Center of the University of Michigan, with which the author has been associated since its establishment. The Survey Research Center was organized in 1946 by a group of social scientists who conducted surveys for the Federal government during World War II at the Division of Program Surveys of the Department of Agriculture under the direction of Rensis Likert. The center is active in several areas other than the study of economic behavior and has sampling and field sections, with a nationwide interviewing staff, which have contributed to the development of sampling and interviewing methods. In addition to training survey specialists, the center conducts surveys designed to study scientific objectives as envisaged by its staff (and financed primarily by foundations). The center also carries out contract research for private business organizations and the Federal government. Close contact with problems confronting government agencies and business organizations is most helpful for many scholarly endeavors. Practical problems of the moment are sometimes best solved through studies of fundamental nature, and basic research needs to be tested through applying its results to actual problems of the day. Contract research by the Survey Research Center is restricted to problems of general interest; the results of all studies undertaken must be publishable rather than confidential in nature. Adhering to this principle the Survey Research Center does not conduct surveys the sole purpose of which is to serve the competitive advantage of the sponsor. Thereby the usual surveys conducted by market research, advertising research, and media research organizations are excluded from the center's program.[7]

The most extensive series of economic surveys conducted by the Survey Research Center are the Surveys of Consumer Finances, made from 1946 to 1959 in cooperation with the Federal Reserve Board and reported in the *Federal Reserve Bulletin*. The largest part of these surveys is devoted to the measurement of the distribution of incomes, assets, debts, and purchases. While these measurements need not be made more often than once a year, measurements of economic attitudes are needed more frequently. The latter are carried out through the Periodic Surveys, which have been conducted by the center at least twice a year since 1951. The Periodic Surveys, which are privately financed, contain many more questions on attitudes and expectations than the Federal Reserve—sponsored surveys, but their samples are smaller.[8] The findings of the Periodic Surveys are published in mimeographed reports and, later in scholarly articles and monographs; brief releases to the press are also issued immediately following the analysis of survey findings. Attitudinal data relevant for business fluctuations and published in this book without reference to previous publications are taken from the Periodic Surveys.

From 1954 to 1957 the center conducted an extensive panel study—five waves of interviews with the same representative urban sample—thanks to a grant received from the Ford Foundation. Occasionally the center also conducts special surveys on specific problems of economic behavior, sponsored by business corporations. In addition to consumer surveys, in which business owners and managers are represented as part of the general public and are interviewed on consumer problems, the center has conducted a limited number of business surveys which have likewise yielded findings utilized in this book.[9]

The surveys mentioned here are nationwide. The universe from which a stratified representative sample is drawn by probability methods consists of all private households in the continental United States. An exception was the 1954–1957 panel study which was restricted to the urban population, that is, to families living in towns and cities with at least 2,500 population, including suburban districts surrounding the cities. The expression "private households" means that the institutional population, members of the Armed Forces, and

[7] See the Report of the Institute for Social Research for 1946 to 1956, of which the Survey Research Center is a part.

[8] The sample size of each Survey of Consumer Finances is approximately 3,000 spending units, that of each Periodic Survey 1,300 to 1,700 families. In the Survey of Consumer Finances the head of each spending unit is designated as respondent; in the Periodic Surveys husband and wife are interviewed alternately in complete families. For each of these successive surveys a different representative sample is drawn (but the Surveys of Consumer Finances occasionally contained some reinterviews).

[9] Business surveys conducted by other organizations—by the SEC and the Commerce Department, the Economic Department of McGraw-Hill, Dun & Bradstreet, National Industrial Conference Board, and in Germany by IFO—have also been mentioned in this book. For a good discussion of business surveys the reader may be referred to a volume published by the Social Science Research Council on *Expectations, Uncertainty, and Business Behavior*, edited by M. J. Bowman.

people permanently living in hotels and large boarding houses are excluded. Occasionally the Survey Research Center conducts economic surveys with samples drawn from more restricted universes. To study bank deposits, for instance, a representative sample of depositors was drawn, or to study unemployment in Detroit in 1958 a representative sample of blue-collar workers in that city was interviewed.

Psychological analysis of consumer and business behavior, through quantitative measurement of the relation of motives, attitudes, and expectations to spending and saving, is a fairly new development. Like most new endeavors it has had its years of struggle characterized less by opposition than by indifference. Although some financial support for economic-psychological surveys could be obtained at a very early stage from governmental agencies and foundations, and somewhat later from some forward-looking large business organizations as well, for several years economic-psychological findings remained unnoticed by most economists and psychologists as well as by policy makers. Thus, as cited in Chapter 3, very little attention was given to findings on cyclical developments during the first few years after World War II. Many economists abstained from reading what they considered psychology, and psychologists showed no interest at all in allegedly economic publications. During a somewhat later stage there was review and criticism—both constructive critique and disparaging attacks—as well as uncritical acceptance. The latter is, of course, most dangerous. When tentative findings about what has happened under certain conditions are treated as laws of human nature or when business analysts consider a few survey questions on expectations and buying intentions as a sure method for forecasting economic trends, the understanding of economic processes and the progress of research are hampered rather than facilitated.

For many years the psychological economists at the Survey Research Center were quite lonely. Although some of their survey questions—as, for instance, those about price expectations—were occasionally inserted in surveys conducted by others, no organization shared with the center the task of conducting *continuing* research on the psychological aspects of economic behavior. In the fifties the situation improved, although both in the United States and in a number of foreign countries (e.g., in Great Britain) economic surveys were more concerned with consumer finances (income, assets, debts, purchases) than with attitudes and expectations. More recently the Survey Research Center was in a position to welcome other organizations which followed it in collecting data on how consumer expectations and buying intentions changed over time.[10] Again in line with the process that often characterizes the spread

[10] Questionnaires mailed to volunteering subscribers of the *Consumer Reports* magazine were broadened and analyzed by the National Bureau of Economic Research in 1957 and 1958 (see the article by Juster). Sindlinger and Co. began with a series of telephone interviews, sponsored by *Newsweek* magazine, with the cooperation of the National Industrial Conference Board in 1958 (see the article by Cohen and Gainsbrugh). Early in 1959 the U.S. Bureau of the Census inserted a few questions about intentions to buy consumer durables into some of its regular quarterly surveys, the main purpose of which is to measure the extent of employment and unemployment; the results have not yet been published.

and acceptance of innovations, the newcomers turned to simplified methods in their attempt to collect data of practical usefulness rather than enlarging and deepening the scope of research. Nevertheless, mail surveys, telephone interviews, and the inclusion of questions about buying intentions in a large survey operation concerned with factual enumeration, as published or introduced in 1958–1959, will all contribute to progress both as they will be successful and as they will yield predictions which are not fully confirmed by later developments.

One warning, however, may not be out of place: even though none of the organizations which have recently begun conducting consumer surveys intends them to do so, some of the readers of their findings may think that the time has come when simple mechanical devices will solve the problem of forecasting consumer purchases or even economic trends. But electronic computers into which the answers to a few simple survey questions are fed will not take over the task of forecasting. In order to understand what is going on and thereby improve our ability to predict, the results of a variety of approaches must be evaluated. Progress in this task requires further innovation and pioneering in new directions.

M. R.

Consumer research, the methods of which have been described in this chapter, must be distinguished from market research, both in its traditional aspects and its newer developments which have received some publicity in recent years under the name of motivation research, or M. R. A brief discussion of the research methods used by industry and the advertising community centered in Madison Avenue is necessary because their methods differ from those used in our studies of motives, described in Chapter 8; and because they have brought forth conclusions at variance with the implications of our studies about the intelligence of consumers and the autonomy of consumer behavior, which have been summarized in Chapter 14.

Consumer studies might be divided three ways: They may deal, first, with variations in the rate of spending and saving as they influence the entire economy, its growth or stagnation as well as cyclical fluctuations. Second, they may concern themselves with fluctuations in purchases of different kinds of goods as, for instance, automobiles, or clothing, or food. Finally, fluctuations in the purchases of individual goods or brands give rise to problems which are studied primarily by market research for the purpose of increasing a particular firm's share in the market. Our studies concern mainly the first area—although studies of the second area supplement some aspects of our discussion—and neglect the third area.[11] Yet we should not forget that consumer discretion and influence, which, as we have shown, grew substantially over the last few decades in the first area, were always pronounced in choosing between individual products and brands.

[11] For a systematic discussion of the different aspects of research on consumer behavior, including market research, and an annotated bibliography of recent empirical studies, see J. N. Morgan, "A Review of Recent Research on Consumer Behavior."

During the past few years traditional market research and advertising research have undergone great changes. A school of researchers became active, opposed to what they derisively called nose-counting studies—for instance, finding out the proportion of young and old among the buyers of various brands—and emphasizing the study of hidden and elusive motives. As these studies became familiar several incorrect impressions became widespread, namely, that the adherents of the new school of research originated studies of motivation among consumers, that they discovered the indirect approaches to such studies, and that the direct question Why? was always inadequate to reveal motives. As for this last, we can but repeat that for the purpose of studying cyclical fluctuations by analyzing variations in the rate of spending on durable goods of *all* consumers, the judicious use of the question Why? yielded valuable clues to motivational forces. The correlation approach—finding out with what an increase or decrease in the rate of spending was associated—was of particular importance. Studies of deep-seated and elusive motives could hardly have served our needs. It is easy to see that in a study of short-run change in sentiment among consumers, attitudes and motives ultimately explainable by sexual matters and differences in upbringing (having had stern or permissive parents, for instance) would be of little importance.

For the purpose, however, of studying decisions of consumers about what specific products to purchase, M. R. workers made great progress in adopting the techniques developed by experimental and clinical psychologists. At the outset, unfortunately, they made use of psychological tests by almost completely ignoring their quantitative nature. More recently, however, the joint utilization of "fantasy questions" and of quantitative techniques has become more common.

Let us preface our discussion of their methods by saying that we are in complete agreement with certain basic statements of M. R. workers: First, buying decisions are influenced by emotional needs of the person as well as by the image he has of a product. Second, people's images of products and brands, as well as of institutions and stores, reflect affective components in addition to, and sometimes even without regard to, cognitive notions. Third, "fantasy questions" probing about what might be are useful and sometimes necessary. Finally, there is more in communication than rational thought.

It does not follow from these statements that the basic questions of market research, Why do people buy a given product? and What kind of person is the buyer of a brand? are adequately answered by the methods frequently used by M. R. Most commonly very small samples, chosen for convenience and accessibility, rather than as a representative sample of the population, are subjected to lengthy intensive and indirect questioning. Use is made of such psychological techniques as the sentence completion test and of various story and picture tests (response to pictures shown, based partly on the well-known TAT tests of clinical psychology) with an interpretation of answers which is strongly influenced by psychoanalytic theory. When used by able research workers, such methods can yield hypotheses which are useful to industry, even though they must be tested later through quantitative research. The methods may also be of importance for a study of economic motives beyond the field of market research, and indeed should sometimes be used.

To illustrate how indirect psychological tests may be used in quantitative research, beyond the area of brand preferences, a few examples taken from Survey Research Center studies may be cited. In each case, a randomly selected large representative sample of the population was contacted and the results were quantified. In a survey of mental health problems, several TAT-type picture cards (showing, for instance, two young men or two young women in serious discussion) were presented to the respondents. Answers to such questions as Who are these people? or What are they talking about? were quantified, and differences in response permitted the ranking of respondents on scales reflecting achievement orientation and its absence, or need for affiliation and its absence. In economic studies, motives for such activities as traveling by plane or long-distance telephoning (placing social rather than business or emergency calls) were clarified by the use of sentence completion tests and pictures. The elusive variable of fear or anxiety in connection with flying, or the attraction of speed in connection with jets, could be studied by such methods. In the case of the study of long-distance telephoning, many people who had little to say in answer to a variety of direct questions were able, through commenting on a very short story (for instance, about a woman who frequently calls her friends in distant cities), to reveal their attitudes toward long-distance telephoning and their motives for making or refraining from making them.

In studies of fluctuations in purchases of automobiles, household appliances, and saving, relatively little progress has been achieved through the use of indirect techniques. Even differences between more consumption-oriented and more frugal personality types could be established by simpler methods. But it is quite probable that in the not-too-distant future the use of indirect methods will contribute to our understanding of consumer behavior. Studies of suburbia and of the impact of communication on consumers should likewise profit from the use of new methods.

Recently the general public became widely acquainted with M. R., partly through Vance Packard's best-selling book *The Hidden Persuaders*, which aroused some hardly justified misgivings and anxieties.[12] Packard made many people believe (1) that motivation researchers do discover people's hidden fears and desires and play upon them for business purposes, and (2) that it is immoral for business firms to appeal to people's unconscious desires rather than to convince them on the basis of quality and function of their products. Little need be said about the second argument—except that appealing to not fully conscious desires is done usually when from a social point of view it does not matter much, for the competing products differ very little, if at all,

---

[12] V. Packard, *The Hidden Persuaders*. In summarizing Packard's major arguments, we follow the discussion by Harry Henry in his book *Motivation Research*, especially p. 226. A well-balanced discussion of motivation research and its psychological foundations may be found in the book, *Motivation and Market Behavior*, edited by R. Ferber and H. G. Wales.

in quality—because the first argument is unacceptable. Motivation research practitioners are not capable of discovering people's hidden fears and desires. Through the use of indirect techniques, some progress may be achieved in clarifying elusive motives—and hunches useful to a producer of a brand may result—but the depth of such probing should not be overestimated. What sometimes is possible through many weeks or months of painstaking collaboration between a trained psychiatrist or clinical psychologist and a patient cannot be done in a few hours by M. R. interviewers—and need not be done for the purposes of consumer research.

Theory and Research

Theory construction and empirical research must go hand in hand. Science is not a collection of facts. Scientific truths are derived from the ordering of facts, which thereby become integral parts of a consistent whole.[13] Observation, as part of scientific endeavor, must be guided by hypotheses or theories. Scientific inquiry consists of a never-ending process of hypothesis, test of hypothesis through controlled and replicable observation, reformulation and revision of hypothesis, testing, and so on.

All-encompassing theories have sometimes been developed on the basis of a few axioms in advance of testing their implications and derivations through observation. Theoreticians have sometimes argued that the smaller the number of axioms and the more elegant and simple the system, the greater its value. Since reality is complex, the axioms and basic propositions must represent unreal and untestable abstractions.

Classical economic theory developed along such lines. Among its basic assumptions are such unrealistic abstractions as complete information, complete mobility, and perfect competition. Nevertheless, the theory has yielded implications which have been most useful for realistic economic analysis. But classical economic theory has not proved to be a complete success; many of its implications and predictions have not proved to be correct. Progress in scientific inquiry is not achieved by considering simplicity of a theory its highest value, but by improving the theory, often through making its basic assumptions more complex and more realistic.[14]

More commonly, scientific endeavor does not begin with an axiomatic system or a full-fledged theory. It starts with low-level hypotheses, relating to operations in just one aspect of the field. Hypotheses represent the creative or intuitive contributions of the scholar, arrived at through reorganizing and restructuring the problem or gestalt in such a way that something new emerges from familiar material. Findings and generalizations from one field of endeavor

[13] See the little book by J. Bronowski, *Science and Human Values*, which beautifully describes the essence of science.

[14] For a fuller discussion, see the author's comments attached to H. R. Bowen's essay, *The Business Enterprise*, as well as the author's paper, "Rational Behavior and Economic Behavior." The point of view not accepted by the author has been emphasized recently by M. Friedman in his *Essays in Positive Economics*.

often serve as hypotheses in another field. Low-level hypotheses are tested through the process of systematic observations characterizing empirical research. Such tests hardly ever result in confirmation of a hypothesis and not often in its rejection. What one usually learns from tests is how to improve, revise, or reformulate the hypothesis and then, as we said before, testing must be taken up again. Such procedures result in empirically validated generalizations—not in laws valid under any and all circumstances—which represent the proximate aim of scientific research.

Theory construction and systematization are parts of the process of testing and revising hypotheses. They need not be delayed until all observations are completed. Through integrating hypotheses relating to apparently different aspects of behavior or to different disciplines, middle-level theories may be constructed. They are valuable insofar as they yield testable derivations.

Survey research, which makes it possible to collect economic, sociological, and psychological data for the same sample of people, is particularly useful at that middle stage of operation. The traditional boundaries of the different social sciences—and probably also of the natural sciences—represent theoretical abstractions rather than boundaries fixed for all time by some natural law. Through utilizing, for an understanding of economic behavior, what was first developed in experimental or social psychology about problem solving, habit formation, or motivation, both economic knowledge and psychological knowledge are promoted.

Survey research also contributes to eliminating the gap between ivory-tower research and applied research. The aim of science is the understanding of nature, which is a most practical goal. Sometimes, it is true, the higher the level of generalization we reach, the more abstract will be our functional relationships, but, as Bronowski emphasized, there need not be deep boundaries between knowledge and its use.

The distant goal to which economic psychology contributes is a theory of social behavior rather than of economic behavior. Integrated principles of motivation, group membership, learning, and decision making must be developed in all areas of human activity, including the behavior toward material resources.

By deriving predictions from hypotheses and theories we make way for the most powerful of scientific tests. This is the means whereby we let nature decide how our hypotheses need to be revised. To be sure, since reality is complex our tests are seldom if ever pure. Nevertheless, scholars must dare to predict, and progress may be achieved both through correct and through incorrect predictions. Prediction is also a practical necessity. Much of behavior, and of economic behavior in particular, is oriented toward the future. Our image of the future determines our actions. This image is derived from past experience, and yet the statement that the past governs the future is correct only in a certain sense. History does not repeat itself. We do not always do what we have done before in similar circumstances, and extrapolation is not a generally valid guide to the future. It is hypotheses and theories, developed in the past, which provide the best predictions and at the same time shape our image of the future.

Survey research has the great advantage of yielding testable predictions. Let us emphasize again that these predictions do not consist of the answers which decision makers give about what they will do or what the future will bring. The raw materials of data collection are transformed by the scientific process. The empirically validated generalizations which result provide an understanding of what is and therefore also of what will be, rather than reproduce reality. Survey research is part of the scientific process and not a method which serves merely to describe reality.

Bibliography

Publications which present research findings of the Economic Behavior Program of the Survey Research Center are marked with an asterisk.

Arrow, K. J. "Mathematical Models in the Social Sciences." In D. Lerner and H. D. Lasswell (Eds.), *The Policy Sciences.* Stanford, Calif.: Stanford University Press, 1951, 129–155.

————. *Social Choice and Individual Values.* New York: John Wiley & Sons, 1951.

Atkinson, J. W. "Motivational Determinants of Risk-taking Behavior." *Psychological Review, 64,* 1957, 359–373.

Boulding, Elise. "Achievement versus Security Orientation and Consumer Behavior." Not yet published.*

Boulding, K. E. *The Image.* Ann Arbor, Mich.: University of Michigan Press, 1956.

Bowen, H. R. *The Business Enterprise as a Subject for Research.* New York: Social Science Research Council, 1955.

Bowman, M. J. (Ed.). *Expectations, Uncertainty, and Business Behavior.* New York: Social Science Research Council, 1958.

Bristol, R. B., Jr. "Factors Associated with Income Variability." *American Economic Review,* Papers and Proceedings, *48,* 1958, 279–291.*

Bronowski, J. *Science and Human Values.* New York: Julian Messner, Inc., Publishers, 1958.

Burns, A. F. *Prosperity without Inflation.* New York: Fordham University Press, 1957.

————. "Some Lessons of the Recent Recession." *New York Commercial and Financial Chronicle,* Nov. 27, 1958.

Butters, J. K., L. E. Thompson, and L. L. Bollinger. *Investments by Individuals.* Boston: Harvard University Press, 1953.

Campbell, Angus, and George Katona. "The Sample Survey: A Technique for Social Science Research." In L. Festinger and D. Katz (Eds.), *Research Methods in the Behavioral Sciences.* New York: The Dryden Press, Inc., 1953, 15–55.

Cannell, C. F., and R. L. Kahn. "The Collection of Data by Interviewers." In L. Festinger and D. Katz (Eds.), *Research Methods in the Behavioral Sciences.* New York: The Dryden Press, Inc., 1953, 327–380.

Cartwright, Dorwin. "Some Principles of Mass Persuasion." *Human Relations, 2,* 1949, 253–267.

Cohen, Morris, and M. R. Gainsbrugh. "Consumer Buying Plans: A New Survey." *National Industrial Conference Board Business Record,* November, 1958.

Committee on Price Determination. *Cost Behavior and Price Policy.* New York: National Bureau of Economic Research, Inc., 1943.

Consultant Committee. *Consumer Survey Statistics.* Federal Reserve Board, 1955.

―――. *Statistics on Saving.* Federal Reserve Board, 1955.

de Janosi, P. E. "Factors Influencing the Demand for Automobiles: A Cross Section Analysis." Doctoral Dissertation, University of Michigan, 1956.*

Enthoven, Alain. "Instalment Credit and Prosperity." *American Economic Review,* 47, 1957, 913–930.

Ferber, Robert. "Factors Influencing Durable Goods Purchases." In L. H. Clark (Ed.), *Consumer Behavior,* Vol. II. New York: New York University Press, 1955, 75–113.

―――― and H. G. Wales (Eds.). *Motivation and Market Behavior.* Prepared under the sponsorship of the American Marketing Association. Homewood, Ill.: Richard D. Irwin, Inc., 1958.

Festinger, Leon. *A Theory of Cognitive Dissonance.* Evanston, Ill.: Row, Peterson & Company, 1957.

Fisher, B. R., and S. B. Withey. *Big Business as the People See It.* Ann Arbor, Mich.: Survey Research Center, 1951.

Foundation for Research on Human Behavior. *Psychological Surveys in Business Forecasting.* Ann Arbor, Mich., 1954, 43 pp.

―――. *Prospects for 1957: Consumer Expectations and Business Capital Appropriations.* Ann Arbor, Mich., December, 1956, 66 pp. mimeo.*

―――. *Consumer Optimism Weakening.* Ann Arbor, Mich., July, 1957, 50 pp. mimeo.*

―――. *Sign Posts to Turning Points.* Ann Arbor, Mich., December, 1957, 101 pp. mimeo.*

―――. *Convenience Goods Purchasing.* Ann Arbor, Mich., 1957.

Friedman, Milton. *Essays in Positive Economics.* Chicago: University of Chicago Press, 1953.

―――. *The Theory of the Consumption Function.* National Bureau of Economic Research. Princeton, N.J.: Princeton University Press, 1957.

Friend, Irwin, and Jean Bronfenbrenner. "Business Investment Programs and Their Realization." *Survey of Current Business,* 30 (12), 1950, 11–22.

―――. "Comments on a Theory of the Consumption Function." In L. H. Clark (Ed.), *Consumer Behavior,* Vol. III. New York: Harper & Brothers, 1958, 456–459.

Galbraith, J. K. *American Capitalism.* Boston: Houghton Mifflin Company, 1952.

Goldsmith, S. F. "The Relation of Census Income Distribution Statistics to Other Income Data." In *Studies in Income and Wealth,* Vol. 23, National Bureau of Economic Research. Princeton, N.J.: Princeton University Press, 1958, 65–107.

―――. "Size Distribution of Personal Income." *Survey of Current Business,* 39 (4), 1959, 9–16.

Henry, Harry. *Motivation Research.* New York: Frederick Ungar Publishing Co., 1958.

Institute for Social Research. *1946–1956: Ten-year Progress Report.* Ann Arbor, Mich., 1956.

Institute of Life Insurance. *The Life Insurance Public,* as portrayed by a nationwide survey by the Survey Research Center of life insurance ownership and attitudes. New York, 1957, 64 pp.*

Jöhr, W. A. *Die Konjunkturschwankungen.* Tübingen: J. C. B. Mohr, 1952.

Juster, F. T. "The Predictive Value of Consumers Union Spending Intentions Data." Conference on the *Quality and Economic Significance of Anticipations Data.* To be published by National Bureau of Economic Research, Princeton University Press.

Kahn, R. L., and C. F. Cannell. *The Dynamics of Interviewing: Theory, Techniques, and Cases.* New York: John Wiley & Sons, Inc., 1957.

Kaplan, A. D. H., J. B. Dirlan, and R. F. Lanzilotti. *Pricing in Big Business.* Washington, D.C.: Brookings Institution, 1958.

Katona, George. *Organizing and Memorizing: Studies in the Psychology of Learning and Teaching.* New York: Columbia University Press, 1940.

――――. *War without Inflation: The Psychological Approach to Problems of War Economy.* New York: Columbia University Press, 1942.

――――. "Psychological Analysis of Business Decisions and Expectations." *American Economic Review, 36,* 1946, 44–63.

――――. "Analysis of Dissaving." *American Economic Review, 39,* 1949, 673–688.*

――――. "Effect of Income Changes on the Rate of Saving." *Review of Economics and Statistics, 31,* 1949, 95–103.*

――――. "Expectations and Decisions in Economic Behavior." In D. Lerner and H. Lasswell (Eds.), *The Policy Sciences.* Stanford, Calif.: Stanford University Press, 1951, 219–232.*

――――. *Psychological Analysis of Economic Behavior.* New York: McGraw-Hill Book Company, Inc., 1951, 347 pp.*

―――― "Changing Assumptions in the Theory of Business Behavior." *Proceedings of the Fifth Annual Meeting of the Industrial Relations Research Association,* 1952.*

―――― and Albert Lauterbach. *The People versus Inflation.* An Education Resource Unit, prepared for the Office of Price Stabilization and the National Education Association. Washington, D.C.: U.S. Government Printing Office, 1952.

――――. "Rational Behavior and Economic Behavior." *Psychological Review, 60,* 1953, 307–318.*

――――, J. B. Lansing, and P. E. de Janosi. "Stock Ownership among American Families." *Michigan Business Review* (Ann Arbor, Mich., University of Michigan), 5 (1), 1953, 12–16.*

―――― and Eva Mueller. *Consumer Attitudes and Demand 1950–1952.* Ann Arbor, Mich.: Survey Research Center, 1953, 119 pp.*

――――. "The Predictive Value of Data on Consumer Attitudes." In L. H. Clark (Ed.), *Consumer Behavior,* Vol. II. New York: New York University Press, 1955, 66–74.*

―――― and Eva Mueller. *Consumer Expectations 1953–1956.* Ann Arbor, Mich.: Survey Research Center, 1956, 143 pp.*

――――. "Attitudes toward Saving and Borrowing." *Consumer Instalment Credit,* Part 2, Vol. 1. National Bureau of Economic Research and Federal Reserve Board. Washington, D.C.: U.S. Government Printing Office, 1957, 450–487.*

――――, Stanley Steinkamp, and Albert Lauterbach. *Business Looks at Banks: A Study of Business Behavior.* Ann Arbor, Mich.: University of Michigan Press, 1957.*

――――. "Federal Reserve Board Committee Reports on Consumer Expectations and Savings Statistics." *Review of Economics and Statistics, 39,* 1957, 40–45.*

———. "The Function of Survey Research in Economics." In M. Komarovsky (Ed.), *Common Frontiers of the Social Sciences.* Glencoe, Ill.: Free Press, 1957, 358–375.*

———. "Public Opinion and Economic Research." *Public Opinion Quarterly, 21,* 1957, 117–128.*

———. "Attitude Change: Instability of Response and Acquisition of Experience." *Psychological Monographs, 72* (10), 1958, 38 pp.*

———. "Business Expectations in the Framework of Psychological Economics (Toward a Theory of Expectations)." In M. J. Bowman (Ed.), *Expectations, Uncertainty, and Business Behavior.* New York: Social Science Research Council, 1958, 59–73.*

———. "The Psychology of the Recession." *American Psychologist, 14,* 1959, 135–143.*

———. "Repetitiousness and Variability of Consumer Behavior." *Human Relations, 12,* 1959, 35–49.*

Katz, Elihu, and P. F. Lazarsfeld. *Personal Influence.* Glencoe, Ill.: Free Press, 1955.

Keynes, J. M. *The General Theory of Employment, Interest, and Money.* New York: Harcourt, Brace and Company, Inc., 1936.

Kimmel, L. H. *Share Ownership in the United States.* Washington, D.C.: Brookings Institution, 1952.

Kish, Leslie. "Selection of the Sample." In L. Festinger and D. Katz (Eds.), *Research Methods in the Behavioral Sciences.* New York: The Dryden Press, Inc., 1953, 175–240.

Klein, L. R. "Estimating Patterns of Savings Behavior from Sample Survey Data." *Econometrica, 19,* 1951, 438–454.*

———. "Assets, Debts, and Economic Behavior." In *Studies in Income and Wealth,* Vol. 14. New York: National Bureau of Economic Research, Inc., 1952, 195–229.*

——— and H. W. Mooney. "Negro-White Savings Differentials and the Consumption Function Problem." *Econometrica, 21,* 1953, 425–456.*

——— (Ed.). *Contributions of Survey Methods to Economics.* Articles by G. Katona, L. R. Klein, J. B. Lansing, and J. N. Morgan. New York: Columbia University Press, 1954.*

——— and Julius Margolis. "Statistical Studies of Unincorporated Business." *Review of Economics and Statistics, 30,* 1954, 33–46.*

——— and J. B. Lansing. "Decisions to Purchase Consumer Durable Goods." *Journal of Marketing, 20,* 1955, 109–132.*

——— and N. Liviatan. "The Significance of Income Variability on Savings Behaviour." *Bulletin of the Oxford Institute of Statistics, 19,* 1957, 151–160.

Kreinin, M. E. "Factors Associated with Stock Ownership." *Review of Economics and Statistics, 41,* 1959, 12–24.*

Lansing, J. B., and E. S. Maynes. "Inflation and Savings in the Consumer Sector." *Journal of Political Economy, 60,* 1952, 383–391.*

——— and J. N. Morgan. "Consumer Finances over the Life Cycle." In L. H. Clark (Ed.), *Consumer Behavior,* Vol. II. New York: New York University Press, 1955, 36–51.*

——— and S. B. Withey. "Consumer Anticipations: Their Use in Forecasting

Behavior." In *Studies in Income and Wealth*, Vol. 17. New York: National Bureau of Economic Research, Inc., 1955, 381–453.*

———— and Ernest Lilienstein. *The Travel Market, 1955: A Report to the Travel Research Association*. Ann Arbor, Mich.: Survey Research Center, 200 pp.*

———— and Leslie Kish. "Family Life Cycle as an Independent Variable." *American Sociological Review*, 22, 1957, 512–519.*

————, E. S. Maynes, and M. E. Kreinin. "Factors Associated with the Use of Consumer Credit." *Consumer Instalment Credit*, Part 2, Vol. 1. National Bureau of Economic Research and Federal Reserve Board. Washington, D.C.: U.S. Government Printing Office, 1957, 487–520.*

————. *The Travel Market 1958*. Ann Arbor, Mich.: Survey Research Center, 1958.*

Lekachman, Robert. "The Non-economic Assumptions of J. M. Keynes." In M. Komarovsky (Ed.), *Common Frontiers of the Social Sciences*. Glencoe, Ill.: Free Press, 1957, 338–358.

Lewin, Kurt, Tamara Dembo, Leon Festinger, and P. S. Sears. "Level of Aspiration." In J. McV. Hunt (Ed.), *Personality and Behavior Disorders*. New York: The Ronald Press Company, 1944.

Likert, Rensis. "The Sample Interview Survey: A Fundamental Research Tool of the Social Sciences." In *Current Trends in Psychology*. Pittsburgh, Pa.: University of Pittsburgh Press, 1947.

————. "Developing Patterns in Management," Part I and Part II. New York: American Management Association, *General Management Series, Nos. 178 and 182*, 1955–1956.

Lininger, Charles, Eva Mueller, and Hans Wyss. "Some Uses of Panel Studies in Forecasting the Automobile Market." *Proceedings of the Business and Economic Statistics Section of the American Statistical Association*, 1957, 409–421.*

Mack, R. P. "Economics of Consumption." In B. F. Haley (Ed.), *A Survey of Contemporary Economics*, Vol. II. Homewood, Ill.: Richard D. Irwin, Inc., 1952, 39–78.

————. "Trends in American Consumption and the Aspiration to Consume." *American Economic Review*, Papers and Proceedings, 46, 1956, 55–69.

Maslow, A. H. *Motivation and Personality*. New York: Harper & Brothers, 1954.

May, F. E. "The Use of Consumer Survey Data in Forecasts of the Domestic Demand for Consumer Durable Goods." Doctoral Dissertation, University of Michigan, 1958.*

Maynes, E. S. "Alternative Concepts of Consumer Saving: A Statistical Study." Doctoral Dissertation, University of Michigan, 1955.*

McClelland, D. C., J. W. Atkinson, R. A. Clark, and E. L. Lovell. *The Achievement Motive*. New York: Appleton-Century-Crofts, Inc., 1953.

Meyer, J. R. "Brief Comments on the Recession." *Review of Economics and Statistics*, 40, 1958, 316–318.

Miner, J. L. *Life Insurance Ownership among American Families, 1957*. Ann Arbor, Mich.: Survey Research Center, 1958.*

Modigliani, Franco, and R. E. Brumberg. "Utility Analysis and the Consumption Function." In K. K. Kurihara (Ed.), *Post Keynesian Economics*. New Brunswick, N.J.: Rutgers University Press, 1954.

———— and A. K. Ando. "Tests of the Life Cycle Hypothesis of Savings." *Bulletin of the Oxford Institute of Statistics, 19*, 1957, 99–124.

Moore, G. H. "Measuring Recessions." *Journal of American Statistical Association*, 53, 1958, 259–317.

Morgan, J. N. "The Structure of Aggregate Personal Saving." *Journal of Political Economy*, 59, 1951, 528–534.*

———. "Consumer Investment Expenditures." *American Economic Review*, 48, 1958, 874–902.*

———. "A Review of Recent Research on Consumer Behavior." In L. H. Clark (Ed.), *Consumer Behavior*, Vol. III. New York: Harper & Brothers, 1958, 93–222.

Morrissett, Irving. "Psychological Surveys in Business Forecasting." In S. P. Hayes, Jr., and R. Likert (Eds.). *Some Applications of Behavioural Research*. Paris: UNESCO, 1957.

Mosteller, Frederick, and P. Nogee. "An Experimental Measurement of Utility." *Journal of Political Economy*, 59, 1951, 371–405.

Mueller, Eva. "A Study of Purchase Decisions." In L. H. Clark (Ed.), *Consumer Behavior*, Vol. I. New York: New York University Press, 1955, 30–87.*

———. "Effects of Consumer Attitudes on Purchases." *American Economic Review*, 47, 1957, 946–965.*

———. "The Desire for Innovations in Household Goods." In L. H. Clark (Ed.), *Consumer Behavior*, Vol. III. New York: Harper & Brothers, 1958, 13–37.*

———. "Consumer Attitudes: Their Influence and Forecasting Value." Conference on the *Quality and Economic Significance of Anticipations Data*. To be published by National Bureau of Economic Research, Princeton University Press.*

———. "Consumer Reactions to Inflation." *Quarterly Journal of Economics*, 73, 1959, 246–262.*

National Bureau of Economic Research. *Investing in Economic Knowledge*. Thirty-eighth Annual Report, New York, May, 1958.

Okun, A. M. "The Value of Anticipations Data in Forecasting National Product." Conference on the *Quality and Economic Significance of Anticipations Data*. To be published by National Bureau of Economic Research, Princeton University Press.

Packard, Vance. *The Hidden Persuaders*. New York: David McKay Company, Inc., 1957.

Paxton, E. T. *What People Want When They Buy a House*. Based on a report of a study conducted by the Survey Research Center for the Housing and Home Finance Agency. U.S. Department of Commerce, 1955.*

Riesman, David. *The Lonely Crowd*. New Haven, Conn.: Yale University Press, 1950.

———. "Abundance for What?" In *Problems of U.S. Economic Development*, Vol. I. New York: Committee for Economic Development, 1958.

Shackle, G. L. S. *Expectations in Economics*. New York: Cambridge University Press, 1949.

Simon, H. A. *Models of Man*. New York: John Wiley & Sons, Inc., 1957.

———. "The Role of Expectations in an Adaptive or Behavioristic Model." In M. J. Bowman (Ed.), *Expectations, Uncertainty, and Business Behavior*. New York: Social Science Research Council, 1958, 49–59.

Sirken, M. G., E. S. Maynes, and J. A. Frechtling. "The Survey of Consumer Finances and the Census Quality Check." In *Studies in Income and*

Wealth, Vol. 23. National Bureau of Economic Research. Princeton, N.J.: Princeton University Press, 1958, 127–169.*

Slichter, S. H. "On the Side of Inflation." *Harvard Business Review*, 35 (5), 1957.

Sobol, M. Gross. "Panel Mortality and Panel Bias." *Journal of American Statistical Association*, 54 (285), 1959, 52–68.*

Survey of Consumer Finances. Annual articles in the *Federal Reserve Bulletin*.*

Survey of Consumer Finances, Methods of. *Federal Reserve Bulletin*, July, 1950.*

Survey Research Center. *The Outlook for Consumer Demand*, Ann Arbor, Mich., July, 1958, 50 pp., mimeo.*

————. *The Outlook for Consumer Demand*, Ann Arbor, Mich., November, 1958, 50 pp., mimeo.*

Tobin, James. "Consumer Debt and Spending." In *Consumer Instalment Credit*, Part 2, Vol. 1. National Bureau of Economic Research and Federal Reserve Board. Washington, D.C.: U.S. Government Printing Office, 1957, 521–551.

————. "On the Predictive Value of Consumer Intentions and Attitudes." *Review of Economics and Statistics*, 41, 1959, 1–12. (See also Comments to this paper by G. Katona, same periodical, 41, 1959, 317.)

Vandome, Peter. "Aspects of the Dynamics of Consumer Behaviour." *Bulletin of the Oxford Institute of Statistics*, 20, 1958, 65–105.

Wertheimer, Max. *Productive Thinking*. New York: Harper & Brothers, 1945.

Whyte, W. H., Jr. "The Web of Word of Mouth." In L. H. Clark (Ed.), *Consumer Behavior*, Vol. II. New York: New York University Press, 1955, 113–123.

————. *The Organization Man*. New York: Simon and Schuster, Inc., 1956.

Wolgast, E. H. "Do Husbands or Wives Make the Purchasing Decisions?" *Journal of Marketing*, 23, 1958, 151–158.*

Index